C000192869

ZAGATSURVEY®
25TH ANNIVERSARY

2005

LONDON
RESTAURANTS

**Edited and Coordinated by
Sholto Douglas-Home
and Susan Kessler**

Editor: Randi Gollin

Published and distributed by
ZAGAT SURVEY, LLC
4 Columbus Circle
New York, New York 10019
Tel: 212 977 6000
E-mail: london@zagat.com
Web site: www.zagat.com

Acknowledgments

We thank Deborah Bennett, Karen Bonham, Caroline
Clegg, Ricki Conway, Alex, Louis and Tallula Douglas-
Home, Barbara Illias, Rosanne Johnston, Larry Kessler, Le
Cordon Bleu, Pamela and Michael Lester, Margaret Levin,
Ben and Sheila Miller, Zoë Miller, Natasha Robinson, Anne
Semmes, Alexandra Spezzotti, Peter Vogl, Susan and
Jeffrey Weingarten, as well as the following members of
our staff: Reni Chin, Larry Cohn, Anu Duggal, Schuyler
Frazier, Jeff Freier, Michael Gitter, Katherine Harris, Natalie
Lebert, Mike Liao, Dave Makulec, Robert Poole, Benjamin
Schmerler, Robert Seixas, Daniel Simmons
and Sharon Yates.

The reviews published in this guide are based on public opinion surveys,
with numerical ratings reflecting the average scores given by all survey
participants who voted on each establishment and text based on direct
quotes from, or fair paraphrasings of, participants' comments. Phone
numbers, addresses and other factual information were correct to the
best of our knowledge when published in this guide; any subsequent
changes may not be reflected.

© 2004 Zagat Survey, LLC
ISBN 1-57006-625-6
Printed in the United States of America

Contents

About This Survey

Here are the results of our *2005 London Restaurant Survey*, covering some 953 restaurants as tested, and tasted, by over 4,000 avid local restaurant-goers.

This marks the 25th year that Zagat Survey has reported on the shared experiences of diners like you and the ninth year we have covered London. What started in 1979 as a hobby involving 200 friends rating local restaurants has come a long way. Today we have more than 250,000 surveyors and have branched out to cover entertaining, golf, hotels, movies, music, nightlife, resorts, shopping, spas, theater and travel. Our *Surveys* are also available on wireless devices by subscription at zagat.com, where you can vote and shop as well.

By regularly surveying large numbers of avid customers, we hope to have achieved a uniquely current and reliable guide. This year's London participants dined out an average of 2.4 times per week, meaning this *Survey* is based on more than 500,000 meals. Of these surveyors, 39% are women, 61% men; the breakdown by age is 17% in their 20s; 34%, 30s; 20%, 40s; 17%, 50s; and 12%, 60s or above. Our editors have synopsized our surveyors' opinions, with their comments shown in quotation marks. We sincerely thank each of these surveyors; this book is really "theirs."

Of course, we are especially grateful to our editor/coordinators: Sholto Douglas-Home, a London restaurant critic for 18 years, and Susan Kessler, cookbook author and consultant for numerous lifestyle publications in the U.K. and U.S.

To help our readers find London's best meals and best buys, we have prepared a number of lists. See Most Popular (page 9), Top Ratings (pages 10–16) and Best Buys (page 17). In addition, we have provided 41 handy indexes and have tried to be concise. Also, for the first time, we have included Web addresses.

To join this or any of our upcoming *Surveys*, just register at zagat.com. Each participant will receive a free copy of the resulting guide when published. Your comments and even criticisms of this guide are also solicited. There is always room for improvement with your help. You can contact us at london@zagat.com. We look forward to hearing from you.

New York, NY
27 August, 2004

Nina and Tim Zagat

What's New

In London's dynamic dining scene, restaurateurs not only compete for customers, they also vie for exposure on the media's radar screen, and the press, ever hungry for tidbits about hot chefs at the trendiest 'in' spots, willingly obliges.

Names in Lights: Chic yearlings like The Strand's Savoy Grill and The Wolseley in Piccadilly merit column inches in countless newspapers as established glamour meccas like Nobu in Old Park Lane and Zuma in Knightsbridge continue to receive media plugs, often off the back of celeb sightings.

Budding Offshoots: Some of this year's most heralded arrivals are new concepts from old hands. A branch of the world-famous Cipriani empire debuted in Mayfair as Claudio Pulze reunited with Sir Michael Caine to unveil Deya near Oxford Street. The Club Gascon team brought the stylish Le Cercle to Sloane Square while the Conran Group topped its list with Plateau and Alan Yau of Hakkasan and Wagamama fame added Yauatcha to his stable, with plans to unwrap another eatery near Carnaby Street before year's end.

New Kid on the Block: Young restaurateur Marlon Abela, who backs a handful of enterprises in the U.S. and France, is making waves with Mayfair revamps of The Greenhouse and Morton's private club, and at press time will introduce Umu, a Kyoto-accented venture in Bruton Place.

Pound-for-Pound: While the average cost of a meal in London rose since the last *Survey* from £32.15 to £35.14, that barely deters respondents, 40% of whom report that they dine out more often than they did two years ago. And with the pace of openings showing no sign of abating, choices abound. Exciting upcoming ventures include: the Chutney Mary–Veeraswamy team's Amaya in Knightsbridge; the transformation of Soho's Mezzo into a Cuban and Spanish duo named Floridita and Meza, respectively; a Gordon Ramsay outpost in the London Marriott; a Nobu branch in the former Mayfair Club site; the Conran Group's Paternoster Chophouse in the City; and Roka, a robata grill from Zuma's Rainer Becker, due to open in the West End at press time.

No Butt-Ends: Many of our surveyors consider smoking one of the most irritating aspects of eating out, with about 76% of them in favour of banning it in eateries. Their wishes are nearing reality as political parties limber up to include restaurant and pub smoking restrictions in their next election manifestos. Proactive chefs and patrons like Bruce Poole, Gordon Ramsay and Antony Worrall Thompson have already instituted this policy in their establishments, confirming that the London scene never stands still.

Wimbledon, London   Sholto Douglas-Home
27 August, 2004

Ratings & Symbols

Name, Address, Tube Stop, Phone*, Fax & Web Site

Zagat Ratings

Hours & Credit Cards

		F	D	S	C
Tim & Nina's Fish Bar	◑ S ⌀	▽ 23	5	9	£9

Exeter St., WC2 (Covent Garden), 020-7123 4567;
fax 020-7123 4567; www.zagat.com

☑ Open seven days a week, 24 hours a day (some say
that's "168 hours too many"), this "chaotic" Covent
Garden dive serving "cheap, no-nonsense" fish 'n' chips
is "ideal" for a "quick grease fix"; no one's impressed by
the "tired, tatty decor" or "patchy service", but judging
from its "perpetual queues", the "no-frills" food and
prices "hit the spot."

Review, with surveyors' comments in quotes

Restaurants with the highest overall ratings and greatest
popularity and importance are printed in CAPITAL LETTERS.

Before reviews a symbol indicates whether responses
were uniform ■ or mixed ☑.

Hours: ◑ serves after 11 PM
◙ closed on Sunday

Credit Cards: ⌀ no credit cards accepted

Ratings: Food, Decor and Service are rated on a scale of
0 to **30**. The Cost (C) column reflects our surveyors' estimate
of the price of dinner including one drink and service.

F	Food	D	Decor	S	Service	C	Cost
23		5		9		£9	

0–9	poor to fair	**20–25**	very good to excellent
10–15	fair to good	**26–30**	extraordinary to perfection
16–19	good to very good	▽	low response/less reliable

For places listed without ratings or a numerical cost estimate,
such as a newcomer or survey write-in, the price range is
indicated by the following symbols.

I	£20 and below	**E**	£36 to £50
M	£21 to £35	**VE**	£51 or more

* When calling from outside the U.K., dial international code + 44,
then omit the first zero of the number.

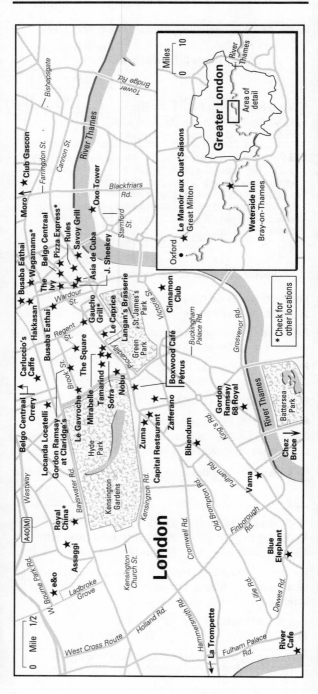

Most Popular map of London restaurants including: Club Gascon, Moro, Oxo Tower, Busaba Eathai, Wagamama*, Belgo Centraal, Pizza Express*, Rules, Savoy Grill, Asia de Cuba, J. Sheekey, The Ivy, Hakkasan, Busaba Eathai, Gaucho Grill*, Le Caprice, Langan's Brasserie, Cinnamon Club, Carluccio's Caffe, Belgo Centraal, Orrery, The Square, Boxwood Café, Pétrus, Locanda Locatelli, Gordon Ramsay at Claridge's, Le Gavroche, Mirabelle, Tamarind, Sofra, Nobu, Gordon Ramsay/68 Royal, Zafferano, Zuma, Bibendum, Capital Restaurant, Royal China*, Assaggi, e&o, Vama, Blue Elephant, La Trompette, Chez Bruce, River Cafe.

Inset map: Greater London — Le Manoir aux Quat'Saisons, Great Milton; Waterside Inn, Bray-on-Thames; Oxford. Area of detail.

Most Popular

1. Nobu
2. Wagamama
3. Ivy
4. Gordon Ramsay/Claridge's
5. Gordon Ramsay/68 Royal
6. J. Sheekey
7. Rules
8. Square
9. Zuma
10. Hakkasan
11. Zafferano
12. Royal China
13. Le Gavroche
14. Asia de Cuba
15. Locanda Locatelli
16. Le Caprice
17. Busaba Eathai
18. Le Manoir/Quat'Saisons*
19. Bibendum
20. Belgo Centraal
21. Orrery
22. Capital Rest.
23. Savoy Grill
24. River Cafe
25. Club Gascon
26. Pizza Express
27. Chez Bruce
28. Mirabelle
29. Carluccio's
30. Gaucho Grill*
31. Tamarind
32. Vama*
33. e&o
34. Pétrus*
35. Langan's Brasserie
36. Waterside Inn
37. Blue Elephant
38. Oxo Tower*
39. Assaggi
40. Moro
41. Sofra*
42. Boxwood Café
43. Cinnamon Club*
44. La Trompette

It's obvious that many of the restaurants on the above list are among the most expensive, but if popularity were calibrated to price, we suspect that a number of other restaurants would join the above ranks. Given the fact that both our surveyors and readers love to discover dining bargains, we have added a list of 80 Best Buys on page 17. These are restaurants that give real quality at extremely reasonable prices.

* Indicates a tie with restaurant above

Top Ratings

Top lists exclude restaurants with low voting.

Top Food

29 Gordon Ramsay/68 Royal	River Cafe
Pied à Terre	Ubon
27 Thyme	Orrery
Chez Bruce	Foliage
Waterside Inn	Gordon Ramsay/Claridge's
Square	Assaggi
Le Manoir/Quat'Saisons	Aubergine
La Trompette	Monsieur Max
Fat Duck	Quirinale*
Le Gavroche	Defune
Kai Mayfair	Hunan
Mosimann's (club)	Sarkhel's
Club Gascon	Mandarin Kitchen
Pétrus*	**25** Zafferano
Capital Rest.	Oslo Court
Nobu	Lahore Kebab
Roussillon	Cafe Spice
Clarke's	Enoteca Turi*
Tsunami	St. John*
26 Vama	Tamarind*

By Cuisine

Asian
25 Champor-Champor
24 Eight Over Eight
east@west
23 e&o
22 Cicada

British (Modern)
27 Chez Bruce
Clarke's
25 St. John
Glasshouse
24 Richard Corrigan

British (Traditional)
24 Grill Room
French Horn
Mark's Club (club)*
Notting Grill
23 Smiths/Top Floor

Chinese
27 Kai Mayfair
26 Hunan
Mandarin Kitchen
25 Hakkasan
Mr. Kong

Chophouses
24 Notting Grill
23 Smiths/Top Floor
22 Rules
Rib Room/Oyster
21 El Gaucho

Eclectic
27 Mosimann's (club)
24 Sugar Club
Lanes
22 Boxwood Café
Oxo Tower

Fish 'n' Chips
24 Sweetings
21 Geales Fish
18 Seashell
17 Fish!
16 Livebait

French (Bistro)
26 Monsieur Max
23 Racine
La Poule au Pot
Bibendum Oyster
22 L'Escargot

French (Classic)
27 Waterside Inn
    Le Gavroche
25 Oslo Court
23 L'Aventure
    Mirabelle

French (New)
29 Gordon Ramsay/68 Royal
    Pied à Terre
27 Thyme
    Square
    Le Manoir/Quat'Saisons

Indian
26 Vama
    Sarkhel's
25 Lahore Kebab
    Cafe Spice
    Tamarind*

Italian
26 River Cafe
    Assaggi
    Quirinale
25 Zafferano
    Enoteca Turi

Japanese
27 Nobu
    Tsunami
26 Ubon
    Defune
25 Tatsuso

Mediterranean
24 L'Oranger
23 Moro
    Eagle
21 Levant
    Monte's (club)

Mexican/Tex-Mex/SW
18 Canyon
17 Santa Fe
16 Cafe Pacifico
14 La Perla

Middle Eastern
25 Noura
23 Al Sultan
    Ishbilia
22 Al Hamra
    Alounak

Modern European
26 Foliage
24 Le Caprice
    Angela Hartnett's
23 Odette's
    Ivy

North American
20 Lucky 7
19 Chelsea Bun
    Christopher's
18 Canyon
    Bodeans

Pacific Rim
24 Sugar Club
21 Oxo Tower Brass.
20 Blakes
    Mju

Pizza
24 Pizza Metro
21 Made in Italy
    Oliveto
20 Red Pepper
    Spighetta*

Seafood
25 J. Sheekey
    One-O-One
24 Wilton's
    Fish Hoek
    Sweetings

Spanish
24 Fino
    Moro
23 Cambio de Tercio
21 Cigala
20 Eyre Brothers

Thai
24 Patara
23 Churchill Arms
    Nahm
22 Blue Elephant
    Mango Tree

Vegetarian
27 Roussillon
24 Rasa
23 Gate
22 Food for Thought
21 Blah! Blah! Blah!

Top Food

By Special Feature

Breakfast
- *24* Angela Hartnett's
- *22* Cinnamon Club
- *19* Tom's Deli
  - Pat. Valerie
  - Wolseley

Brunch
- *26* Clarke's
- *25* Lundum's
- *24* Le Caprice
- *21* Providores/Tapa
- *19* Villandry

Cheeseboards
- *29* Gordon Ramsay/68 Royal
  - Pied à Terre
- *27* Square
  - Pétrus
- *25* Tom Aikens

Child-Friendly
- *26* River Cafe
- *24* Pizza Metro
- *22* Blue Elephant
  - Boxwood Café
- *21* La Famiglia

Hotel Dining
- *27* Pétrus
  - Berkeley Hotel
  - Capital Rest.
  - Capital Hotel
  - Nobu
  - Metropolitan
- *26* Foliage
  - Mandarin Oriental
  - Gordon Ramsay
  - Claridge's

In-Store Eating
- *24* Books for Cooks
- *19* Nicole's
- *18* Fifth Floor
  - Cafe at Sotheby's
  - Carluccio's (Fenwick)

Lunch Spots
- *27* Club Gascon
  - Nobu
- *25* Zafferano
  - Hakkasan
- *24* Zuma

Meet for a Drink
- *25* Hakkasan
- *24* Zuma
  - Fino
- *22* Asia de Cuba
  - Cinnamon Club

Newcomers/Rated
- *24* Morgan M
  - east@west
- *20* 1492
  - Plateau
- *19* Wolseley

Newcomers/Unrated
- Cipriani
- Le Cercle
- Rasoi Vineet Bhatia
- Yauatcha
- Zetter

Offbeat
- *24* Books for Cooks
- *23* St. John Bread/Wine
- *22* Asia de Cuba
- *21* Providores/Tapa
- *20* Spoon+

Olde England
- *24* Wilton's (1742)
  - Sweetings (1889)
- *23* Ritz (1906)
- *22* Rules (1798)
- *19* Simpson's (1828)

Outdoor
- *26* River Cafe
- *23* Smiths/Top Floor
  - Ritz
  - La Poule au Pot
- *21* Le Pont de la Tour

People-Watching
- *27* Nobu
- *25* Hakkasan
- *24* Zuma
- *23* Ivy
- *19* San Lorenzo

Private Clubs - Members Only
- *27* Mosimann's
- *24* Mark's Club
- *23* Harry's Bar
- *22* George
- *20* Annabel's

Top Food

Private Rooms

27 Square
    Pétrus
26 Gordon Ramsay/ Claridge's
24 Zuma
    Oriental

Pub Dining

23 Churchill Arms
    Eagle
21 Lansdowne
20 Wells
    Cow Din. Rm.

Room with a View

27 Nobu
26 Foliage
23 Smiths/Top Floor
22 Putney Bridge
21 Le Pont de la Tour

Small Plates

27 Thyme
    Club Gascon
24 Fino
    Moro
    east@west

Sunday Lunch/Town

27 Chez Bruce
26 River Cafe
    Orrery
25 Zafferano
23 Bibendum

Sunday Lunch/Country

27 Waterside Inn
    Le Manoir/Quat'Saisons
    Fat Duck
24 French Horn
23 Gravetye Manor

Tasting Menus

29 Gordon Ramsay/68 Royal
    Pied à Terre
27 Square
    Pétrus
    Nobu

Tea Service

    Berkeley Hotel
    Capital Rest.
    Connaught Hotel
    Lanesborough Hotel
    Ritz Hotel

Theatre District

25 J. Sheekey
24 Richard Corrigan
    Savoy Grill
    east@west
23 Neal Street

Wine Bars

21 Cellar Gascon
20 L'Estaminet
18 Ebury Wine Bar
    Motcombs
17 Julie's

By Location

Belgravia

27 Pétrus
25 Zafferano
    Salloos
    One-O-One
23 Nahm

Bloomsbury/Fitzrovia

29 Pied à Terre
25 Hakkasan
24 Fino
    Rasa
22 Passione

Canary Wharf/Docklands

26 Ubon
23 Royal China
    Quadrato
20 Gaucho Grill
    Plateau

Chelsea

29 Gordon Ramsay/68 Royal
26 Vama
    Aubergine
25 Tom Aikens
    Toto's

Chiswick

27 La Trompette
26 Monsieur Max (Hamp. Hill)
24 Fish Hoek
19 Silks & Spice
17 Giraffe

City

25 Lahore Kebab
    Cafe Spice
    Tatsuso
24 Sweetings
22 Don

Top Food

Clerkenwell
25 St. John
24 Moro
23 Eagle
22 Cicada
19 Clerkenwell Din.

Covent Garden
25 J. Sheekey
24 Savoy Grill
   east@west
23 Neal Street
   Ivy

Hampstead
23 Jin Kichi
20 Gaucho Grill
   Wells
19 ZeNW3
   Opera

Islington
24 Morgan M
23 Metrogusto
   La Trouvaille
22 Frederick's
21 Almeida

Kensington
27 Clarke's
24 Zaika
23 Churchill Arms
22 Timo
   Memories of China

Knightsbridge
27 Mosimann's (club)
   Capital Rest.
26 Foliage
24 Zuma
   Patara

Marylebone
26 Orrery
   Defune
25 Locanda Locatelli
24 Mandalay
23 Royal China

Mayfair
27 Square
   Le Gavroche
   Kai Mayfair
   Nobu
26 Gordon Ramsay/Claridge's

Notting Hill
26 Assaggi
24 Osteria Basilico
   Books for Cooks
   Notting Grill
23 e&o

Piccadilly
23 Yoshino
22 Terrace
21 Bentley's
   Osia
   Fakhreldine

Shoreditch/Hoxton
23 St. John Bread/Wine
21 Viet Hoa
   Fifteen
20 Eyre Brothers
   Great Eastern Din.

Smithfield
27 Club Gascon
23 Smiths/Top Floor
22 Le Café du Marché
21 Cellar Gascon
20 Smiths/Dining Rm.

Soho
24 Richard Corrigan
   Sugar Club
   Alastair Little
   Red Fort
23 La Trouvaille

South Kensington
25 Lundum's
24 Patara
   L'Etranger
23 Star of India
   Bibendum

St. James's
24 Quilon
   Wilton's
   L'Oranger
   Le Caprice
23 Ritz

In the Country
27 Waterside Inn
   Le Manoir/Quat'Saisons
   Fat Duck
24 French Horn
23 Gravetye Manor

Top Decor

28 Ritz
27 Les Trois Garcons
Le Manoir/Quat'Saisons
26 Hakkasan
Criterion Grill
Mosimann's (club)
Chintamani
Belvedere
Sugar Hut
25 Rules
Lanesborough
Wolseley
Gordon Ramsay/68 Royal
Blue Elephant
Blakes
Oxo Tower*
Wapping Food*
Waterside Inn
Levant
La Porte des Indes
Lundum's

Gravetye Manor
Oxo Tower Brass.
Le Gavroche
Pasha
24 Gordon Ramsay/Claridge's
Momo
Lanes
Savoy Grill
Grill Room
Mark's Club (club)
Mint Leaf
Putney Bridge
Pétrus
Ye Olde Cheshire
Asia de Cuba
Spoon+
23 Home House (club)
Annabel's (club)
Benares
Notting Hill Brass.*
Harry's Bar (club)

Outdoors

Belvedere
Coq d'Argent
Inn The Park
La Famiglia
La Poule au Pot
Le Colombier

Le Pont de la Tour
Oxo Tower
Ritz
River Cafe
Smiths/Top Floor
Spoon+

Romance

Andrew Edmunds
Blakes
Club Gascon
Criterion Grill
La Poule au Pot
Lundum's

Momo
Odin's
Pétrus
Richard Corrigan
Ritz
Tom Aikens

Rooms

Asia de Cuba
Aurora
Cinnamon Club
Criterion Grill
Hakkasan
Les Trois Garcons

Momo
Plateau
Ritz
Sketch
Wolseley
Zuma

Views

Blue Print Cafe
Coq d'Argent
Foliage
Le Pont de la Tour
Nobu
Oxo Tower

People's Palace
Putney Bridge
Smiths/Top Floor
Thai on the River
Ubon
Windows on World

Top Service

29	Gordon Ramsay/68 Royal		Gordon Ramsay/Claridge's
28	Mark's Club (club)		Square
27	Lanes		Roussillon
	Mosimann's (club)		Oriental
	Waterside Inn		Mandalay
	Le Gavroche	24	Savoy Grill
	Gravetye Manor		Aubergine
26	Le Manoir/Quat'Saisons		Monte's (club)
	Pétrus		Wilton's*
	Grill Room		Harry's Bar (club)
	Oslo Court		Tom Aikens
	Ritz		Annabel's (club)
	Lundum's		Clarke's
	Fat Duck		Monsieur Max
	Quirinale		Goring Din. Rm.
	Capital Rest.		French Horn
	Foliage		Tatsuso
25	Le Soufflé	23	J. Sheekey
	George		Champor-Champor
	Pied à Terre		La Trompette

subscribe to zagat.com

Best Buys

Top Bangs for the Buck

1. Food for Thought
2. Churchill Arms
3. Books for Cooks
4. Chelsea Bun
5. Mandalay
6. Lucky 7
7. Tokyo Diner
8. Pepper Tree
9. Wagamama
10. Ed's Easy Diner
11. Lahore Kebab
12. Gallipoli
13. Pat. Valerie
14. Troubadour
15. Nyonya
16. Little Bay
17. Busaba Eathai
18. New Culture Rev.
19. Blah! Blah! Blah!
20. Masala Zone
21. La Porchetta Pizza
22. Tas
23. Mildreds
24. Joy King Lau
25. Pizza Express
26. Arkansas Cafe
27. Geales Fish
28. Ye Olde Cheshire
29. Duke of Clarence
30. Bodeans
31. Alounak
32. Chowki Bar
33. Eagle
34. Giraffe
35. Bankside
36. Bierodrome
37. Yoshino
38. Malabar Junction
39. Viet Hoa
40. Porters

Other Good Values

Anglesea Arms
Aperitivo
Ask Pizza
Belgo Centraal
Buona Sera
Cafe Japan
Carluccio's
Cellar Gascon
Chiang Mai
Chuen Cheng Ku
Duke of Cambridge
ECapital
Efes Kebab
Four Seasons Chin.
Golden Dragon
Harbour City
Havelock Tavern
Ikkyu
Joe's Rest.
Khan's
Kulu Kulu Sushi
Le Cercle
Made in Italy
Malabar
Maroush
Memories of India
Moshi Moshi
Mr. Kong
Noto
Pizza Metro
Pizza on Park
Restaurant 7
Royal China
Seashell
Soho Spice
Tom's Deli
Truc Vert
Two Brothers Fish
202
Yauatcha

subscribe to zagat.com

Restaurant Directory

Abbaye　　　16　13　15　£23
55 Charterhouse St., EC1 (Farringdon), 020-7253 1612
■ "No need to escape on the Eurostar" for your "mussel
fix" – or "good wholesome" "comfort food" – "when
Belgium is right on your doorstep" chime customers of this
"charming", two-floor Clerkenwell venue; the rustic, "warm
atmosphere" and "excellent selection of beers" make it
"reliable" for a "post-shopping chill out" and "enjoyable
boozy evenings", plus there's live jazz twice a week.

Abbeville, The　　　–　–　–　M
67-69 Abbeville Rd., SW4 (Clapham South), 020-8675 2201;
fax 7924 6536
"Surprisingly unpopulated by children considering it's in
the heart of Clapham's nappy valley", this "nice" gastro-pub
serves "good" Traditional British cooking at reasonable
prices "with a smile", making it "great for paper-reading
and a nosh" on weekends; whilst it can get "jammed" in
the evenings, a recent expansion may improve matters.

Abbey Road Pub & Dining Room　16　13　12　£25
(fka Salt House)
63 Abbey Rd., NW8 (St. John's Wood), 020-7328 6626;
fax 7625 9168
◢ After a recent name change (from Salt House) and
"complete makeover (again!)", customers are of two minds
about this St. John's Wood gastro-pub under the same
ownership as the Salusbury Pub & Dining Room; admirers
are smitten by the "solid, well-executed" Italian cooking
and "lovely atmosphere", but nonbelievers observe that
whilst "potential exists", they're spooked by the "*Addams
Family*" re-fit of this once-"cosy" spot.

Abeno Museum　　　–　–　–　M
47 Museum St., WC1 (Holborn), 020-7405 3211
This "unknown gem" in "nice, cosy" premises around the
corner from the British Museum in Bloomsbury "specialises
in *okonomiyaki*" ("rice batter omelettes") "prepared on a
grill atop your table" – which, along with a "reasonably
priced" menu of "original" Kansai regional dishes, makes
it an "original" "alternative Japanese restaurant" and "fun
for a group"; P.S. "their sushi is great too."

Abingdon, The　　　20　17　19　£31
54 Abingdon Rd., W8 (Earl's Ct./High St. Kensington),
020-7937 3339; fax 7795 6388; www.theabingdon.ukgateway.net
■ Still an "eternal favourite", this "popular hangout" in
Kensington staffed with "relaxed yet efficient" service
"consistently delivers" a "high standard of" "trusty,
delicious" Modern European dishes and "tasty", "clever"
"daily choices" "from a frequently revised menu"; this
"place feels as though it's been around forever", making it a
"first choice for a casual evening out" or "anytime of day."

A Cena
∇ 20 | 18 | 18 | £33

418 Richmond Rd., Twickenham (Richmond), 020-8288 0108
■ "They keep it simple and it works" at this "friendly" spot near Richmond Bridge run by former professional polo player Tim Healy, and his wife Camilla; the "wholesome, unpretentious" Northern Italian cooking saves "trekking into Central London", and it's especially "worth going" at lunch when there's a £10 prix fixe lunch menu.

Adam Street 🗷
∇ 18 | 19 | 19 | £30

9 Adam St., WC2 (Charing Cross), 020-7379 8000; fax 7379 1444;
www.adamstreet.co.uk
🗹 "In what looks like an old wine cellar" beneath the Strand (with stone walls and arches dating back to the 18th century) lies a private club with two bars, a dance floor and a "surprisingly relaxed" restaurant serving "tasty" Modern British fare; filled with "wheelers and dealers", it's an "efficient place to conduct business"; still, an adam-ant few claim it's more suited to relaxed nocturnal pursuits; N.B. nonmembers welcome at lunch.

Admiral Codrington, The
17 | 17 | 16 | £29

17 Mossop St., SW3 (South Kensington), 020-7581 0005;
fax 7589 2452
🗹 A "dream local", this "chic, chatty" Chelsea gastro-pub has a "light, airy" restaurant at the rear offering "modern twists on old comfy classics" from a "comprehensive" Modern European menu, fronted by "enthusiastic service"; an "irregular Prince William haunt", this "bright" "landmark" setting with "comfy booths" is "cosy in winter" and "great on balmy summer evenings thanks to the retracting roof"; if a few feel prices are "quite dear" and deem the crowd "quite Sloaney", even they admit it's a "fun place."

Admiralty, The
19 | 19 | 17 | £41

Somerset House, The Strand, WC2 (Temple), 020-7845 4646;
fax 7845 4647
🗹 "Bring your grandmother rather than your girlfriend" to this high-ceilinged, "lovely setting, reminiscent of a country house dining room" within the Strand's historic Somerset House where the Modern British "menu allows you to be experimental or go for the classics" and the "staff are discreet, but right on the ball"; but a fleet of foes find it "too expensive for average food" and "stuffy unless you're an admiral" ("can charm one minute, depress the next").

Alastair Little ●🗷
24 | 14 | 21 | £45

49 Frith St., W1 (Leicester Sq./Tottenham Court Rd.),
020-7734 5183; fax 7734 5206
■ "Buzzy upstairs, intimate", "almost domestic" downstairs, this "pleasurable Soho hideaway" with "attentive service" serves "celestial" Modern British fare that "still hits the mark", even though "Alastair [Little] is no longer behind the

stove" (or the business after resigning in 2003 and leaving his former co-owner, Kirsten Pedersen in charge); the "understated" setting may be "a bit too much like eating in someone's house" for a few, but most maintain the "only problem is deciding" what to order from the menu "filled with delicious options."

Alba ☒　　　　　∇ 15 ‖ 13 ‖ 15 ‖ £32

107 Whitecross St., EC1 (Barbican/Moorgate), 020-7588 1798;
fax 7638 5793

◪ An "oasis in the desert" of options near the Barbican reveal supporters who rally round this "secret" find for a quick, casual meal of "good", reasonably priced fare inspired by the Piedmont region, coupled with an exclusively Italian wine list; N.B. the comfy, unpretentious setting was recently spruced up with a light refurb.

Al Bustan　　　　　19 ‖ 13 ‖ 18 ‖ £31

68 Old Brompton Rd., SW7 (South Kensington), 020-7584 5805;
fax 8563 1036

◪ "Tasty" Lebanese cooking that "never disappoints", plus "friendly service" and a "gregarious chef-owner" make this simply decorated bi-level South Kensington restaurant, transplanted from Belgravia to the former Hilaire space a few years ago, a "regular for many in the neighbourhood"; whilst "great ingredients" shine in "well done dishes", including "delicious mezze starters", a few bridle at the "bill that comes out higher than you expect."

Al Duca ☒　　　　　20 ‖ 16 ‖ 18 ‖ £37

4-5 Duke of York St., SW1 (Green Park/Piccadilly Circus),
020-7839 3090; fax 7839 4050;
www.alduca-restaurant.co.uk

◪ For "pasta *paradisio* in lovely St. James's", duck into this "Piccadilly gem tucked off Jermyn Street" entreat enthusiasts enamoured by the "inventive" cooking "with flair", "smart wine list", "crisp styling" of the room and "helpful staff"; the "wonderful food" and "true Italian feel" "make for a delightful dinner" or "business lunch"; but a few declare this duca "won't blow your socks off", citing "tight quarters" and "spotty service."

Al Hamra ◗　　　　　22 ‖ 15 ‖ 19 ‖ £34

31-33 Shepherd Mkt., W1 (Green Park), 020-7493 1954;
fax 7493 1044; www.alhamrarestaurant.com

◪ "We find ourselves drawn back every time we're in the mood for Lebanese" food concur cohorts of this "very crowded", "friendly" "mezze heaven" in Mayfair; it's "a great place to" try "top-notch" specialties so "forget the menu", "take the captain's recommendations" and "keep it coming"; but the less-impressed balk at the "brusque service" and £20 minimum order prices that seem "more for sheiks."

Allium   _ _ _ VE
Dolphin Square Hotel, Chichester St., SW1 (Pimlico),
020-7798 6888; www.allium.co.uk
In the "unexciting Dolphin Square Hotel complex" in Pimlico
that previously housed Rhodes in the Square, veteran chef
Anton Edelmann has launched his first venture since leaving
the Savoy Hotel after two celebrated decades, bringing
along head chef Peter Woods, formerly of the Belvedere;
boasting a "light, imaginative" Modern European menu and
a "dark interior", it's a "restaurant with a cool difference",
including displays of modern art from the Contemporary
Art Society; N.B. closed Mondays.

Alloro ⊠   20 17 18 £48
19-20 Dover St., W1 (Green Park), 020-7495 4768; fax 7629 5348
☑ "Bravo for the food" that's "worth every penny" proclaim
admirers of this "civilised", "grown-up" yet "always
buzzing" Mayfair Italian offering "imaginative dishes
enhanced by solicitous service" that "shines" and an
"outstanding wine list" managed by a "helpful sommelier";
whilst it may be a "trendy, chichi, very 'now' sort of place",
the "very fine" cooking is "interesting too"; but a few
gripers grouch it's "expensive" for "nothing exciting" and
"lacking in atmosphere."

Almeida   21 19 21 £41
30 Almeida St., N1 (Angel/Highbury & Islington), 020-7354 4777;
www.conran-restaurants.co.uk
☑ "Top" Classic French "nosh" and "professional service"
"pitched just right" in a "relaxed atmosphere" with a "see-
through kitchen" make this "buzzy" "favourite Conran"
eatery in Islington "ideal for a visit to the Almeida Theatre";
the "set dinner is a great bargain" whilst the "hearty, rich
food" "married to excellent wine selections" are "well
executed"; but to a minority "when they are good, they are
very, very good and when they're not, they're ordinary."

Alounak ◑   22 10 15 £19
10 Russell Gardens, W14 (Olympia), 020-7603 1130
44 Westbourne Grove, W2 (Bayswater/Queensway),
020-7229 4158; fax 7792 1219
■ "Who cares about the [basic] decor" and "packed" tables
when there's "awesome", "consistently good Persian food
in huge portions" and "freshly baked bread" to be had at
this "convivial culinary cache" in Olympia and Westbourne
Grove; it's a "great family" location for a "cheap and
cheerful" meal (especially as "you can BYO") and "no
reservations mean people are in quick, out quick" too.

Al San Vincenzo ⊠   ▽ 26 17 22 £44
30 Connaught St., W2 (Marble Arch), 020-7262 9623
■ The combination of a "cosy living-room atmosphere",
"excellent" rustic Italian cooking and "welcoming"

proprietors Vincent and Elaine Borgonzolo "who care very much" ensure a "lovely experience" at this discreet Bayswater eatery "hidden" near Hyde Park; the "warm", "wonderful" vibe prompts patrons to promise "we'll be back"; N.B. evening reservations recommended.

Al Sultan   23 | 15 | 19 | £33
51-52 Hertford St., W1 (Green Park), 020-7408 1155; fax 7408 1113; www.alsultan.co.uk
■ Sultans and subjects alike say the "brilliant food, especially the exquisite mezze" and "excellent kebabs", makes this "very consistent" Lebanese "favourite" next to Mayfair's Curzon cinema an "excellent alternative"; the simple, "traditional" "decor is nothing to write home about, but they have all the classics" along with "friendly, multilingual service."

Al Waha ●   ▽ 23 | 11 | 19 | £30
75 Westbourne Grove, W2 (Bayswater/Queensway), 020-7229 0806; www.waha-uk.com
■ "Middle Eastern food becomes a grown-up, yet retains the charm of youth" at this casual, "family-friendly" Bayswater Lebanese where "lesser-known dishes" and "fantastic" classics are "outstanding"; the simple decor may explain why some prefer "their local home delivery service."

Anchor & Hope   ▽ 20 | 14 | 14 | £22
36 The Cut, SE1 (Waterloo), 020-7928 9898
☑ "Forget the gastro-pub label, this place is fantastic" fawn fans who find this newcomer near Waterloo, run by a team formerly at the Eagle, "wonderful, even with the crush"; the "inventive", "well-executed" Modern British cooking and spare decor leave you with a "warm, cosy" glow – "how many restaurants make you feel this way?"; those with little hope of anchoring a table retort it was "probably a good find before it was discovered."

Andrew Edmunds   22 | 18 | 20 | £33
46 Lexington St., W1 (Oxford Circus/Piccadilly Circus), 020-7437 5708
■ "Ideal for romancing", this "delightful" Soho "hot spot" "dripping with candles and cosy corners to hide in" "charms" "canoodlers" with "hearty" Modern European cooking; it's a "superb place to spend very little money", plus it makes you "feel like you're the first" to uncover a "well-kept secret"; "book a table upstairs" because downstairs "takes the meaning of intimate to a new level (you may as well sit on your neighbour's lap")."

Angela Hartnett's MENU   24 | 23 | 23 | £66
The Connaught Hotel, Carlos Pl., W1 (Bond St./Green Park), 020-7592 1222; fax 7292 1223; www.gordonramsay.com
☑ "The epitome of what" an "extremely civilised" London "experience" can be, this Nina Campbell–designed Mayfair

hotel dining room is a "fantastic combo of old- and new-world style" and now home to Gordon Ramsay's protégé, Angela Hartnett, whose Modern European cooking with Med accents can "exceed her mentor's"; whilst some "miss the old room" and claim the cooking is "nice, but not amazing", most maintain this no-smoking venue "keeps enough of the Connaught tradition to make it extraordinary."

Anglesea Arms | 18 | 14 | 12 | £24 |

35 Wingate Rd., W6 (Goldhawk Rd./Ravenscourt Park), 020-8749 1291; fax 8749 1254

◪ "A great local that would be even better if it were less crowded" is the consensus on this "lovely, casual gastropub" in Shepherd's Bush with a "warm atmosphere" and "friendly" staff; the "innovative" daily changing Modern British menu offers "rather innovative dishes", plus there's also "fun summer dining" on the outside patio; but some are up in arms about the "hit-or-miss service" and the "no-booking policy" – it's a "struggle to get a table for dinner."

Annabel's ●🏷 | 20 | 23 | 24 | £71 |

Private club; inquiries: 020-7629 1096

◪ "Eternally wonderful", especially after an "elegant" makeover last year, this 42-year-old Mayfair private club is still the "haunt of the great and the good", attracting "the gorgeous rich", "the overly rich and those aspiring to be rich" with "sexy ambience", a dance floor and Classic Anglo–French fare that's "surprisingly" "yummy"; sure, some decry it as a "repository of over-funded socialites", nevertheless, few would pass up an opportunity "to be seen" at this "celebrity-filled cellar."

Annie's | ▽ 19 | 24 | 20 | £33 |

162 Thames Rd., W4 (Kew Bridge B.R.), 020-8994 6848; fax 8744 5579
36-38 White Hart Ln., SW13 (Barnes Bridge B.R.), 020-8878 2020; fax 8876 8478

■ The "slightly bizarre decor" – mismatched baroque/rococo furniture and "big tables and chairs" – creates an "excellent ambience" that feels like you're dining in someone's front room at this Chiswick "gem" and its younger Barnes sib from Lorraine Angliss (formerly manager at Bill Wyman's Sticky Fingers); the "interesting" Modern British menu and "really good service" make this "nice hideaway" the "ultimate reliable local."

Aperitivo | 20 | 16 | 19 | £27 |

41 Beak St., W1 (Oxford Circus/Piccadilly Circus), 020-7287 2057 🏷
30 Hawley Crescent, NW1 (Camden Town), 020-7267 7755
www.aperitivo-restaurants.com

■ Thanks to the "brilliant concept" of "tasty, simple" "well-executed Italian tapas", "food is always a talking point" at this "informal" venue with "modern surroundings" "tucked away" off Regent Street and its new Camden Town offshoot; "the perfect-sized portions" allow you to "eat as much or as little as you like", making it "fun for dining with friends", especially "over a good glass of *vino*."

Approach Tavern, The
– – – M

47 Approach Rd., E2 (Bethnal Green), 020-8980 2321

Bethnal Green's "great, little unpretentious boozer" with a working fireplace and a jukebox is "comfortable for your every mood", with "friendly staff" serving "above-average [Modern British] gastro fare" that's "not overpriced like some" similar pub-based places; to complete the ever-approachable picture, there's a garden for summer dining and an upstairs gallery featuring the work of several artists.

Arancia ⊠
– – – M

52 Southwark Park Rd., SE16 (Bermondsey), 020-7394 1751; fax 7394 1044

An "oasis in poorly served" Bermondsey, this "local place" satisfies appetites with "massive portions" of "surprisingly good and adventurous" Italian fare at prices that offer "great value" (including a bargain £7.50 two-course prix fixe); the weekly changing menu, "relaxed atmosphere" and "nice staff" also make it "well worth a visit."

Archipelago ⊠
▽ 21 29 26 £55

110 Whitfield St., W1 (Goodge St./Warren St.), 020-7383 3346; fax 7383 7181

■ "The care and attention to detail is evident" at this Fitzrovia "experience" where the "witty", "sumptuous decor" is "matched" with "unique" Eclectic globe-trotting cooking "unlike anything anywhere else"; it's "full of wonderful surprises", from the "unusual" food – "think crickets, reindeer and other odd fare" – to the "original presentation of each dish", plus staff are "pleasant"; P.S. "they also cater to those with less exotic tastes."

Ark
20 19 20 £36

122 Palace Gardens Terrace, W8 (Notting Hill Gate), 020-7229 4024; fax 7792 8787

◪ "Dinner in a Nissen hut might" not float everyone's boat, but Louise Mayo's quirky Kensington "hideaway" is a "favourite haunt" of many (especially for an "intimate" encounter), encore enthusiasts who climb onboard for the "inventive" Italian menu and wine list and "charming service"; a few feel it's "expensive for what it is", but for most this "good neighbourhood joint" is "here to stay."

Arkansas Cafe
15 9 17 £16

Old Spitalfields Mkt., 107B Commercial St., E1 (Liverpool St.), 020-7377 6999; fax 7377 6999

■ "Characterful American" chef-owner "Bubba [Helberg] still rocks" promise patriots who insist his Spitalfields

Market "BBQ joint", a lunch-only "landmark" (now into its third decade), is well "worth a pilgrimage"; it doesn't look like a "proper restaurant" and it's sure "not a haute cuisine experience", but it's a "fun place" for "good comfort food" including a "selection of various beefs."

Armadillo ⊠　　　　　　　　– | – | – | M

41 Broadway Mkt., E8 (Bethnal Green), 020-7249 3633;
www.armadillorestaurant.co.uk
Beyond the unassuming glass frontage of this former shop in Hackney lies a characterful eatery with a cream, brown and blonde-wood modern interior and small rear patio where Brazilian chef-patron Rogerio David offers a perky, weekly changing menu of unusual, "wonderful Latin American" fare accompanied by a wine list dominated by Chilean and Argentinean choices; N.B. dinner only, but snacks are served at lunchtime.

Artigiano　　　　　　　18 | 17 | 14 | £37

12A Belsize Terrace, NW3 (Belsize Park/Swiss Cottage),
020-7794 4288; fax 7435 2048; www.etruscagroup.co.uk
◪ An authentic Oscar reportedly bestowed by a real recipient "forms an added attraction" at this "stylish", "friendly" Modern Italian, a "firm local favourite" of the "well-heeled Belsize Park crowd"; the "authentic", "well-executed" fare ("good selection of fish and pasta"), multi-coloured lighting and glass frontage reveal "impeccable attention to detail"; still, a few draw the conclusion that it's a "bit expensive for what it is."

Ashbells　　　　　　　16 | 19 | 12 | £37

29 All Saints Rd., W11 (Ladbroke Grove/Notting Hill Gate),
020-7221 8585; www.ashbells.co.uk
◪ Bringing "a breath of fresh air" to Notting Hill, this "eccentric" belle from South Carolina–born chef-owner Ashbell McElveen seduces admirers with "down-home" Southern cooking that's "close to the real thing" ("grits just like mama makes them") served in a "generously decorated" setting; whilst many find it "finger licking good" ("brunch in particular"), vowing "I'll be back soon, y'all", detractors chime "it's definitely not" "all it's cracked up to be."

ASIA DE CUBA ❶　　　　　22 | 24 | 19 | £46

St. Martin's Lane Hotel, 45 St. Martin's Ln., WC2
(Leicester Sq.), 020-7300 5588; fax 7300 5540;
www.chinagrillmanagement.com
◪ "Love the excitement, drama" and "beautiful library decor" gush gazillions gratified by this "fashionable" "definite 'in' spot" ("trendoid heaven") in Theatreland's St. Martin's Lane Hotel; it's a "place to go to be among the pretty people" with the added pull of "perfect-for-sharing" ("portions are quite big") Asian-Cuban fusion dishes from NY-trained chef Owen Stewart and "bento boxes ideal for

pre-theatre"; but the less-impressed sniff you're "paying through the nose for a meal" that's all "sizzle and flash."

Ask Pizza | 14 | 13 | 14 | £18 |

145 Notting Hill Gate, W11 (Notting Hill Gate), 020-7792 9942
222 Kensington High St., W8 (High St. Kensington), 020-7937 5540; fax 7937 5540
219-221 Chiswick High Rd., W4 (Turnham Green), 020-8742 1323 ◖
121-125 Park St., W1 (Marble Arch), 020-7495 7760; fax 7495 7702
48 Grafton Way, W1 (Warren St.), 020-7388 8108; fax 7388 8112 ◖
Unit 23-24 Gloucester Arcade, SW7 (Gloucester Rd.), 020-7835 0840 ◖
345 Fulham Palace Rd., SW6 (Hammersmith/Putney Bridge), 020-7371 0392
300 King's Rd., SW3 (Sloane Sq.), 020-7349 9123
160-162 Victoria St., SW1 (St. James's Park/Victoria), 020-7630 8228; fax 7630 5218
216 Haverstock Hill, NW3 (Belsize Park/Chalk Farm), 020-7433 3896; fax 7435 6490 ◖
Additional locations throughout London
■ "No matter the location", expect "dependable pizzas", "affordable", "well-prepared pasta" and "solicitous, quick service" at this "casual" "Italian-themed chain" that has "everything for everyone's tastes"; even if the "samey" experience is "nothing to write *a la casa* about", most agree it's "perfect for pre- or post-cinema grub" or "catching up with friends."

ASSAGGI ⌧ | 26 | 16 | 22 | £46 |

39 Chepstow Pl., W2 (Notting Hill Gate), 020-7792 5501; fax 7792 9033
■ "If only it were bigger" sigh those who begrudge the "need to book weeks in advance" at this "small, buzzy" Italian "treat" of a trattoria where "every morsel is a wonder" and "unhurried, knowledgeable" staff who "clearly like what they do" explain the "varied menu with passion"; the "flawless", "*fantastico*", "simply prepared" cooking along with the "unassuming", "comfortable, no-fuss", "homelike atmosphere" above a pub convey a "Sardinia-in-Notting-Hill" feel.

Atlantic Bar & Grill ◖⌧ | 16 | 20 | 15 | £42 |

20 Glasshouse St., W1 (Piccadilly Circus), 020-7734 4888; fax 7734 5400; www.atlanticbarandgrill.com
☑ Recently refurbished, Oliver Peyton's "cavernous", art-filled Piccadilly haunt "holds its own" as a "sexy" "subterranean mecca" for "divine" Med–Modern British fare from former Monte's chef Ben O'Donoghue; "the grand feel" ("imagine you're in the dining room of a luxurious

liner") makes it "great" for "expense-accounters" or "Essex girls" on a "noisy night out", with a range of "areas to suit every level of inebriation"; but critics snipe it's "overpriced."

AUBERGINE ⊠   26 22 24 £60

11 Park Walk, SW10 (Gloucester Rd./South Kensington), 020-7352 3449; fax 7351 1770; www.atozrestaurants.com

◪ "Worth the money and the wait" to get a reservation is the consensus on this "intimate", "refined" Chelsea venue where William Drabble's "inventive" New French cooking is "an absolute delight", and certainly "not for amateurs", and "service is primo"; a minority find it "a tad fussy", "way pricey" (the "wine list can take the bill to the stratosphere!") and claim it's "lost its sparkle", but they're out-gunned by the "loyal" who insist it "still delivers"; P.S. "best to go for the great value set lunch" at £32.

Aura Kitchen & Bar ⊠   ▽ 16 17 13 £47

48-49 St. James's St., SW1 (Green Park), 020-7499 6655; www.the-aura.com

■ In a "converted basement" on a busy Piccadilly corner, this dinner-only restaurant/bar serves "simple, efficient" Eclectic dishes with a Med accent; but "that's not what this place is all about" confide insiders who stay on past mealtime, watching as the "tables get thrown to the side", a "dance floor appears" and the premises "turn into a superb bar and nightclub"; N.B. members only at weekends.

Aurora ⊠   21 21 19 £50

Great Eastern Hotel, 40 Liverpool St., EC2 (Liverpool St.), 020-7618 7000; fax 7618 7001; www.aurora-restaurant.co.uk

◪ Dining "is a businesslike affair" ("quiet" for "closing your swaps, deals or takeovers") at this "grand room" with a "beautiful" stained-glass dome ceiling inside the City's Great Eastern Hotel where Conran Group's new chef, Alan Pickett (ex Orrery), prepares "imaginative" Modern European dishes, accompanied by an "excellent wine list and cheeseboard"; "friendly service" and a "knowledgeable sommelier" further illuminate its status as a "good upmarket" "experience"; still, some sceptics find it "too expensive for what it is."

Avenue ●   - - - E

7-9 St. James's St., SW1 (Green Park), 020-7321 2111; fax 7321 2500; www.egami.co.uk

It's "like being on a fashion runway" coo catwalkers who slink into this "sleek, minimalist" St. James's behemoth (part of the group that owns Kensington Place, et al.) "for lunch with business acquaintances or friends"; the "elegant" servers and "creative" Modern European cooking ensure it has a loyal following, plus there's even an "excellent" set menu for under £18 worth purring about.

Axis ⌀   21 | 21 | 21 | £42 |

One Aldwych Hotel, 1 Aldwych, WC2 (Charing Cross/
Covent Garden), 020-7300 0300; fax 7300 0301;
www.onealdwych.co.uk

■ "Go for the food and still enjoy the scene" at this
"happening" basement dining room in Theatreland's One
Aldwych Hotel advise admirers of the "brilliant" Modern
British–Eclectic menu, "well-dressed crowd", "attentive
service" and "modernist" setting decorated "with a frisson
of chic" and dominated by a large mural of a skyline; the
"well-upholstered interior" "soaks up superfluous clatter"
making it "a place to come as a treat or to impress a client"
and "a good choice" for pre- or post-theatre; N.B. live jazz
on Tuesdays and Wednesdays.

Aziz   ▽ 19 | 20 | 18 | £29 |

30-32 Vanston Pl., SW6 (Fulham Broadway), 020-7386 0086;
fax 7386 0086

◪ "Noshtastic" concur customers who claim this "strong"
"contributor to the gastronomisation of Fulham Broadway"
offers "a cut above the standard" North African–Middle
Eastern cooking, with a "broad selection" that includes an
"excellent value" £15 prix fixe lunch; foes find the fare
"rather bland", but it's still early days for this yearling,
which has the added benefit of a deli/cafe next door.

Babylon   16 | 22 | 16 | £39 |

The Roof Gardens, 99 Kensington High St., W8
(High St. Kensington), 020-7368 3993; www.roofgardens.com
◪ "The view is divine" from atop Sir Richard Branson's Roof
Gardens in Kensington, a "real experience" with a "Zen
garden", "amazing" terrace and "lovely bar with tropical
fish tanks"; the "great-value lunch" and "good brunch"
come recommended, still, most feel the "expensive" Modern
European "menu bites off more than it can chew"; but
"who cares about the food" – go for the "decor straight
out of *Wallpaper* magazine"; N.B. diners can access the
private nightclub (for a fee) on Thursdays and Saturdays.

Balans ◑   15 | 13 | 16 | £22 |

187 Kensington High St., W8 (High St. Kensington),
020-7376 0115; fax 7938 4653
60 Old Compton St., W1 (Leicester Sq./Piccadilly Circus),
020-7439 2183; fax 7734 2665
239 Old Brompton Rd., SW5 (Earl's Ct.), 020-7244 8838;
fax 7244 6226
www.balans.co.uk

◪ "You don't have to be gay to enjoy the lively atmosphere"
at this "campy" all-day cafe-chain in Soho, Earl's Court and
Kensington full of "trendy people (young and old)" where
"eye-candy waiters" are one of "the best things on the
menu"; it's "perfect for Sunday brunch" and the otherwise
"dependable" Modern British fare is "not too demanding

on the palate or imagination"; P.S. Compton Street is open all night and very "convenient for Soho's bars and clubs."

Balham Kitchen & Bar   17 20 16 £30
15-19 Bedford Hill, SW12 (Balham B.R.), 020-8675 6900; fax 8673 3965; www.balhamkitchen.com

◪ "Book ahead" because "the Soho House mob have done it again" with this "true diamond in the rough" of Balham, comprising a "very busy bar", "comfortable", snug area (with open fire) and Modern British "menu of perfect comfort food" that works well for kids; but dissenters disappointed by the occasionally "lax service" and "bit too cool for school" vibe are also done in by the din of "pumping music", shouting "what? can't hear you."

Baltic   21 22 18 £37
74 Blackfriars Rd., SE1 (Southwark), 020-7928 1111; fax 7928 8487; www.balticrestaurant.co.uk

■ "A surprising gem" in an "out-of-the-way location", Jan Woroniecki's (Wòdka's owner) "stylish" spot in a former coach builder's workshop in Southwark offers "a refreshing change", with Eastern European fare "cooked to please the English palate", all served by "personable" staff; the "crowd is so divine", the bar so "cool" and the "superb vodkas" "so numerous" you may not "remember what you ate"; N.B. now open for lunch on Saturday.

Bam-Bou ⊠   18 22 18 £36
1 Percy St., W1 (Tottenham Court Rd.), 020-7323 9130; fax 7323 9140; www.bam-bou.co.uk

◪ "All-in-all, it's a grown-up experience" at this Fitzrovia townhouse ("many floors, many rooms") that's a "perfect date spot", with "dramatic", "colonial ambience", "candlelit whispery corners", a Vietnamese/ Southeast-Asian "menu that encourages adventure" and "fantastic" service; Gary Lee's "original" "high-end" cooking is "absolutely delicious" plus the bar is "great to lounge in" with "good nibbles" with which "to wash down your tailor-made cocktails", but a minority feel it's "not as amazing as it used to be."

Bangkok ⊠   ▽ 19 11 18 £27
9 Bute St., SW7 (South Kensington), 020-7584 8529

◪ Still "one of the best Thai restaurants in the area" after over 37 years, this "reliable gem" down a South Kensington side street remains a "favourite" for a few; but the less-enthused claim the cooking has "its ups and downs" and find the "dining area crowded and rushed", concluding "there are far better [places] elsewhere."

Bank Aldwych   18 19 18 £38
1 Kingsway, WC2 (Holborn), 020-7379 9797; fax 7240 7001; www.bankrestaurants.com

◪ The clearly "spectacular glass ceiling transforms" this "cavernous" Aldwych eatery with a "cutting-edge" "interior into something magical" attest admirers who adore the "keen service" and "delish" Modern British cooking and count on this "safe pair of hands for business" lunches, "great brekkies" and "relaxed pre- or post-theatre meals" (the "£15 set menu is one of the bargains of London"); but detractors declare "don't bank on it" "for an evening of romance or privacy" as it can seem "soulless"; N.B. the Decor rating may not reflect a light post-*Survey* refurb.

Bankside   18 | 17 | 16 | £21

32 Southwark Bridge Rd., SE1 (London Bridge), 020-7633 0011; fax 7633 0011; www.banksiderestaurants.co.uk
◪ Though "quiet, comfy and cosy", this L-shaped location in Southwark also "feels quite trendy inside" with the "brilliant idea of buzzers at each table to attract staff attention", plus the "interesting" Modern British cooking and "particularly attractive" set menus offer "excellent value for money in central London" (along with "reasonably cheap wine"); but a few balk that this bank's menu "can be a bit limiting."

Bank Westminster &   18 | 19 | 16 | £33
Zander Bar ☒

45 Buckingham Gate, SW1 (St. James's Park), 020-7379 9797; fax 7240 7001; www.bankrestaurants.com
■ "Sit in" the "sunny conservatory" at this Victoria Bank sibling with an "enormous window looking onto an exquisite courtyard" and "you'll be transported to another time" agree acolytes who also find the Modern British cooking at "fair prices" (there's a £15 set menu) "surprisingly enjoyable"; the "always packed" 48-metre-long bar with "charming staff and "tasty cocktails" is "martini-tastic" and "excellent after work", with a weekend DJ too.

Banquette   ▽ 22 | 23 | 24 | £41

Savoy Hotel, The Strand, WC2 (Covent Garden/ Embankment), 020-7420 2392; fax 7592 1601; www.the-savoy-group.com
■ The "corridor" space overlooking the Savoy Hotel's busy forecourt in the Strand has been revamped into a "cool", no-smoking "'50s-style diner" with smart cream-coloured banquette seating that offers a "wonderful location" for "people-watching" or "after the theatre"; the "interesting", "light" Modern European menu of "British favourites are given a tasty contemporary spin", making for a "refreshing change" from the hotel's other dining options.

Barnsbury   – | – | – | M

209-211 Liverpool Rd., N1 (Angel), 020-7607 5519; fax 7607 3256; www.thebarnsbury.co.uk
"A great bet away from the Upper Street throngs", this "excellent gastro-pub" with original oak panelling and fireplaces has a "laid-back atmosphere (love the wine

glass chandeliers!)" and a "really good value" Modern British menu that "tends to the rustic", and includes "a mean Sunday roast"; "the icing on the cake: friendly, attentive service" and perhaps some of the "best chips in town"; N.B. a garden opened post-*Survey*.

Beiteddine ◑　　　　　　　▽ 17 ‖ 16 ‖ 16 ‖ £47 ‖
8 Harriet St., SW1 (Knightsbridge/Sloane Sq.), 020-7235 3969; fax 7245 6335
■ Named after a 19th-century palace, this low-key, "nice and good" Lebanese "tucked away in a side street" in Knightsbridge has a "pleasant atmosphere" and "authentic cuisine", with one fan voting it "the home of London's best kibbeh nayeh" (raw lamb); N.B. the takeaway and delivery options also have its followers.

Belair House　　　　　　　▽ 14 ‖ 22 ‖ 14 ‖ £45 ‖
Gallery Rd., Dulwich Village, SE21 (West Dulwich B.R.), 020-8299 9788; fax 8299 6793; www.belairhouse.co.uk
◪ "A haven of civilisation" in "Dulwich's desolate culinary landscape", this Georgian Grade II listed building (dated 1785) set in Belair Park offers terrace dining and Classic French "cooking that's still up there", making it a "perfect spot to bring mum for Sunday lunch"; still, a few believe it offers "style with erratic substance", concurring it "needs to raise its game if it is to attract the sophisticated local clientele"; N.B. there's live jazz once a week.

BELGO CENTRAAL/NOORD ◑　　18 ‖ 16 ‖ 16 ‖ £23 ‖
50 Earlham St., WC2 (Covent Garden), 020-7813 2233; fax 7209 3212
72 Chalk Farm Rd., NW1 (Chalk Farm), 020-7267 0718
www.belgo-restaurants.com
◪ May be "habit forming" fawn followers of this Covent Garden and Chalk Farm duo's "tried-and-tested [Belgian] formula", replete with "dungeonesque" decor, "big communal tables", "trappist monk waiters", "wicked mussels" and "amazing" beers; whilst cynics scowl about the "narrow" seafood menu and "absurdly optimistic waiting times", the "reasonable prices" and "cheerful service" ensure most just "take it for what it is: a fun, casual place."

BELVEDERE, THE　　　　　22 ‖ 26 ‖ 22 ‖ £47 ‖
Holland Park, off Abbotsbury Rd., W8 (Holland Park), 020-7602 1238; fax 7610 4382; www.whitestarline.org.uk
■ It's "hard to imagine a nicer place" for a "leisurely Sunday lunch" than Marco Pierre White's "opulent" Holland Park setting with its "old-world beauty" and "fantastic terrace for summer lunches" "in the middle of Holland Park", perhaps "one of London's prettiest"; "it's a super supper place" too, with an "upscale" Modern British–New French menu, and though it's "not cheap", prices are mitigated by a "good value" set menu for under £20; N.B. at press time,

former L'Escargot chef Billy Reid took over the kitchen, and is expected to introduce a new menu.

Benares   23   23   20   £47

12 Berkeley Sq., W1 (Green Park), 020-7629 8886; fax 7491 8883;
www.benaresrestaurant.com

■ "Tranquil surroundings calm the senses" while the "memorable" cooking – an "exotic Indian adventure" – "fires the taste buds" at Atul Kochhar's (ex Tamarind) "sleek", "sophisticated" Mayfair newcomer; the "smiling, friendly staff are passionate about the food" and though it's "not cheap", the "fab" "bargain" £13.50 "lunch deal" alone is "worth a visit"; but the less-enamoured declare it's more "hype than substance" with "pushy", "amateur service" that detracts from "the experience."

Bengal Clipper ●   19   18   16   £28

11-12 Cardamom Bldg., 31 Shad Thames, SE1 (London Bridge/
Tower Hill), 020-7357 9001; fax 7357 9002;
www.bengalclipper.co.uk

■ "Your curry ship comes into port" at this "large, attractive dining room in an old warehouse" at Butlers Wharf that's "surprisingly nice", with a "good, solid" Indian menu of "well-spiced fare"; a few wisecrack about service that can be "completely at sea" and "no view of the river", but most appreciate other touches, such as the "great pianist" (Tuesday–Saturday) and "cheap Sunday deal" for the "excellent buffet."

Benihana   17   14   19   £35

37 Sackville St, W1 (Green Park/Piccadilly Circus), 020-7494 2525;
fax 7494 1456
77 King's Rd., SW3 (Sloane Sq.), 020-7376 7799;
fax 7376 7377
100 Avenue Rd., NW3 (Swiss Cottage), 020-7586 9508;
fax 7586 6740
www.benihana.com

◪ "The novelty never dies" say supporters of this "lively", "kitschy retro" Japanese chain trio where "dextrous, knife-wielding" teppanyaki chefs "chop and cook" providing an "entertaining" "floor show" and "meal all in one" that's "enthralling for youngsters" and "fun" with a "bunch of friends"; though some insist "there are no surprises" so "it never disappoints", others feel the "amusement fades with each visit", declaring it's a "dated" concept.

Ben's Thai   14   10   14   £18

93 Warrington Crescent, W9 (Maida Vale/Warwick Ave.),
020-7266 3134; fax 7221 8799

◪ "Although you won't be swept to the beaches of Phuket", this "crowded" "local favourite" above a Maida Vale pub with "friendly" service still rustles up "more than reliable Thai in a non-Thai setting" that works for a "nice Sunday lunch"; but it's a "little too cheek by jowl for some tastes", and cynics complain that the fare is "not always consistent."

Bentley's ◑   21 | 19 | 21 | £44 |
11-15 Swallow St., W1 (Piccadilly Circus), 020-7734 4756; fax 7287 2972

▣ "Fresh seafood", a "clubby feel" and "professional service" lure loyalists to this Piccadilly "old-timer" (est. 1916) that's more of a "safe choice than a spectacular one", with a Traditional British menu of "classic favourites"; a minority suggest it's "stuffy" and "stodgy" and object to "expense-account prices", but all concur this stalwart venue is one of London's "most English restaurants."

Berkeley Square Café ☒   19 | 17 | 20 | £44 |
7 Davies St., W1 (Bond St.), 020-7629 6993; www.berkeleysquarecafe.com

▣ "Don't let the name fool you", this "delightful discovery" in "serene" bi-level Mayfair premises is a "high-end business lunch venue by day" and a "grown-up", "charmingly romantic restaurant by evening", with "attentive, but not overbearing service"; it's a "professional outfit", from Steven Black's "excellent" New French menu to the "stylishly comfortable" setting that feels like a "welcome oasis"; still, a few squawk it's "not cheap."

Bertorelli   16 | 15 | 16 | £30 |
11-13 Frith St., W1 (Leicester Sq./Tottenham Court Rd.), 020-7494 3491; fax 7439 9431 ◑
19-23 Charlotte St., W1 (Goodge St./Tottenham Court Rd.), 020-7636 4174; fax 7467 8902 ☒
44A Floral St., WC2 (Covent Garden), 020-7836 3969; fax 7836 1868 ◑☒
www.santeonline.co.uk

▣ Fans "count on this" "bright, lively" trio of Italian bistros in Soho, Covent Garden (recently revamped) and Fitzrovia (the original) for "robust", "reliable cooking" that's a "treat without being expensive"; some feel the chain "seems to have lost its way", citing "hit-or-miss" meals and "slow service", but most endorse it as a "useful" "standby for the theatre" or "after ballet", and "tourists love" that it was in the Gwyneth Paltrow movie *Sliding Doors*.

BIBENDUM ◑   23 | 23 | 21 | £54 |
Michelin House, 81 Fulham Rd., SW3 (South Kensington), 020-7581 5817; fax 7823 7925; www.bibendum.co.uk

■ "Decorated with vintage ads and stained-glass windows" featuring "Bib himself seated on a bicycle", this "classy" Brompton Cross stalwart in the "historic", "whimsical Michelin building" showcases Matthew Harris' "simply outstanding" New French cooking "supplemented" with an "awesome wine list" and "first-class service"; the "classic dishes are so "delicious" they "outshine almost all in Paris itself", prompting some patrons to "worry they'll look like" the "tubby" "tyre logo" man "when finished" and others to exclaim it's "highly recommended for a special occasion."

Bibendum Oyster Bar   23 | 21 | 20 | £34 |
Michelin House, 81 Fulham Rd., SW3 (South Kensington), 020-7589 1480; fax 7823 7925; www.bibendum.co.uk
■ "The care is there, just less of the price" applaud admirers of this Brompton Cross seafood bistro on the ground floor of the "beautiful art deco" Michelin House; this "very laid-back" "alternative to Bibendum" upstairs is a "terrific weekend lunch venue" with "nice service" and "after a long day of shopping, oysters", "excellent salads" and "well-executed" "light dishes with delicious champagnes and wines hit the spot"; P.S. "pick up fresh fish for dinner at the same time!"

Bierodrome   16 | 15 | 15 | £19 |
67 Kingsway, WC2 (Charing Cross/Holborn), 020-7242 7469; fax 7242 7493 ☒
44-48 Clapham High St., SW4 (Clapham North), 020-7720 1118; fax 7720 0288
173-174 Upper St., N1 (Highbury & Islington), 020-7226 5835; fax 7704 0632
www.belgo-restaurants.com
■ "As its name implies", this "*très* casual", Belgo-owned trio of "moules-frites hangouts" is "all about the beer", "Belgium brews to be precise"; sure, it's a "cheerful" "after-work watering hole" ("not the place for deep, meaningful conversation") but you also "can't go wrong with" the "hearty food" so at the very least, "order chips to get you through the night"; N.B. kids eat for free at weekends when accompanied by two adults.

Big Easy ◑   18 | 15 | 16 | £26 |
332-334 King's Rd., SW3 (Sloane Sq.), 020-7352 4071; fax 7352 0844; www.bigeasy.uk.com
■ "Louisiana it isn't, but you're not going to get any closer this side of the Atlantic" to an "Americana experience" declare loyalists who head to this "laid-back" King's Road place for "huge portions" of "good ol'" Southern-style "country eats"; it's an "ideal place" "for a quick dinner for two" or an "office party", so "get your hands dirty, put down some drinks", listen to the "loud, live music downstairs" and "have fun."

Bistrot 190 ◑   16 | 19 | 16 | £36 |
Gore Hotel, 190 Queen's Gate, SW7 (Gloucester Rd./ South Kensington), 020-7581 5666; fax 7589 8127; www.gorehotel.com
◪ Now under the ownership of South Kensington's Gore Hotel and boasting a light revamp, this "comfortable", bright

dining room that's "as cosy as home" offers a midpriced Modern European menu that's "ok", but "to be honest, nothing stands out", with some preferring the "nice bar" across the hall, with its "roaring fire and huge armchairs"; proximity to the Royal Albert Hall makes it handy for a pre- or post-performance meal.

Black & Blue

17 | 17 | 17 | £26

215-217 Kensington Church St., W8 (Notting Hill Gate), 020-7727 0004; fax 7229 9359
90-92 Wigmore St., W1 (Bond St.), 020-7486 1912; fax 7486-1913
105 Gloucester Rd., SW7 (Gloucester Rd.), 020-7244 7666; fax 7244 9993
205-207 Haverstock Hill, NW3 (Belsize Park), 020-7443 7744; fax 7443 7744

■ A "cheap, cheerful" "place for Atkins devotees to get their beef fix", this "friendly" quartet around town may "not have the most varied menu", but makes a "nice discovery" for "huge portions" of "delicious meat", including the "best burgers around"; the only "downside is that it's always so busy" and with no reservations taken there's often a "cumbersome wait for tables"; N.B. the Wigmore Street branch opened post-*Survey.*

Blah! Blah! Blah! 🗷⫫

21 | 15 | 21 | £21

78 Goldhawk Rd., W12 (Goldhawk Rd.), 020-8746 1337

■ "Not just for veggies", this "fab, funky" Shepherd's Bush candlelit venue with "smiley service" makes up for its "cellar"-like, "studenty decor" with "tasty", "genuinely different" vegetarian fare that even pleases "huge meat fans" and "proves you don't need frills to serve good food"; sure, "the cash-only policy is a pain", but the option to "BYO" ensures the bill will be "cheap."

Blakes ◐

20 | 25 | 21 | £67

Blakes Hotel, 33 Roland Gardens, SW7 (Gloucester Rd./ South Kensington), 020-7370 6701; fax 7373 0442; www.blakeshotels.com

◪ "Hidden in a nondescript street in South Ken", the "very au courant" dining room at Anouska Hempel's "romantic" hotel is somewhere discreet to "take your 'niece' to"; new chef Paul Day takes up where long-standing Neville Campbell left off, serving "downright delicious" Eclectic-International cooking that's "as upscale as fusion gets", and even if it can be "ridiculously overpriced", the "superb wine list" and "excellent service" compensate; P.S. they do a "good breakfast" too.

Blandford Street 🗷

18 | 15 | 16 | £39

5-7 Blandford St., W1 (Bond St.), 020-7486 9696; fax 7486 5067; www.blandford-street.co.uk

◪ "Friendly owner" Nick Lambert's "quiet, modern" eatery in Marylebone may have been better known when previously run by Stephen Bull, but it still enjoys a following who appreciate the "carefully put-together" Modern European menu with strong British accents and "nice service"; but bashers deride it as "nothing to write home about."

Bleeding Heart ⊠   23 | 19 | 20 | £41

19 Greville St., EC1 (Farringdon), 020-7404 0333;
fax 7831 1402
Bleeding Heart Yard, off Greville St., EC1 (Farringdon),
020-7242 8238; fax 7831 1402; www.bleedingheart.co.uk
■ The New French "cooking with no pretensions" "never lets you down" fawn fans of this Holborn "gem" "in a secluded courtyard"; the "fabulous wine list", "authentic" Gallic feel and "knowledgeable staff" are "all spot on", whether you "hide away" in the "charming" ground-floor bistro or head to the "more intimate downstairs" that's "ideal for business"; N.B. the nearby Tavern sibling in Bleeding Heart Yard serves spit-roasted Suffolk pork.

Bloom's   16 | 8 | 13 | £22

130 Golders Green Rd., NW11 (Golders Green), 020-8455 1338;
fax 8455 3033; www.bloomsrestaurant.co.uk
☑ Traditionalists craving "old-style, old-school" kosher fare, from "good salt beef" to "typical Eastern European Jewish food" get their "fix" at this "established" 40-year-old "institution" in Golders Green where "the same waiters have been there" for decades; still, "despite its local reputation", most maintain it "badly needs a transfusion of New York"–style pastrami, concurring "this is no Carnegie Deli."

Bluebird   16 | 19 | 14 | £39

350 King's Rd., SW3 (Sloane Sq.), 020-7559 1000; fax 7559 1111;
www.conran.com
☑ "Another temple for Conran Group fans", this "airy", "bustling" room overlooking King's Road draws flocks of fans with "friendly service" and "yummy" Modern European dishes including "seafood classics"; but a few fly at "arrogant" staff and a "lightweight" "formula", concluding it "needs a bit of oomph"; P.S. downstairs there's a food emporium (run by Sainsbury's) and an "excellent coffee shop" with outside seating.

BLUE ELEPHANT ◗   22 | 25 | 21 | £39

3-6 Fulham Broadway, SW6 (Fulham Broadway), 020-7385 6595;
fax 7386 7665; www.blueelephant.com
■ "London's answer to Las Vegas" is this "kitschy", "Eden-esque" "little piece of tropical Thailand in the middle of Fulham" dressed up "B-movie-style" to feel like "your own rainforest" with "lush" plants, fountains and a "bridge over a koi- and carp-filled pool"; the "food is exotic, delightful and beautifully presented" by "attentive" servers, making it "awe-inspiring" for a "romantic evening *à deux*" and a

"great place to impress" business clients; yes, it's "full of surprises – including the bill at the end."

Blue Print Cafe 18 | 20 | 19 | £38 |
Design Museum, Butlers Wharf, 28 Shad Thames, SE1 (London Bridge/Tower Hill), 020-7378 7031; fax 7357 8810; www.conran.com
☑ "Get a table by the window and relax as river life passes you by" at Conran Group's "fashionable, modern" spot attached to the "must-visit Design Museum" offering one of the "best views of Tower Bridge in town" with "good" Modern European cooking and "delicious wines" "to match"; still, many are "not impressed", finding the fare "a bit up and down", but even they admit "it's all worth it" if you score a seat over the Thames.

Bodeans 18 | 14 | 16 | £19 |
10 Poland St., W1 (Oxford Circus), 020-7287 7575; fax 7287 4342
169 Clapham High St., SW4 (Clapham Common), 020-7622 4248
www.bodeansbbq.com
☑ "For a proper stateside experience", "homesick expats" and "those craving Texas-style BBQ" head to this "meat lover's" basement "paradise" near Oxford Street where staff are "chirpy" and there's "American football on TV" – or to the "ground-floor deli, a favourite for a quick bite"; "we ate, ate and ate some more" sigh carnivores sated by portions "big enough to feed the hungriest of punters"; still, a few feel "the search for good 'cue in London continues"; N.B. a Clapham branch opened post-*Survey*.

Boisdale ⊠ 21 | 20 | 18 | £42 |
15 Eccleston St., SW1 (Victoria), 020-7730 6922; fax 7730 0548 ●
Swedeland Ct., 202 Bishopsgate, EC2 (Liverpool St.), 020-7283 1763
www.boisdale.co.uk
■ "If you want the full Scottish treatment this is your place" claim clan fans of Ronald McDonald's "eccentric" Victoria venue (and its younger Bishopsgate sibling); it "feels like a gentlemen's club" with an "extensive whisky and wine list", the "lingering smell of cigars", "tartan on acid decor", "good jazz" nights and "traditional" Hibernian-accented British cooking, including "fantastic game" and haggis; N.B. the City venue awaits a license to stage more regular music nights.

Bombay Bicycle Club ⊠ 22 | 15 | 16 | £27 |
95 Nightingale Ln., SW12 (Clapham South), 020-8673 6217; fax 8673 9100
■ "Fabulous", "authentic but expensive" Indian cooking "with a big dollop of class" is the draw for those who circle round to this "friendly" British colonial-style Clapham eatery that makes a "great local for a casual night out"; but even 'cycling' enthusiasts can't help but wonder "how can the

food be so good and the service" so "incredibly slow"?, prompting most to "cheat and go for the delivery service."

Bombay Brasserie ●   22 20 20 £37
Courtfield Rd., SW7 (Gloucester Rd.), 020-7370 4040;
fax 7835 1669; www.bombaybrasserielondon.com
◩ "It's hard to stay on top over the decades", but admirers of this "comfortable", "airy" South Kensington "institution" say it "remains a good night out" with a "strong menu" of "better-than-ever" Indian cooking and refurbished "quaint colonial" decor and conservatory that's a "throwback to the days of the Raj" ("feels like Churchill and Gandhi are sitting beside you"); still, critics carp that it's "relatively expensive" and find "service snooty."

Books for Cooks ⊠   24 15 15 £14
4 Blenheim Crescent, W11 (Ladbroke Grove/
Notting Hill Gate), 020-7221 1992; fax 7221 1517;
www.booksforcooks.com
■ There's "never a dearth of great reading material" at this "cook's haven" near Portobello Road where the open test kitchen serves an Eclectic menu of "gourmet bites that take a small bite out of the pocket" using "original, tasty" recipes derived from its bookshelves; for a "foodie" "treat", "browse through the latest Nigella tome", then have a "delicious lunch", but arrive early because this "teeny, tiny" spot gets "crowded"; N.B. prams are discouraged due to space constraints.

Boxwood Café   22 20 21 £50
Berkeley Hotel, Wilton Pl., SW1 (Knightsbridge), 020-7235 1010;
fax 7235 1011; www.gordonramsay.com
◩ "Gordon "Ramsay at his unpretentious best" is the take on this "hopping", "happening" yearling with a "chic, new look" that makes this former Vong tri-level space of Knightsbridge's Berkeley Hotel "feel as if it could be in *Sex and the City*"; "sublime" Eclectic dishes that "pack a punch", "unobtrusive service", a "dramatic" setting and a "smart crowd" add up to an "experience worth every pence" – "if this is a new trend, trend on!"; still, a few balk at the "basement gloom" and "variable service"; N.B. lighter fare is now available too.

Brackenbury, The   21 15 17 £34
129-131 Brackenbury Rd., W6 (Goldhawk Rd./Hammersmith),
020-8748 0107; fax 8741 0905
◩ "Small, cosy" and "child-friendly" with "easygoing staff", this "homely style" "neighbourhood place" in Hammersmith is still a "favourite" of many who maintain that the "well-presented", seasonally changing Modern British tucker is "cooked with a sure hand", offering "value for the money"; still, a disgruntled minority say it "needs an injection of creativity and energy" as it's "not as good as it used to be";

N.B. a change of ownership and post-*Survey* refurb may
impact the above scores.

Bradley's   22 | 15 | 19 | £39
*25 Winchester Rd., NW3 (Swiss Cottage), 020-7722 3457;
fax 7435 1392*
■ "A class haven for gastronomes" "without making the
trip to Central London", this "lively Swiss Cottage local"
is "worth taking the trouble to find" for a "really good
meal" of Modern British cooking; devotees delight in the
"delicious, unpretentious food at honest prices" paired
with an "unusual New World wine list", "friendly staff and
relaxing atmosphere", concluding it's an "excellent place"
"to eat and chat."

Brasserie Roux ◐   21 | 21 | 21 | £39
*Sofitel St. James London, 8 Pall Mall, SW1 (Piccadilly Circus),
020-7968 2900; fax 7747 2242; www.sofitel.com*
■ "Elegant" yet "relaxed", this immensely high-ceilinged
"top-rate" Sofitel St. James' hotel dining room in a former
banking hall boasts celebrated chef Albert Roux's name on
the door and some of his "innovative" signature dishes
on the "reasonably priced" French brasserie menu; "with
tables spaced to allow conversation" and "old-school
service without the stuffiness", this "perfect dinner venue"
makes a "welcome addition" to the area, especially for
"pre-theatre at the Haymarket" (with a £15 prix fixe menu).

Brasserie St. Quentin   20 | 18 | 18 | £36
*243 Brompton Rd., SW3 (Knightsbridge/South Kensington),
020-7589 8005; fax 7584 6064;
www.brasseriestquentin.co.uk*
■ "The genuine brasserie article", this quarter-century-old
"bustling" "perennial" with "tight, well-run service" is now
back in the hands of former owner Hugh O'Neill; the "quaint"
Knightsbridge premises offer "a bit of France within walking
distance of Harrods" and a "side-order of people-watching"
whilst the "incredibly durable" Gallic menu boasts "a
couple of stunning surprises", prompting *amis* to conclude
it's "fun" "for hanging out and acting Continental."

Brian Turner Mayfair   22 | 18 | 20 | £55
*Millennium Mayfair Hotel, 44 Grosvenor Sq., W1
(Bond St.), 020-7596 3444; fax 7596 3433;
www.millenniumhotels.com*
■ "By gum, it's champion!" applaud those pleased that
Yorkshire's "great chef", Brian Turner, is "back in action"
(after closing Turners a few years ago) and off to a "really
promising" start at this "minimalist" Millennium Mayfair
dining room specialising in "delish" British dishes; "absolute
enjoyment" echo enthusiasts taken by the "professional
service" and "well-priced" menu that's "more casual than
many fancy hotel restaurants."

Brinkley's
17 | 15 | 15 | £30

*47 Hollywood Rd., SW10 (Earl's Court), 020-7351 1683;
fax 7376 5083*

■ The Modern British "menu might not be cutting edge,
but the cooking is very reliable" reveal regulars of this
"favourite neighbourhood standby" in Chelsea; it's a "solid
place" "to meet friends and have a laugh", and thanks
to the covered rear conservatory it's especially "great
during summer nights"; "don't forget to wander around the
adjoining wine shop – the corkage allows you to go to town
on something special" to share with your table.

Browns
15 | 15 | 15 | £26

*47 Maddox St., W1 (Bond St./Oxford Circus), 020-7491 4565;
fax 7497 4564* ⓢ
*82-84 St. Martin's Ln., WC2 (Leicester Sq.), 020-7497 5050;
fax 7497 5005*
*Shad Thames, SE1 (London Bridge), 020-7378 1700;
fax 020- 7407 0929*
9 Islington Green, N1 (Angel), 020-7226 2555; fax 7359 7306
*Hertsmere Rd., E14 (Canary Wharf/West India Quay),
020-7987 9777; fax 7537 1341*
8 Old Jewry, EC2 (Bank), 020-7606 6677; fax 7600 5359 ⓢ
www.browns-restaurants.com

◪ "Still as popular as ever", this "jolly", "lively but low-
decibel" UK chain with "cheery service" offers "British
comfort at comfortable prices", including "basic yummy
mains", making it "swell for families with young kids" and
a "good bet" for a "quick biz lunch" or "mum's day out"; to
some, it's a little "middle-of-the-road" with a "dated menu",
but then again, "the nice thing" about the place is that
"not much changes."

Brunello
– | – | – | VE

*Baglioni, 60 Hyde Park Gate, SW7 (Gloucester Rd./
High St. Kensington), 020-7368 5900 ;
www.baglionihotellondon.com*

Situated opposite Kensington Palace, on the ground floor of
the opulent new Baglioni hotel, part of the top-end European
chain, this chic dining room, hung with a chandelier,
bathed in natural light and clad in padded leather, is the
setting for chef Stefano Stecca's (ex Green Olive) intricate,
expensive Modern Italian–Eclectic menu, complemented
by a similarly pricey wine list; for a cheaper approach, order
aperitivo (light snacks) around the elegant bar.

Builders Arms
18 | 19 | 14 | £23

*13 Britten St., SW3 (Sloane Sq./South Kensington),
020-7349 9040; fax 7351 3181; www.geronimo-inns.co.uk*

■ Whether hosting a "big post-party nosh-up", "having
brunch over the Sunday paper" or "chilling with a couple of
beers", this "popular" gastro-pub (with "quieter" seating at
the rear) is "cosy anytime"; the Modern British food offers

"good value" and the photos and "fireplace add to the charm"; yes, "smoke is an issue" and so are "noisy crowds", still for most it's a "great neighbourhood venue."

Buona Sera ❶   17 | 17 | 16 | £22
22-26 Northcote Rd., SW11 (Clapham Junction B.R.), 020-7924 1666; fax 7228 1114
289A King's Rd., SW3 (Sloane Sq.), 020-7352 8827; fax 7352 8827
◪ "Good, no-nonsense Italian food" at "reasonable prices" delivered by "cute", "speed-is-of-the-essence" staff adds up to a *buona* "night out with friends" – "hence the buzz" at this "loud" South London duo; "book well ahead" at the "busy-all-week" Battersea branch, and ladies, if "you're climbing up the stairs to a booth with a date" at the "fun" Chelsea branch with "double-decker seating" (it "gives dining a unique slant"), be advised that the ascent and seating is "heels- and skirt-unfriendly."

BUSABA EATHAI   22 | 19 | 15 | £19
106-110 Wardour St., W1 (Piccadilly Circus/Tottenham Court Rd.), 020-7255 8686; fax 7255 8688
22 Store St., WC1 (Goodge St.), 020-7299 7900; fax 7299 7909
◼ With its "finger on the pulse", these "ultra-cool, ultra-chill" "winners" in Soho and Bloomsbury (the newer branch on Store Street) "set the benchmark for casual Thai dining" "on the hop" with "inventive, subtle" cooking at "affordable" prices, served to communal tables where "your elbows end up in a stranger's dish when it's busy"; there are no bookings so "be prepared to queue", "which isn't so bad because it's a chance to watch the hipsters pass by"; P.S. "let's hope they don't wake up and double the prices."

Busabong, The ❶   ▽ 22 | 17 | 23 | £28
1A Langton St., SW10 (Fulham Broadway/Sloane Sq.), 020-7352 7414; fax 7352 7534; www.busabong.co.uk
◼ "Zillions of choices of reliable, authentic Thai fare" to "suit all tastes" and "extremely welcoming service" make this unassuming World's End townhouse especially "good for family gatherings"; "if you go to the top floor" you'll find an "intimate dining area" where "you can kick off your shoes", settle into a cushion seat and "dine on the floor"; P.S. it's also "excellent for takeaways."

Bush Bar & Grill ❶   16 | 19 | 13 | £29
45A Goldhawk Rd., W12 (Goldhawk Rd./Shepherd's Bush), 020-8746 2111; fax 8746 7114; www.bushbar.co.uk
◼ "Two words: great food" – plus a "good buzz" – make this "super-trendy", "stylish oasis" with Modern British fare and an "airy feel" a "genuinely surprising find in Shepherd's Bush"; whilst it's a tad "too cavernous to be fully relaxed" for a few, a £15 pre-theatre set menu offering three courses, an "excellent happy hour" and "inevitably hip service" more than compensate.

Butlers Wharf Chop House   19 | 19 | 18 | £38

Butlers Wharf, 36E Shad Thames, SE1 (London Bridge/
Tower Hill), 020-7403 3403; fax 7403 3414; www.conran.co.uk

☑ "Chop, chop!" cheer customers who converge on this
"relaxed" riversider, part of "Conran's Tower Bridge
empire", for "meat, an obvious choice", and "hearty",
Traditional British fare; you "can't beat an outside table in
the sun", particularly for a "summer's Thameside lunch",
plus "service is faultless" and the "view never fails to
impress"; if a few consider it "overpriced", there's always
the "tasty" snack menu in the bar that's "one of the best
bargains in town."

Cactus Blue ◑   13 | 16 | 13 | £29

86 Fulham Rd., SW3 (South Kensington), 020-7823 7858;
fax 7823 8577

☑ "Go for the charming bar, exotic cocktails" and "fun
atmosphere" at this "loud, trendy" Chelsea cantina – that's
"what this pickup joint is all about" confide insiders; sure,
the "adequate" South American–Pacific Rim fare "fills the
cuisine void in London", but it's the "cool ambience" and
"great live music certain nights" (Thursday–Saturday) that
ensure this place gets "very crowded."

Cafe at Sotheby's ⊠   18 | 16 | 16 | £28

Sotheby's Auction House, 34 New Bond St., W1 (Bond St./
Oxford Circus), 020-7293 5077

■ It's "always a pleasure" to "mingle with the art crowd",
"high bidders" and "LWL's (ladies who lunch)" over
"interesting" Modern British fare at this "tiny" weekday-
only spot with its "nice surroundings" within the famous
Mayfair auctioneers; it has a "resounding enjoyability
about it", making it "good for a quick bite" (including
"the best lobster sandwich in town") or a "convenient"
"getaway" for afternoon tea, hence it's "always booked";
N.B. no dinner served.

Café Boheme ◑   17 | 18 | 17 | £26

13-17 Old Compton St., W1 (Leicester Sq./Tottenham Court Rd.),
020-7734 0623; fax 7434 3775; www.cafeboheme.co.uk

☑ With its "mixture of hip and old-world" ambience
bolstered by "big comfy sofas" and "great live music", this
"fun", "lively" French bistro in Soho is "a great fallback"
that's still "fun after all these years"; the "reasonably
priced" "main courses are always tasty" and "friendly"
servers "let you sit there for hours" watching the "nice eye
candy"; still, a few suggest "go more for a drink than food."

Café des Amis ◑⊠   17 | 16 | 15 | £31

11-14 Hanover Pl., WC2 (Covent Garden), 020-7379 3444;
fax 7379 9124; www.cafedesamis.co.uk

■ "One is truly among friends" at this "Covent Garden
niche", a "pleasant" place "tucked away" down a side

street serving "dependably good" New French fare; the recently refurbished "decor is richly minimal with a strong punch of warm colour", making it a "pleasure to be there" for a "reasonable" prix fixe pre- or post-theatre dinner, plus there's a "fun, lively" wine bar downstairs boasting a "wonderful selection"; one caveat: "service is sometimes more casual than you would like."

Cafe Fish 19 14 16 £28
36-40 Rupert St., W1 (Piccadilly Circus), 020-7287 8989; fax 7287 8400; www.santeonline.co.uk
☑ Catch "very fresh" "fish with just enough flair" at this "relaxed", "lively" Soho spot; "simple preparation" and "efficient service" make it "useful for pre-theatre" so "take advantage of the £10 set menu" and remember, there's even a "pianist at times" (Sunday–Wednesday); still, the "basic decor" reminiscent of an "East End pie and mash shop" can "be off-putting", hence for some it's "not a place to linger for an evening."

Cafe Japan 22 8 19 £24
626 Finchley Rd., NW11 (Golders Green), 020-8455 6854; fax 8455 6854
■ "A must for every sushi lover", this "hole-in-the-wall, homely Japanese" in Golders Green serves "generous portions" that earns high praise: it "doesn't get fresher and more authentic"; there's disappointment "they have disposed of the hot food menu", but when it comes to "raw fish", many feel it's "worth the trek"; N.B. only open for dinner Wednesday–Sunday and weekend lunch.

Cafe Lazeez 19 15 17 £26
21 Dean St., W1 (Leicester Sq.), 020-7434 9393; fax 7434 0022 ● 🖂
93-95 Old Brompton Rd., SW7 (Gloucester Rd./ South Kensington), 020-7581 9993; fax 7581 8200 ●
88 St. John St., EC1 (Farringdon), 020-7253 2224; fax 7253 2112 🖂
☑ "Extremely good modern Indian" dishes offering a "combi of tastes" are "beautifully presented" at this "friendly", "unassuming" trio in Soho, South Ken and Clerkenwell; whilst some say staff are "equally attentive to customers' needs and requests, making it" an option for "couples who want some privacy", a few find that "service can border on diffident on occasion."

Cafe Med 16 16 15 £27
184A Kensington Park Rd., W11 (Ladbroke Grove/ Notting Hill Gate), 020-7221 1150; fax 7229 5647
320 Goldhawk Rd., W6 (Stamford Brook), 020-8741 1994; fax 8741 9980
22-25 Dean St., W1 (Tottenham Court Rd.), 020-7287 9007; fax 7287 3529 ● 🖂

(continued)

(continued)
Cafe Med

21 Loudoun Rd., NW8 (St. John's Wood), 020-7625 1222; fax 7328 1593 ●

370 St. John St., EC1 (Angel), 020-7278 1199; fax 7833 9046
■ "Intimate yet friendly", this "fun", "loungey" "crowd-pleaser" about town makes a "good, dependable fallback" for a "casual meal" of "interesting" Med-Eclectic fare, especially "when you can sit outside on the large terrace" or sidewalk; it's "good for groups or girls chatting" and "very child friendly – a find in London" – plus you always get a "nice" "welcome"; if a few find the "food uninspiring", they're drowned out by loyalists who retort "what more do you want?"

Cafe Pacifico ● 16 14 14 £23
5 Langley St., WC2 (Covent Garden), 020-7379 7728; fax 7836 5088; www.cafepacifico-laperla.com
■ "Don't go with your wife, go to flirt" jest frequenters of this "noisy, lively" "little hideaway" in Convent Garden, offering "a taste of Mexico" along with "fab" cocktails; the vibe is "chaotic, yet service is relaxed", and what's more, "you won't leave hungry"; but others come to this "fun" cantina "only for the party atmosphere and margaritas – declaring "too bad" the "so-so food" "isn't authentic."

Cafe Rouge 13 12 13 £22
31 Kensington Park Rd., W11 (Ladbroke Grove), 020-7221 4449; fax 7792 3064
98-100 Shepherd's Bush Rd., W6 (Shepherd's Bush), 020-7602 7732; fax 7603 7710
227 Chiswick High Rd., W4 (Chiswick Park), 020-8742 7447; fax 8742 7557
15 Frith St., W1 (Tottenham Court Rd.), 020-7437 4307; fax 7437 4442
34 Wellington St., WC2 (Covent Garden), 020-7836 0998; fax 7497 0738
39 Park Gate Rd., SW11 (Clapham Junction/Sloane Sq.), 020-7924 3565; fax 7924 3773
40 Abbeville Rd., SW4 (Clapham South), 020-8673 3399; fax 8673 2299
27-31 Basil St., SW3 (Knightsbridge), 020-7584 2345; fax 7584 4253
120 St. John's Wood High St., NW8 (St. John's Wood), 020-7722 8366; fax 7483 1015
10 Cabot Sq., 29-35 Mackenzie Walk, E14 (Canary Wharf), 020-7537 9696; fax 7987 1232 ☒
www.caferouge.co.uk
Additional locations throughout London
◪ "Just the thing for a nice meal before theatre and just after" or a "quickie" "lunch stop", this "friendly", "reliable" French bistro outfit "that doesn't feel like a chain" has a "big menu" that includes "all the classic comfort foods" –

but "don't expect haute cuisine at these prices"; still, it's a "highly variable experience" for others who find it a "bit samey" and a "bit tired."

CAFE SPICE NAMASTE ☒   25 | 18 | 21 | £31 |
16 Prescot St., E1 (Aldgate/Tower Hill), 020-7488 9242; fax 7488 9339; www.cafespice.co.uk
■ "If you're an Indian food fanatic", Cyrus Todiwala's "inventive, upscale cuisine" served in this "lively", "charming" "edge-of-town location" near Tower Bridge "is what you travel to London for"; the "very different menu offering new choices with old favourites" including a "nice assortment of beverages and surprisingly diverting desserts" is so "out of this world" it "sparks many return trips" – in fact, most "can't wait to go back."

Cambio de Tercio ●   23 | 17 | 22 | £37 |
163 Old Brompton Rd., SW5 (Gloucester Rd./South Kensington), 020-7244 8970; fax 7373 8817
■ "Olé!" – it's "like going to Spain, but quicker than EasyJet" concur compadres of this "casual" South Kensington eatery; the "excellent" "cuisine as good as you can find in Madrid" and "brilliant wine list" ensure it's "always enjoyable", plus the "helpful", "friendly service brings us back again and again"; P.S. the tapas bar across the street under the same ownership is a "favourite."

Camden Brasserie   ▽ 19 | 11 | 18 | £28 |
9-11 Jamestown Rd., NW1 (Camden Town/Chalk Farm), 020-7482 2114; fax 7482 2777
◪ The move 100 metres down the road "has not affected quality or service" at this "welcoming" Med brasserie (over 20 years old), a "fine place in Camden to while away a few hours"; whilst a few suggest the latest space is "lacking that extra special something" and is "not atmospheric", amends are made with the "well-prepared" dishes "served with charm"; P.S. it's a "kids' favourite."

Cantaloupe ●   17 | 13 | 13 | £25 |
35-42 Charlotte Rd., EC2 (Old St.), 020-7729 5566; fax 7613 4111; www.cantaloupe.co.uk
■ "Housed in a cavernous warehouse" and offering "imaginative", "tasty and down-to-earth Mediterranean dishes" "at reasonable prices", this "chilled out" restaurant/bar "can still hold it's own in Shoreditch"; the "very, very busy", "lively atmosphere" and "accommodating service" make it a "fun place to have lunch" and "good for Friday and Saturdays", especially for a "boozy night out."

Cantina del Ponte   13 | 15 | 13 | £32 |
Butlers Wharf Bldg., 36C Shad Thames, SE1 (London Bridge/Tower Hill), 020-7403 5403; fax 7403 4432; www.conran.com
■ "On a good day or night, you cannot ask for better than a table outside or by the window" at this Conran Group

Italian in Butler's Wharf, a "cheap alternative to grander
cousins along the riverbank" offering an "early dinner
special" for £11 and "fantastic views of Tower Bridge"; still,
foes deem the fare "standard" and profess "poor service
prevents the cantina experience from being enjoyable."

Cantina Vinopolis   16   18   17   £35

*Vinopolis Museum, 1 Bank End, SE1 (London Bridge),
020-7940 8333; fax 7940 8334; www.vinopolis.co.uk*

◪ "You need food after a tour" of the Vinopolis Museum
of Wine under the South Bank's railway arches, and this
huge, brick-walled "special treat–type place" next door
with high ceilings and an open kitchen is the answer, with
an "affordable" wine list ("many by the glass") and a
Mediterranean-Eclectic menu offering "interesting fare";
if a few whine it's a "bit inconsistent" and "expensive",
most tout it as a "pleasant surprise."

Canyon   18   23   17   £37

*Tow Path, Riverside, near Richmond Bridge, Richmond
(Richmond), 020-8948 2944; fax 8948 2945;
www.canyonfood.co.uk*

◪ "Not to be missed on a summer's day" so "book a table
outside" at this "riverside gem" near Richmond Bridge for
a "superb brunch" or "any meal of the day"; it's a "fab place
to meet friends", "enjoy" a "romantic" evening or just
"people-watch", so "relax" and peruse the "hip menu" of
Eclectic-American options and "interesting wine list";
whilst a few feel the "food does not live up to the setting"
even they admit the "location is unbeatable."

CAPITAL RESTAURANT, THE   27   22   26   £65

*The Capital Hotel, 22-24 Basil St., SW3 (Knightsbridge),
020-7589 5171; fax 7225 0011; www.capitalhotel.co.uk*

■ "Très cher, très chic, très jolie" gush admirers of this
"gourmand's paradise" in the "posh" Capital Hotel where
"everything is as smooth as silk", from chef Eric Chavot's
"spectacular", "tantalising" New French cooking that
"remains a beacon of innovation" to the "intimate hush-
hush dining room" decorated like an "elegant music box"
to "impeccable service" that "fulfills every need"; if a
few feel the setting is "dowdy", a post-*Survey* refurbishment
that strives to create a 1940s Parisian feel may alter that
point of view.

Caraffini ●🗵   21   16   21   £36

*61-63 Lower Sloane St., SW1 (Sloane Sq.), 020-7259 0235;
fax 7259 0236; www.caraffini.co.uk*

■ There's a "large feel-good factor" at work at this "always
lively", "unpretentious" Chelsea trattoria offering "reliable
Italian fare from a menu that goes way beyond the usual",
along with a "limited wine list" and a "warm welcome" from
the "doting owners" and "helpful staff"; it's a "real treat"

that leaves you "satisfied", indeed, "every neighbourhood should have a cheery Caraffini."

Caravaggio ☒   17 | 16 | 16 | £43 |
107-112 Leadenhall St., EC3 (Bank/Monument), 020-7626 6206; fax 7626 8108; www.etruscagroup.co.uk
◪ A "City hangout" for "pin-striped clientele", this "expense-account Italian" is "cracking for a long business lunch" and "always reliable for dinner"; loyalists bank on the "classy atmosphere", "solid" cooking and "friendly" staff, suggesting "sit upstairs" to take in the recently extended gallery; it's a less-perfect picture for a few who find it "overpriced" with "patchy service", concluding "it seems less in favour" now.

CARLUCCIO'S CAFFE   18 | 14 | 14 | £21 |
5-6 The Green, W5 (Ealing Broadway), 020-8566 4458; fax 8840 8566
St. Christopher's Pl., W1 (Bond St.), 020-7935 5927
Fenwick, New Bond St., W1 (Bond St.), 020-7629 0699; fax 7493 0069 ☒
8 Market Pl., W1 (Oxford Circus), 020-7636 2228; fax 7636 9650
3-5 Barrett St., W1 (Bond St.), 020-7935 5927; fax 7487 5436
The Brewhouse, Putney Wharf, SW15 (Putney Bridge), 020-8789 0591; fax 020-8789-8360
236 Fulham Rd., SW10 (Fulham Rd.), 020-7376-5960; fax 020-7376-3698
2 Nash Ct., E14 (Canary Wharf), 020-7719 1749; fax 7513 1197
12 West Smithfield, EC1 (Farringdon), 020-7329 5904; fax 7248 5981
305-307 Upper St. , N1 (Angel/Highbury & Islington), 020-7359-8167; fax 020-7354-9196
www.carluccios.com
◪ "*Fantastico*", "hearty" dishes "with loads of authenticity" that "speak Italian on the plate" attract supporters to celebrity chef Antonio Carluccio's chain of "bright", "packed" all-day cafes–cum–food shops where "service remains surprisingly caring"; if a few grumble it "rarely disappoints, rarely dazzles", most concede it's a "good-value alternative", especially for "fueling up whilst shopping in Central London"; N.B. the branch in The Brewhouse at Putney Wharf opened post-*Survey*.

Carpaccio ◖☒   24 | 19 | 19 | £42 |
4 Sydney St., SW3 (South Kensington), 020-7352 3433
◪ From the owners of Como Lario and Ziani comes this "irresistible", "buzzing" Modern Italian on a busy South Ken corner; the "excellent, upscale menu" and "smiling staff" working between "crowded, noisy tables" make it "nice for lunch" or a "fun time with friends"; but it wears a bit thin for a few who find it "expensive for the quantity"; N.B. plans were underway at press time to add a private room with a fireplace, fountain and bar.

Casale Franco ◑
▽ 17 | 16 | 12 | £29

134-137 Upper St., N1 (Angel/Highbury & Islington), 020-7226 8994; fax 7359 1114

◪ Despite an "uninviting entrance" down an Islington alley, "once inside this charming", theatrical spot owned by Franco Pensa, a "fun night is guaranteed", with "real Italian food", homemade pizza and "wonderful service" (but, alas, a few fume that "you are sometimes ignored if you aren't a regular"); N.B. there's courtyard dining in warm weather.

Cecconi's
21 | 20 | 20 | £56

5A Burlington Gardens, W1 (Green Park/Piccadilly Circus), 020-7434 1500; fax 7494 2440; www.cecconis.co.uk

◪ "Discreet enough" for a "business or pleasure lunchtime rendezvous" "but definitely fun for a date", this "stylish venue", now under Soho House's management, boasts "delicious" Italian dishes "with a sophisticated twist", a "wonderful wine list", "attentive service" and a "grown-up feel post-refurb"; "great cocktails" shaken and stirred at "one of the nicest bars in Mayfair" seal the deal: it may be "pricey, but it's worth it for a treat."

Cellar Gascon ◑⊠
21 | 20 | 19 | £30

59 West Smithfield, EC1 (Barbican/Farringdon), 020-7796 0600; fax 7796 0601

■ "A yummy and relatively inexpensive way to sample the delights" of Southwestern France declare Cellar dwellers who "just turn up" for "nibbles" from the "very tapas"-style New French menu at this "cosy", "informal" Smithfield wine bar, a sibling of Club Gascon next door; "its small size means it fills up fast but if you secure a seat", you're sure to find "knowledgeable bar staff" who "dispense wine advice and bonhomie in equal measure"; P.S. it's "perfect for pre-Barbican."

Chamberlain's ⊠
– | – | – | E

23-25 Leadenhall Mkt., EC3 (Bank/Monument), 020-7648 8690; www.chamberlains.org

Ah, "finally, a good restaurant in the City" sigh some about this "bustling", bright seafooder with a "wonderful setting" and "good service" in a three-level Victorian building in Leadenhall Market; it's "nice" "for those with a penchant for watching the world from the comfort of [alfresco] tables" in the summer; still, some say it's "expensive" and find "there aren't enough choices."

Champor-Champor ⊠
25 | 21 | 23 | £33

62-64 Weston St., SE1 (London Bridge), 020-7403 4600; www.champor-champor.com

■ "How can something so exotic flourish" in such a "dining desert" near London Bridge muse lovers of this "jewel" offering a "characterful experience", from "beautifully served", seasonally changing Malaysian-Asian dishes "bursting with flavour" to "cosy, quirky" surroundings decorated with tribal artefacts and "now larger than before"; it was once a "well-kept secret" but "word seems to be out and tables are hard to secure" so "reservations are a must."

Chelsea Bun   19 | 11 | 16 | £14
70 Battersea Bridge Rd., SW11 (Sloane Sq.), 020-7738 9009
Limerstone St., SW10 (Sloane Sq.), 020-7352 3635;
fax 7731 4821
■ "Leave your fancy dress at home" and "go hungry" advise bun-sters who insist these "cheap 'n' cheerful cafes" in Chelsea and Battersea are the "ultimate places to satisfy your brunch cravings"; the "vast menu" "combines greasy spoon American breakfast" dishes in "hearty" "portions that builders will like", whilst providing the "perfect solution for hangovers" "the morning after."

Cheyne Walk Brasserie ●   ▽ 24 | 20 | 21 | £40
50 Cheyne Walk, SW3 (Sloane Sq./South Kensington),
020-7376 8787; fax 7376 5878
■ Occupying the former La Chaumiere space, this "damned good" French bistro, still owned by local property developer Robert Bourne, is "not only about fine food – it's a feel-good place" applaud acolytes who've walked this way; "it feels hip – both old and new simultaneously" – having retained the open fire grills in the centre of the room whilst introducing a "refreshingly simple" Gallic menu; P.S. the "groovy" salon/lounge upstairs, looking out to the river, is "great for a casual party."

CHEZ BRUCE   27 | 20 | 23 | £50
2 Bellevue Rd., SW17 (Balham/Wandsworth Common B. R.),
020-8672 0114; fax 8767 6648
■ "A treat" with "everlasting appeal" that "never fails to impress and delight", gush lovers of chef-owner Bruce Poole's "cosy, intimate", no-smoking "gem hidden" by Wandsworth Park; the "sophisticated" Modern British cooking "continues to be excellent and imaginative", "the setting is smart" (the "understated elegance shines through") and "staff are helpful" – yes, this "outstanding experience" "lives up to the hype."

Chez Gérard   16 | 15 | 15 | £30
1 Watling St., EC1 (Mansion House/St. Paul's), 020-7213 0540 ⊠
8 Charlotte St., W1 (Goodge St./Tottenham Court Rd.),
020-7636 4975; fax 7637 4564 ●
31 Dover St., W1 (Green Park), 020-7499 8171;
fax 7491 3818 ●
Opera Terrace, The Market, 1st fl., 45 E. Terrace, WC2
(Covent Garden), 020-7379 0666; fax 7497 9060 ●
(continued)

(continued)
Chez Gérard

119 Chancery Ln., WC2 (Chancery Ln.), 020-7405 0290;
fax 7242 2649 ⌧
9 Belvedere Rd., SE1 (Waterloo), 020-7202 8470;
fax 7202 8474
14 Trinity Sq., EC3 (Tower Hill), 020-7480 5500; fax 7480 5588 ⌧
64 Bishopsgate, EC2 (Bank/Liverpool St.), 020-7588 1200;
fax 7588 1122 ⌧
www.santeonline.co.uk

☑ "In a city where good steak is rare, as in hard to find", this "above-average" French chain is "still a regular pleaser", with "consistently satisfying" bistro cooking and a "lively (but not too lively) atmosphere"; it "works in a pinch" as a "pre-opera rendezvous spot", a "stolid luncher" and "for an after-work date"; still, cynics say it "underwhelms at every opportunity", dismissing it as "formulaic slap dash."

Chiang Mai   21 12 17 £23

48 Frith St., W1 (Leicester Sq./Tottenham Court Rd.), 020-7437 7444;
fax 7287 2255

☑ "Yum!" – an "enjoyable" "Thai eatery that's light on the wallet" chime Chiang-ians who claim this "super-friendly family-run place in" Soho is "the place to go" when craving "tasty" dishes, "plus some lesser-known specialities"; a pre-*Survey* redo of the "remarkable setting" seems to have gone unnoticed by many who still say the "decor and ambience leave you wanting."

CHINTAMANI ●⌧   21 26 20 £43

122 Jermyn St., SW1 (Piccadilly Circus), 020-7839 2020;
fax 7839 7700; www.chintamanilondon.co.uk

■ "The place has good vibes" agree admirers hooked on the "intriguing Turkish food" and "fabulous", "funky" contemporary Ottoman setting, "amazing" right down to sultan-style details like dramatic curtains and spice-coloured cushions; "it's a bit pricey, but worth it for the nouveau mezze" and other specialities – including wines – rarely "found outside Turkey"; P.S. a DJ keeps the "very nice atmosphere" spinning at weekends.

Chor Bizarre ●   22 22 20 £32

16 Albemarle St., W1 (Green Park), 020-7629 9802; fax 7493 7756;
www.chorbizarre.com

☑ "Dining here is no chore" agree acolytes of this "atmospheric" venue in Mayfair with a "quirky" marketlike decor that "transports you far away from London", plus "scrumptious" "nontraditional fare" paired with "fabulous wine suggestions"; if a few find it "nothing special" they're overruled by many who deem it "charming"; P.S. Chai Bazaar in the basement is "great" for high tea with an £8.50 set price menu offering 30 varieties.

Chowki Bar & Restaurant ◗   20   15   18   £22
2-3 Denman St., W1 (Piccadilly Circus), 020-7439 1330;
fax 7287 5919; www.chowki.com
■ "It's fun to taste dishes from the various Indian regions",
plus the "rotating menu" "keeps selections interesting"
at Kuldeep Singh's "hip" bi-level Mela sibling, "a great
place" "for a cheap bite" in Piccadilly; the "modern decor
is refreshing" and the "innovative" fare is "elegantly
presented"; if a few find "service could be faster" most
retort they "go the extra mile to make guests feel welcome."

Christopher's Covent Garden   19   15   17   £40
18 Wellington St., WC2 (Covent Garden), 020-7240 4222;
fax 7240 3357; www.christophersgrill.com
◪ "Light, airy, sophisticated" and "ridiculously high
ceilinged", thanks to its historic setting in a Grade II listed
Victorian building near Covent Garden, Christopher Gilmore's
first-floor eatery is a "first-class choice for business", with
a "simple" menu of Contemporary American "surf 'n'
turf" "comfort food"; whilst a few feel "service can be
iffy", punters counter "dining before the theatre is quick";
P.S. there's a "great" ground-floor bar serving snacks.

Chuen Cheng Ku ◗   18   11   14   £19
17 Wardour St., W1 (Leicester Sq./Piccadilly Circus),
020-7437 1398; fax 7434 0533
■ The "parade" of "passing trolleys captures the feeling of
Hong Kong" at this "dim sum heaven" in Chinatown where
the "minimal" "decor is best forgotten" in favour of "fast
and furious" dining on multiregional Chinese fare that
wagon welcomers consider "one of the few bargains"
around; the "place is popular with tourists, families and
locals", so roll in "early on weekends – it's crowded!"

Churchill Arms   23   16   14   £13
119 Kensington Church St., W8 (High St. Kensington/
Notting Hill Gate), 020-7727 4242
■ "Famous in the area, and deserves to be so", this "cosy
conservatory" that's "somewhat incongruously" at the
"back of a busy pub" in Kensington serves "amazing",
"authentic" Thai food for, well, "the price of a pint" – and
there's "no skimping on the portions either"; if the "wait for
a table", "quirky decor" and "slow service" lack appeal,
"don't forget the takeaway option."

Chutney Mary ◗   24   22   21   £42
535 King's Rd., SW10 (Fulham Broadway), 020-7351 3113;
fax 7351 7694; www.realindianfood.com
■ "Still evolving after all these years" (15 to be precise), the
"refurbished 'Mary'" is the "king of King's Road" boasting
"inviting decor", "accommodating service" and "sublime
Indian" cooking with a "different zest" that reveals some
"flavours that exist nowhere else in the West"; "get a table

in the conservatory" as the "gentle, refined" setting is "perfect" for a "dream date complete with chutney."

Chutney's ❶   ∇ 22 | 13 | 16 | £16
124 Drummond St., NW1 (Euston Sq.), 020-7388 0604; fax 7209 0627
■ Insiders sweet on this low-key vegetarian in Euston just overlook the "bad-throwback-to-the-'80s decor" because the "great service" and "innovative", "regularly changing" Indian cooking "reflecting available fresh" produce compensate; special praise goes to the "seriously good value" £5.95 lunch buffet – "the only better bargain in London is a one-day bus pass!"

Cicada   22 | 16 | 16 | £28
132-136 St. John St., EC1 (Farringdon), 020-7608 1550; fax 7608 1551; www.cicada.nu
◪ "More down to earth than [older sibling] e&o", this Clerkenwell haunt with an opium-den-style setting attracts an "oh-so-cool media crowd" with "flavoursome" Pan-Asian cooking, "perfectly crafted" drinks and a "buzzing" atmosphere; "it's hard to find an alternative that offers such a reliable evening", especially for "an easy eclectic dinner" or on a "summer night"; if a few feel it's "disappointing", most insist it's "always satisfying."

Cigala   21 | 13 | 16 | £32
54 Lamb's Conduit St., WC1 (Holborn/Russell Sq.), 020-7405 1717; fax 7242 9949; www.cigala.co.uk
◪ "Modest", "authentic Spanish home cooking and a superb wine list" "arranged by grape varieties" add up to "a distinctive culinary experience" at chef-patron Jake Hodges' premises with "sparse decor" and popular pavement dining; still, cynics snipe "you might expect more in Bloomsbury", deeming it "uncomfortable."

Cinnamon Club ⊠   22 | 23 | 19 | £46
The Old Westminster Library, Great Smith St., SW1 (St. James's Park/Westminster), 020-7222 2555; fax 7222 1333; www.cinnamonclub.com
■ "The spice is right" – this is "what high-end Indian food is all about" gush fans of the "clever" cuisine at this "stylish" two-level setting in the Old Westminster Library "with important people throughout the dining room" (it is near Parliament, after all); "worth every penny", the "winning formula" extends to the private "Bollywood-style downstairs bar that's the height of ultrachic"; but others say it's "fine – if someone else is footing the bill"

Cipriani   – | – | – | VE
25 Davies St., W1 (Bond St.), 020-7399 0500; fax 7399 0501; www.cipriani.com
This world-famous restaurant, with outposts from Venice to New York to Hong Kong, makes its London debut with a

classy, elegant Mayfair venue co-owned by the Cipriani
family and Renault's Formula One wizard, Flavio Briatore; a
sophisticated Italian menu comes at high-end prices, but
well-balanced, daily changing prix fixe menus and an
afternoon tea and pastries option widens its accessibility
from midday till 11 PM.

Circus ●☒　　　　　　　20 | 21 | 20 | £40

*1 Upper James St., W1 (Piccadilly Circus), 020-7534 4000;
fax 7534 4010; www.egami.co.uk*
■ "Bright and white" with "unfussy" Modern European
dishes and "excellent service", this Soho "experience"
"delivers more than you'd expect"; the "appealing menu
and surroundings" make it "enjoyable for a meal with the
after-work crowd" and "fine for business (take the mistress
elsewhere")"; if a few feel it's "become less hip", the "slick"
downstairs bar is "still fun", with a DJ Thursdays–Saturdays.

Citrus ☒　　　　　　　18 | 17 | 20 | £29

Park Lane Hotel, 112 Piccadilly, W1 (Green Park), 020-7290 7364
■ "Surprised it is not busier", say those familiar with this
"comfortable", "cheerful" Park Lane Hotel dining room in
Piccadilly with patio tables that "look out onto Green Park";
"well-prepared", "complex" Mediterranean fare appeals
to most (including a £15 prix fixe option), although some
feel the "menu needs updating."

City Miyama ☒　　　　　▽ 22 | 13 | 17 | £34

17 Godliman St., EC4 (St. Paul's), 020-7489 1937; fax 7236 0325
☑ "Authentic tastes in a cramped room" captures this
"friendly" bi-level Japanese near St Paul's Cathedral,
where "terrific teppanyaki" and "sushi are top class, even
compared to Japan"; the set menu options "are good for a
quick lunch" or dinner, though a few pout that "you sure do
pay for" the regular menu options.

CLARKE'S　　　　　　　27 | 20 | 24 | £53

*124 Kensington Church St., W8 (Notting Hill Gate), 020-7221 9225;
fax 7229 4564; www.sallyclarke.com*
■ "So worth it for an experience in calm enjoyment" encore
enthusiasts enthralled by this "surprisingly romantic"
Kensington "throwback where Sally Clarke shows up and
cooks" four-course Modern British meals from seasonal
"fresh ingredients"; the "flat-out fabulous" "food is not
fussy" – "what a treat" "not to be faced with a menu"
(though there are lunch/brunch choices) – this is "dinner
on the roll of the dice" so call first to see if it "suits your
tastes"; N.B. the adjacent cafe/deli opens at 8 AM.

Clerkenwell Dining Room & Bar ☒　19 | 16 | 21 | £43

*69-73 St. John St., EC1 (Farringdon), 020-7253 9000;
fax 7253 3322; www.theclerkenwell.com*
☑ "Delivers on the upmarket promise well", say supporters
of chef-patron Andrew Thompson's "relaxed", "friendly"

Clerkenwell spot in "simple", "modern" premises with Modern European cooking that offers "an adventure on your plate" (including "desserts to die for"); a minority feel it "lacks edge" compared to others in the "St. John dining scene", but most are "impressed" enough to "go again."

CLUB GASCON ☒   27 21 22 £58
57 West Smithfield, EC1 (Barbican/Farringdon), 020-7796 0600; fax 7796 0601

■ "Not for the faint-hearted, nor the faint-financed", this "foie gras lovers' paradise" by Smithfield Market where "tapas meets haute cuisine de Gascony" (and the "French contingent flock") "deserves all the accolades" for its "impeccable" New French fare and "superb regional wine list"; frustrations about it being "fiendishly difficult to get a table" and then "spending more than intended" matter little to the majority who laud this "unique dining experience" as "the kind of high-end innovation London nurtures so well."

Collection, The ◗   16 21 12 £41
264 Brompton Rd., SW3 (South Kensington), 020-7225 1212; fax 7225 1050; www.the-collection.co.uk

◪ There's a "great atmosphere again at this reborn South Kensington" brasserie where the Modern British–Eclectic cooking in the "scene-y" upstairs restaurant is "surprisingly good for a hip spot"; still, dissenters are miffed by the "disappointing service" and maintain that "one goes there to drink" in the "long" "happening bar" and gaze at the collection of "beautiful people."

Como Lario ☒   14 13 17 £40
18-22 Holbein Pl., SW1 (Sloane Sq.), 020-7730 2954; fax 7730 9046; www.comolario.uk.com

◪ "A local classic" for "basic Italian nosh" from the owners of Carpaccio and Ziani, this "hidden gem at Sloane Square" with "friendly", "fun staff" is "still going strong" after nearly 50 years (under different owners); the "tables are too close together" for some who lament it's "not what it used to be", but for most it's a "reliable" "good value" venue; N.B. a post-*Survey* revamp may impact the above Decor score.

Coq d'Argent   18 21 16 £49
No. 1 Poultry, EC2 (Bank), 020-7395 5000; fax 7395 5050; www.conran.com

◪ "You're elevated above the hustle-bustle of the City" at the Conran Group's "discreet" rooftop dining room and garden, with "stunning views" across London and "high-flying atmosphere" ("if your broker isn't answering the phone, you'll find him here" "power-lunching"); although most appreciate the regional New French "expense-account fare", some feel "it's better for a drink on a summer's day on the incredible terrace."

Costas Grill ⌧⇪ – | – | – | M
12-14 Hillgate St., W8 (Notting Hill Gate), 020-7229 3794
"Now it's the turn of the grandchildren to serve" at this "family-run", "delightful little hole-in-the-wall" in Notting Hill that's been dishing out "enjoyable Greek-Cypriot specialities" since 1951; "the decor is so dreadful it's almost trendy", but never mind, you get "decent food at a decent price" so "join the crowd in the vine-covered back garden in the summer or relax indoors in the winter."

Cow Dining Room, The 20 | 15 | 15 | £32
89 Westbourne Park Rd., W2 (Westbourne Park), 020-7221 0021; fax 7727 8687
■ "The formula keeps on working" at Tom Conran's "wonderful time warp" in Notting Hill, comprised of an "old-fashioned", "quiet upstairs dining room" serving "simple", "upscale" Modern British fare with Irish and French accents; on the ground floor, the "cosy" bar attracts "the coolest crowd", with a few tables for snacks like "awesome oysters and prawns, washed down with champagne and Guinness"; P.S. "can get crowded on weekends."

Crazy Bear, The ⌧ – | – | – | VE
26-28 Whitfield St., W1 (Goodge St.), 020-7631 0088; fax 7631 1188; www.crazybeargroup.co.uk
Buoyed by the success of his popular Crazy Bear hotel near Oxford, an over-the-top, vividly coloured citified country escape, owner Jason Hunt brings his eccentric sensibility to Fitzrovia with this ambitious new Thai restaurant boasting a ground-floor, art deco–style dining room with cream ostrich swivel chairs and a wide-ranging upscale menu; downstairs there's a hip sunken bar with banquettes, leather-clad walls and a huge cigar selection.

CRITERION GRILL ⌧ 18 | 26 | 16 | £41
224 Piccadilly, W1 (Piccadilly Circus), 020-7930 0488; fax 7930 8380; www.whitestarline.org.uk
◪ Reminiscent of the "set of *Aida*", this "spectacularly restored" neo-Byzantine Piccadilly dining room is "great for impressing visitors" but thereafter opinions on this 10-year-old Marco Pierre White–owned venue are divided: fans deem the New French–Modern European fare "excellent", with service from "superbly drilled troops", whilst cynics are let down by food that "could be up a notch" and "uncoordinated" staff ("we almost had to send up flares to get noticed!"); N.B. at press time, plans were underway to modernise the decor and simplify the menu.

Crivelli's Garden ▽ 13 | 16 | 12 | £20
National Gallery, Sainsbury Wing, Trafalgar Sq., WC2 (Charing Cross/Piccadilly Circus), 020-7747 2869; fax 7747 5800
◪ It garners few comments, but visitors to the National Gallery in Trafalgar Square find this "convenient" venue "a

good spot to take a break from a long day", with a "standard" menu of New French–Mediterranean fare, including "soups, salads" and the like (catered by the Red Pepper Group); but it hasn't grown on everyone – a few feel the cooking "does not do justice to the location"; N.B. closed for dinner except Wednesdays.

Cru   ▽ 22 | 21 | 16 | £32
2-4 Rufus St., N1 (Old St.), 020-7729 5252; fax 7729 1070; www.cru.uk.com
■ "Fun and funky", this "rustic", "loungey" restaurant/bar in a Hoxton warehouse attracts oenophiles "looking to explore a great list at good prices", along with a "selection of snacks", "specialty platters" and "grown-up" Med fare; the "open kitchen adds to the atmosphere", and service is "friendly", prompting fans to muse "what more could you want?"; N.B. check for the regular wine tasting evenings run by Katheryn Thal.

Dan's   ▽ 15 | 15 | 18 | £37
119 Sydney St., SW3 (Sloane Sq./South Kensington), 020-7352 2718; fax 7352 3265
■ "A real Chelsea restaurant patronised by real Chelsea people", this 25-year-old spot with "very nice staff" offering "above-average, fairly priced" Modern British fare is most appreciated for its "nice garden", which is "a lovely spot" for the "good two-course" £14.50 set price lunch, "great for brunch" and "comes into its own on summer evenings"; still, a minority feel it "looks a bit scruffy."

Daphne ●⊠   – | – | – | M
83 Bayham St., NW1 (Camden Town), 020-7267 7322; fax 7482 3964
Expect "a lovely welcome" at this "dependable Greek taverna" "slightly off the hippie-tourist beaten Camden track"; "fully enjoy" this "old favourite" that's "great for an evening with friends" by "securing a roof garden table on a sunny day", where you can "sip retsina whilst nibbling at a selection of simple, authentic and freshly cooked dishes."

Daphne's ●   22 | 20 | 20 | £45
112 Draycott Ave., SW3 (South Kensington), 020-7589 4257; fax 7225 2766; www.daphnes-restaurant.co.uk
■ "The occasional celeb spices things up" at this Brompton Cross" "favourite of the see-and-be-seen", owned by the Ivy–Le Caprice team, which has "an air of sophistication" and "tasty" Modern Italian fare; the setting is "ideal for couples" – they "pull out the stops for a romantic meal" – though for some "the prices make this a treat, rather than a regular" romp.

Daquise   17 | 8 | 16 | £18
20 Thurloe St., SW7 (South Kensington), 020-7589 6117
■ "In a scene from 1950s Warsaw", you'll find "characters arguing solutions to the world's problems" at this "elegantly

run-down" South Kensington "time warp", appreciated for its "interesting", "inexpensive", "hearty" cooking – it's like "leaving London for the price of a good Polish dinner."

Deca ☒　　　　　　　22 | 18 | 20 | £45

23 Conduit St., W1 (Bond St./Oxford Circus), 020-7493 7070; fax 7493 7090; www.decarestaurant.com

■ "Assured and accomplished" with "professional staff" and a "lovely upstairs room" offering "great views to Conduit Street", this "comfortable" Incognico sibling run by Nico Ladenis' daughter Natasha is a "sure bet" for "tasty" New French fare, and what's more, the £12.50 set lunch is a "veritable bargain"; whilst a few find it "perfect for the theatre", others advise it "can be a little quiet on Saturday" so "go when the business crowd is there."

De Cecco ☒　　　　　▽ 17 | 19 | 20 | £32

189 New King's Rd., SW6 (Parsons Green), 020-7736 1145; fax 7371 0278; www.simpsonsofmayfair.com

■ There's a "buzzy atmosphere" that's especially "great on weekends" at this "reliable", refurbished and expanded Parsons Green haunt where "very friendly, quick service" and "divine" Italian seafood classics like the house specialty of lobster spaghetti and a "solid wine list" get the thumbs up; P.S. you "must book when Chelsea are playing at home."

DEFUNE　　　　　　　26 | 15 | 21 | £53

34 George St., W1 (Baker St./Bond St.), 020-7935 8311; fax 7487 3762

☑ "Marylebone's best-kept secret" with "efficient service" say supporters of the "Japanese haute-cuisine" "feast for the palate" on offer at "modernist" bi-level premises that include a ground-floor sushi bar and downstairs teppanyaki room; but cynics cite "language difficulties with staff", a "cold ambience" "lacking in atmosphere" and gripe it's a "delightful evening . . . until" the "whopping bill" arrives.

Del Buongustaio　　　　　– | – | – | M

283-285 Putney Bridge Rd., SW15 (East Putney/Putney Bridge), 020-8780 9361; fax 8780 9361; www.delbuongustaio.com

A post-*Survey* change of ownership at this "simple", rustic-looking Putney Bridge Italian has seen an injection of new ideas on the menu from a new Napoli-born chef, which may please pouters who felt the cooking "used to be better" in the site's '90s heyday; P.S. the next door pasticceria is "nice for a panini and cappuccino."

Deya ☒　　　　　　　– | – | – | E

34 Portman Sq., W1 (Marble Arch), 020-7224 0028

This new venue boasts the thoroughbred backing of Claudio Pulze (of Zaika fame) and Sir Michael Caine, the movie star's first dining venture since the now-defunct Canteen in 1992; spread across two grand rooms, the high-ceilinged premises on the corner of Portman Square feature chef

Sanjay Dwivedi's contemporary Indian menu, characterised by ghee-free, delicate, healthy dishes, including a well-balanced, five-course vegetarian tasting menu.

Dibbens ⊠ | – | – | – | M |
2-3 Cowcross St., EC1 (Farringdon), 020-7250 0035; fax 7250 3080
Martin Dibben's "low-key", little-known "gem tucked away" by Smithfield Market is one of the "classier places" in the area, serving "decent" Modern British fare, which along with "excellent attention" from the staff makes it a "great place to entertain clients" or enjoy a "discreet dinner for two"; N.B. a pianist and singer perform on Friday nights.

dim t | ▽ 19 | 17 | 15 | £21 |
1A Hampstead Ln., N6 (Hampstead), 020-8340 8800; fax 8648 1671
▣ This "funky", casual Highgate newcomer makes a "great chill-out" spot, with a "diverse, delish" menu of "tasty dim sum" and other Pan-Asian dishes (the choose-your-own stir-fry option is popular) along with 16 varieties of tea; most appreciate this "new addition" to the area's "otherwise dreary restaurant scene", but aren't happy about the "hassle to get a table" on busy evenings.

Dish Dash | 15 | 15 | 15 | £25 |
11-13 Bedford Hill, SW12 (Balham B.R.), 020-8673 5555; www.dish-dash.com
▣ "Go for the music, cocktails, swordfish kebabs" and "interesting, tapas-style" Persian dishes including "great vegetarian" options as it's "not the spacious or private dining" that cuts a dash for most at this "crowded, chaotic" restaurant/bar in Balham; but a few find their hopes done in by the din ("requires a tolerance for noise") and food that's "a bit expensive for what should be cheap and cheerful."

Diverso ● | 20 | 17 | 17 | £43 |
85 Piccadilly, W1 (Green Park), 020-7491 2222; fax 7495 1977
▣ "Molto Italiano, molto delizioso" applaud fans of the fare at this discreet, comfortable Green Park venue with rustic decor; "grab a table by the window" and "enjoy" a "quiet dinner" (even as a "solo diner on business trips") whilst choosing from an "above-average wine list"; but a handful of "disappointed" visitors maintain it's "mediocre" and shrug "why bother?"

Don, The ⊠ | 22 | 20 | 22 | £42 |
The Courtyard, 20 St. Swithins Ln., EC4 (Bank/Cannon St.), 020-7626 2606; fax 7626 2616
■ "Very well Don" applaud admirers of Bleeding Heart's "baby" sibling near Cannon Street set in the "old" circa-1798 House of Sandeman sherry importer's warehouse where "eclectic" Modern European–French cooking and a "fantastic wine" and port selection now take centre stage; "cosy surroundings" ("try the cellar" bistro – "superb" for "private parties") and "knowledgeable staff" who "enjoy

discussing every aspect of the menu" make it a "clear treat for lunch" and "even for a romantic dinner."

Draper's Arms, The   20 | 18 | 18 | £28 |
44 Barnsbury St., N1 (Highbury & Islington), 020-7619 0348; fax 7619 0413
■ "Light and airy" with a "good balance of atmosphere, attentive service" and "super" Modern European food, this first-floor dining room above a "friendly" Islington gastro-pub is "becoming a destination (which spoils it for locals)"; although it's "increasingly popular" ("the presence of telly or film personalities is so common as to be unremarkable"), the "food remains top-notch" on account of chef Mark Emberton whose dishes are "ambitious in conception and execution", plus there's a garden that's "bliss in summer."

Drones   19 | 19 | 19 | £47 |
1 Pont St., SW1 (Sloane Sq.), 020-7235 9555; fax 7235 9566; www.whitestarline.org.uk
Private club; inquiries: 020-7491 0576
☑ "See, be seen, be cosseted" declare devotees who deem Marco Pierre White's "intimate" Belgravia eatery with a "chic" setting, replete with "great old [Cornel Lucas] photos of celebs" and "soundly produced" Modern European fare a "wonderful" place and "very nice" for Sunday lunch; still, sceptics suggest the dishes need "zest"; N.B. the Mayfair venue is a private dining club in a converted barbershop owned by MPW and entrepreneur Piers Adam.

Duke of Cambridge   18 | 12 | 12 | £23 |
30 St. Peter's St., N1 (Angel), 020-7359 3066; fax 7359 1877; www.singhboulton.co.uk
☑ "Feel you've done your bit for the environment" at this "hugely popular" Islington "gastro-pub with a difference" where "everything is organic – including the cola", beer and wine; the front bar is "dedicated to drinking with large tables", whilst in the "airy", no-smoking rear dining room, "friendly" servers create a "well-fed experience", with "innovative" Modern British cooking; still, a few feel it's "too busy to linger or get the attention" of staff with "attitude cubed."

Duke of Clarence, The   14 | 14 | 15 | £17 |
148 Old Brompton Rd., SW5 (Gloucester Rd./South Kensington), 020-7373 1285
☑ "After the Bram Stoker aberration, the Duke returns" to this South Kensington venue, transformed by the Builders Arms team from an eccentric concept eatery to a "warm, attractive" gastro-pub with sofas so "comfortable" they may "make you doze off"; opinions on the Modern British fare range from "good" to "mediocre", but for most it works as a "relaxing traditional Sunday lunch" venue, especially if you sit "next to the fire."

Eagle, The　　　　　23 ⃓ 13 ⃓ 12 ⃓ £19 ⃓
159 Farringdon Rd., EC1 (Farringdon), 020-7837 1353; fax 7689 5882
◪ "Leading the charge as one of the best gastro-pubs", this "charmingly scruffy" "institution" in Clerkenwell offers daily changing, "good-value Mediterranean nosh" characterised by "big flavours, rough edges and hearty portions"; "get there early and go often to try as much as you can" from the "eclectic, interesting" offerings; brickbats are aimed at the "forgetful", "slow service", but most feel "the formula works" – just "be in the mood to fight for a table."

E&O　　　　　23 ⃓ 19 ⃓ 17 ⃓ £40 ⃓
14 Blenheim Crescent, W11 (Ladbroke Grove), 020-7229 5454; fax 7229 5522; www.eando.nu
◪ Expect "food that outshines the hype" at Will Ricker's "sexy", "slick", "celeb-spotting" Notting Hill "hot spot", where the "delicious" Pan-Asian cooking, including "popcorn shrimp so addictive it should be a controlled substance", will have you "thinking about it for days afterwards"; yes, it's "absolutely fabulous in every way, daaarling!" – but even fans feel "staff are not geared towards serving mere mortals"; P.S. there's also a "see-and-be-seen" bar serving signature "watermelon martinis."

east@west ◐⊠　　　　　24 ⃓ 21 ⃓ 22 ⃓ £54 ⃓
(fka West Street)
13-15 West St., WC2 (Leicester Sq.), 020-7010 8600; www.egami.co.uk
◪ Though still owned by the team behind Kensington Place, Avenue, et al., this tri-level Theatrelander has undergone another reincarnation, this time with West Street morphing into an "exciting" newcomer with "professional staff" and Australian chef Christine Manfield at the helm preparing "delicious small portions" of Pan-Asian fare – which can "leave you happy but hungry"; below the "unhurried" dining room are two floors of bars serving "exotic" cocktails.

Eat & Two Veg　　　　　14 ⃓ 15 ⃓ 17 ⃓ £20 ⃓
50 Marylebone High St., W1 (Baker St.), 020-7258 8595; www.eatandtwoveg.com
◪ The vegetarian "cooking is so inventive, you hardly notice the absence of meat" laud lovers of the "wholesome stuff" on offer at this all-day, "modern 'diner'" in Marylebone; some think it's "crazy for a health-conscious restaurant to allow smoking", but on balance, this fun, "unpretentious" spot has a loyal following, especially "for Sunday brunch: the seating keeps young children confined!"

Ebury Dining Room & Brasserie　　▽ 12 ⃓ 15 ⃓ 12 ⃓ £34 ⃓
11 Pimlico Rd., SW1 (Sloane Sq./Victoria), 020-7730 6784; fax 7730 6149; www.theebury.co.uk
■ In a converted Pimlico pub, this "nice addition to the neighbourhood" comprises a "trendy", "loud" bar/brasserie

with a relaxed sofa area serving Eclectic fare (including a "fresh seafood" bar), and quieter first-floor quarters, which offer dining that "leans towards the business" crowd, with "interesting" New French dishes prepared by chef Michael Nadra.

Ebury Wine Bar & Restaurant   18 | 17 | 18 | £31

139 Ebury St., SW1 (Sloane Sq./Victoria), 020-7730 5447; fax 7823 6053; www.eburywinebars.co.uk

■ "Still going strong" in its fourth decade, this "cute little wine bar" in a "sleepy area of bed and breakfasts" near Victoria Station is "fine for a glass" of *vino* and a "bite to eat" from a "solid" Eclectic menu; though "nothing is spectacular, everything is good" and it offers "good value in this part of town"; it's "a tad noisy and cramped" for some, but most "continue to enjoy it."

ECapital ●   ▽ 22 | 16 | 18 | £23

8 Gerrard St., W1 (Leicester Sq./Piccadilly Circus), 020-7434 3838; fax 7434 9991

☑ "Regional delicacies like beggars chicken" and other "delicious" Shanghai specialties are "worth fighting Bruce Lee for" say acolytes of this "minimalist" Chinatown eatery with a new dining room upstairs; whilst some say the "queue out the door tells its own tale", others insist it's "never overly busy – either way, its a "very tasty" experience; N.B. the shutters come down on the kitchen at midnight.

Eco   ▽ 19 | 13 | 13 | £17

4 Market Row, SW9 (Brixton), 020-7738 3021; fax 7720 0738 ⊠
162 Clapham High St., SW4 (Clapham Common), 020-7978 1108; fax 7720 0738
www.ecorestaurants.com

■ "Book early for the weekends" at this "old favourite" of Clapham-ites, appreciated as much for the "thin pizzas", "delicious salads", pasta and other "great" Italian fare as the "nice buzz" – but beware, "it can get loud" and "smoky"; the older of the two, "hidden in Brixton Market", is BYO and "you can utilise outside tables" for lunch as it's closed for dinner.

Edera   21 | 17 | 19 | £38

148 Holland Park Ave., W11 (Holland Park), 020-7221 6090

☑ "The best thing to happen to Holland Park since Holland Park" gush lovers of this "great addition to the [A-Z Group] family", a "bustling" Modern Italian "find" with a "creative" set menu offering "fantastic value without sacrificing on choice"; if a few feel the "ingredients fail to mesh in any meaningful way" they're overruled by most who pledge "I'd go back in a heartbeat"; N.B. the name translates to 'ivy' in English.

Ed's Easy Diner　　　　　　　15　14　15　£14

12 Moor St., W1 (Leicester Sq./Tottenham Court Rd.),
020-7439 1955; fax 7494 0173
London Trocadero Ctr., 19 Rupert St., W1 (Piccadilly Circus),
020-7287 1951; fax 7287 6998 ◗
362 King's Rd., SW3 (Sloane Sq.), 020-7352 1956; fax 7352 4660
O₂ Ctr., 255 Finchley Rd., NW3 (Finchley Rd.), 020-7431 1958;
fax 7431 9837
www.edseasydiner.co.uk

■ "You feel you're in *Grease*" at this quartet of "totally kitsch", American-themed "funky retro diners" with "fun jukeboxes" ("bring your 20p's"), "truly great malted milkshakes", "hearty", "good cheap burgers, hot dogs" and other "instant comfort food" fare ("don't miss the chili fries"); go for a "quick bite whilst shopping" or for a "post-movie meal", and remember: the "family-friendly surroundings" make it "a fave with children."

Efes Kebab House　　　　　　　18　11　15　£22

175-177 Great Portland St., W1 (Great Portland St.),
020-7436 0600; fax 7636 6293 ◗
80 Great Titchfield St., W1 (Oxford Circus), 020-7636 1953;
fax 7323 5082 ▨

■ The "great combination of kebabs with belly dancing" is a "Turkish delight" for "any occasion" at the younger Great Portland Street sibling of this Middle Eastern duo, and while the Great Titchfield Street original does not have the "sexy" dancers, it does boast "fine traditional recipes" that have made it a barely kept "secret" for over 25 years ("it's on my speed dial!") along with "teeth-shattering coffee."

1880　▨　　　　　　　−　−　−　VE

The Bentley, 27-33 Harrington Gardens, SW7 (Gloucester Rd.),
020-7244 5361; www.thebentley-hotel.com

It's early days for the Bentley, an impressive hotel in South Kensington (transformed from four private houses) and its "opulent" basement dining room spotlighting "perfect service" and "inventive", albeit "mucho expensive" New French–Modern European cooking; chef Andrew Turner, previously at Brown's Hotel's defunct 1837, is "back with what he knows best", attracting admirers with an "excellent cheese trolley" and tasting menus; N.B. there's also an elegant all-day brasserie called Peridot on the ground floor.

1802　　　　　　　▽　18　19　11　£21

1 West India Quay, Hertsmere Rd., E14 (Canary Wharf/
West India Quay), 0870-444 3886; www.searcys.co.uk

■ A "welcome addition to Canary Wharf", this old tea-sorting house, named after the date the West India Quay first opened, is now a "sleek", "airy" loft-style space with a "fabulous outside" riverside patio, a "good", daily changing Modern British menu courtesy of the caterers Searcy's and "nice ambience" "for after-work drinks" ("very funky, especially compared to the chain bars"); it's "a break from the norm" – in fact, it "even has its own historic" Museum in Docklands next door.

Eight Over Eight   24 | 20 | 17 | £41 |
392 King's Rd., SW3 (Sloane Sq.), 020-7349 9934;
www.eightovereight.nu
◪ "You could point at the menu blindfolded and be sure of getting something delicious" at Will Ricker's "e&o sibling" in Chelsea (formerly the Man in the Moon pub), a "super-cool room" where a "smart crowd" of "bright young things" have latched on to the "edgy" Pan-Asian dishes; the "great vibe" makes it "perfect for a first date", "gossip with the girls" or "star spotting", but snipers snarl it's "a triumph of style over substance" and aim a stiletto at "pretty rather than efficient service."

El Blason ⌧   17 | 13 | 18 | £35 |
8-9 Blacklands Terrace, SW3 (Sloane Sq.), 020-7823 7383;
fax 7589 6313
◪ Owner Carlos Ulloa "remembers everyone" and ensures there's "always a party" at this "hangout" in the backstreets behind King's Road "recommended" for "excellent" Spanish fare, including "the best tapas and paella"; "el blah, blah, blah" grumble the disgruntled few who deem the food "average to middling" and the digs "characterless."

Electric Brasserie, The   19 | 19 | 15 | £31 |
191 Portobello Rd., W11 (Ladbroke Grove/Notting Hill Gate),
020-7908 9696; fax 7908 9595; www.the-electric.co.uk
◪ "Still has a buzz all day long", yes, this "Portobello Road hot spot lives up to its reputation" as a "hip haunt" for "delicious no-frills" Eclectic brasserie fare and "prime celeb spotting" amongst "footballers' wives and the odd footballer!"; still, some snipe that "food is secondary to the vibe" and advise don't be shocked by "abrupt service as it's usually manic"; P.S. "catch a showing" at the comfy cinema or go for the "snug upstairs" private members club, both in the same complex and owned by Soho House.

El Gaucho   21 | 14 | 15 | £32 |
88 Ifield Rd., SW10 (Earl's Court), 020-7823 3333 ⌧
30 Old Brompton Rd., SW7 (South Kensington), 020-7584 8999
Chelsea Farmers Mkt., 125 Sydney St., SW3 (Sloane Sq./
South Kensington), 020-7376 8514 ⇴
◪ "If you're in the mood for meat", this "lively" Argentinean trio in Chelsea and South Ken offers a "speciality" of "melt-in-your-mouth beef" and "tasty side dishes", as well as a "good wine selection"; even if el gripers grouch "don't expect much from the decor and service", and suggest "a few vegetarian options wouldn't hurt", most concede, "for steak lovers", it's "superb"; N.B. Farmers Market closes at 6 PM, and Ifield Road is dinner only.

Elistano ⬤ 18 13 16 £30
25-27 Elystan St., SW3 (South Kensington), 020-7584 5248; fax 7584 8965

◪ "They do pack them in" at this "cheerful", unassuming trattoria near Chelsea Green where "they make you feel like one of the family"; it's "still super popular" as an "affordable" spot for "homey" Italian fare, and while it "can get a bit noisy, that's part of the fun" (plus it's alleviated by "nice pavement dining in summer"); but a few feel that service can "go down the drain" "when they're busy" and insist it's "too loud for conversation."

El Pirata ⬤ 🖾 – – – M
5-6 Down St., W1 (Green Park), 020-7491 3810; www.elpirata.co.uk

Peruse the "long list of tapas items" then "order a little bit of everything" – "all very tasty" – "so you can get a good array of flavours" suggest supporters who also say this "noisy", "casual", "attractive" Spaniard "on a side street near Park Lane" is "great for a full meal"; walk up or head down the "spiral staircase – there's seating on both levels" – and join the "fun, lively crowd" that find it "better than many of the fancy places."

Embassy ⬤ 🖾 18 18 17 £50
29 Old Burlington St., W1 (Piccadilly Circus), 020-7851 0956; fax 7734 3224; www.embassylondon.com

◪ "Beg for asylum, you'll want to stay" quip ambassadors of chef-patron Garry Hollihead's restaurant-cum–private lounge near Bond Street, with its "fashionable young crowd" ("wrinklies tolerated, but not much in evidence") and "excellently executed" Modern European menu of "high-end dishes"; but to the less diplomatic, the "bland and stiff" setting is "sooo has-been", with many appreciating it more for the "convenience of being above a great club."

Emporio Armani Caffe 🖾 17 18 18 £29
Emporio Armani, 191 Brompton Rd., SW3 (Knightsbridge), 020-7581 0854; fax 7823 8854

■ A "great place to grab" a "delicious lunch" of "good" Italian fare "while doing damage to the credit card", this narrow in-store cafe on the first floor of Emporio Armani's Knightsbridge store attracts a "very chichi" "smart young set"; the "food's a secondary consideration to the scenery and scene" say a few sceptics, but most concede it's a "useful place in the neighbourhood"; N.B. last orders at 5:30 PM.

Engineer, The 20 17 17 £30
65 Gloucester Ave., NW1 (Chalk Farm), 020-7722 0950; fax 7483 0592; www.the-engineer.com

◪ "Still hip and hopping" – and "still reigns as a top gastro-pub" say admirers on track with this airy Primrose Hill spot boasting an "imaginative" Modern British menu with a "great Sunday brunch"; the "casual atmosphere enhances good gossipy conversation", making it "recommended" for "summer outdoor eats" "with a group of friends" ("nowhere better on a nice night"); but others derailed by "prices that are not quite justified" snipe it's "slipping."

ENOTECA TURI 🗗　　　　　　25 ｜ 17 ｜ 18 ｜ £37
28 Putney High St., SW15 (Putney Bridge), 020-8785 4449; fax 8780 5409
■ The "wonderful patron keeps the place buzzing" agree admirers who turn up at [Giuseppe] Turi's "small, but accommodating" neighbourhood "find" for "excellent" Modern Italian dishes supported by an "outstanding wine list"; the "unpretentious food" is "well presented", plus "service is helpful" – in short, "always a good experience."

Enterprise, The　　　　　　19 ｜ 20 ｜ 20 ｜ £34
35 Walton St., SW3 (Knightsbridge/South Kensington), 020-7584 3148; fax 7584 2516; www.christophersgrill.com
■ Expect "some entertaining eavesdropping as the tables are close together" at this "buzzy", "people-watching" Chelsea gastro-pub confide insiders who also make it their business to enjoy the "always reliable" Eclectic fare and "interesting wines", all delivered by "efficient staff"; it's "relaxed and casual at the same time", making it a "great meeting point" – and a "good place to go back to."

Esarn Kheaw　　　　　　▽ 25 ｜ 8 ｜ 15 ｜ £28
314 Uxbridge Rd., W12 (Shepherd's Bush), 020-8743 8930; fax 7243 1250
◪ "Underrated, except by those who know Thai food", this "low-key", "über-authentic haunt" in Shepherd's Bush is "not much to look at in terms of decor" and "not for everyone", particularly those with "delicate European palates"; nevertheless, the "knowledgeable staff are willing to adapt dishes to suit your taste", and for most, the "fantastic food" is "to die for."

Essenza ◖　　　　　　▽ 23 ｜ 17 ｜ 16 ｜ £34
210 Kensington Park Rd., W11 (Ladbroke Grove), 020-7792 1066
◪ The Notting Hill "show ponies have decided not to graze here yet", so this "nice, cosy joint" – formerly Zilli and now run by the Mediterraneo crew – remains a "lovely" "local gem" and a "good alternative" for those in-the-know, with an "incredible" Modern Italian menu that offers "excellent value for money" and "friendly staff"; but a nonchalant few shrug it's "ok, just nothing special."

Exmouth Grill　　　　　　– ｜ – ｜ – ｜ E
55-57 Exmouth Market, EC1 (Farringdon/Angel), 020-7837 0009
Roosting on the spot previously held by a low-key Greek taverna, this casually bohemian Clerkenwell venue has a small dining area offering a simple Modern European

menu dominated by grilled meats and fish with a wide choice of 'pick and mix' accompaniments; there's also an eclectically decorated bar area with comfy leather sofas and crushed-velvet banquettes, plus a handful of pavement tables on Exmouth Market.

Eyre Brothers ☒

20 | 19 | 18 | £46

70 Leonard St., EC2 (Old St.), 020-7613 5346;
fax 7739 8199

🗖 A "little-known diamond in the area" offering "hospitable" attention from patrons David and Rob Eyre, founders of the Eagle pub, this "chic, sleek" Shoreditch venue may be "out of the way, but worth the visit" attest admirers lured by the "interesting", "authentic" Spanish-Portuguese menu boasting "big, robust flavours" – like "magnificent Mozambique prawns"; if a handful huff that it's "overpriced" with "spotty service", they're in the minority.

Fairuz ●

21 | 15 | 20 | £28

27 Westbourne Grove, W2 (Bayswater/Queensway),
020-7243 8444; fax 7243 8777
3 Blandford St., W1 (Baker St./Bond St.), 020-7486 8108;
fax 7935 8581

■ The "startlingly fresh" Lebanese fare is "outstanding", the "wine list is strong" and the "staff are very helpful", especially "if you don't know what to order" at this "comfortable" Marylebone standby and younger Bayswater sibling; "it's one of the few places where you can enjoy a village atmosphere", so dig into the "tasty meats" and "wonderful mezze", sample the "must-try freshly made juices" and bask in the "nice experience."

Fakhreldine ●

21 | 17 | 20 | £27

92 Queensway, W2 (Bayswater/Queensway), 020-7243 3177;
fax 7313 9071
1st fl., 85 Piccadilly, W1 (Green Park), 020-7493 3424;
fax 7495 1977
www.fakhreldine.co.uk

■ Named after Prince Fakhreldine II, a prominent figure in Lebanese history, this first-floor Green Park stalwart is "possibly the most stylish Lebanese in town" since its redecoration last year; the "fine" Middle Eastern cooking, including some of the "best kebabs in London by a mile", is "innovative and traditional at the same time" laud loyal subjects who suggest you "order anything for satisfaction guaranteed"; N.B. the Queensway branch is takeaway only.

FAT DUCK, THE

27 | 20 | 26 | £78

High St., Bray, Berkshire, 01628 580333; fax 01628 776188;
www.fatduck.co.uk

🗖 Try to "make sure your taste buds are in shape for an encounter" with the "inventive" "theatre" on stage at "magic chef" Heston Blumenthal's New French Berkshire

venue (about 40 minutes west of London); if a few feathers
are ruffled by his "relentless quest for unusual flavours"
(some question whether he is a "mad scientist" or "culinary
genius"), most diners report that the "fabulously executed",
"playful" combinations at this "charming hideaway" offer
"real gastronauts an experience they'll never forget."

ffiona's　　　　　　　　21　16　22　£33
51 Kensington Church St., W8 (High St. Kensington/
Notting Hill Gate), 020-7937 4152
▰ "If she takes a shine to you, the world is your oyster" fawn
fans of "lovely hostess" Ffiona Reid Owen and her "cosy",
"romantic" "local haunt" in Kensington that "continues to
deliver" a "marvellous" Modern British menu of "home
quality" "comfort food"; this "icon" "makes you feel like
you're in your best friend's living room, but with superior"
cooking, so "let her pick for you – and take her ribbing in
stride"; still, sceptics pout she's a "little pushy" and deem
the food "indifferent."

Fifteen ◑　　　　　　　　21　18　19　£51
15 Westland Pl., N1 (Old St.), 0871-330 1515; fax 020-7566 1778;
www.fifteenrestaurant.com
▰ "Brilliant job, well done" encore enthusiasts of Jamie
Oliver's "fun", "funky" no-smoking Hoxton dining project,
which offers training apprenticeships to youngsters in
need, and where it's "impossible to get a reservation"
thanks to "rustic" Mediterranean dishes of "exquisite
simplicity" in "massive portions"; but cynics snipe that at
these "wallet-thumping prices" "it should knock your socks
off"; P.S. "try a late lunch" if you can't book dinner – or the
new ground-floor trattoria for a more casual meal.

Fifth Floor　　　　　　　　18　16　17　£41
Harvey Nichols, 109-125 Knightsbridge, SW1 (Knightsbridge),
020-7235 5250; fax 7823 2207; www.harveynichols.co.uk
▰ The "fun of Harvey Nichols, but with food!" yes, the
famous Knightsbridge store's dining room, now boasting a
"snazzy" new decor (with "lighting that subtly changes
colours as you dine"), is "a favourite place to meet up" "after
a shopping spree" for Simon Shaw's "divine" Modern British
cooking; "civil" waiters, "knowledgeable sommeliers" and
a "buzzy" bar complete the picture; but a few feel "prices
are sky high" and while the "crowd is posh, the fare is not."

Fifth Floor Cafe　　　　　　　17　15　15　£27
Harvey Nichols, 109-125 Knightsbridge, SW1 (Knightsbridge),
020-7823 1839; fax 7823 2207
▰ "Weary *Sex and the City* girls" "catch a breather while
shopping" at this "lively, chic" Knightsbridge in-store cafe
that's as "loud" and "as busy as ever" and still a "people-
watching" paradise; an all-day Med menu of "delicious"
"basics" is "efficiently served" by "rushed" staff, and

there's a small terrace for warm-weather dining – "good
luck getting a table though."

Fina Estampa 🅱   ▽ 21 | 15 | 21 | £28 |
150 Tooley St., SE1 (London Bridge), 020-7403 1342; fax 7403 1342
■ "Huge portions" of "unusual", "authentic" Peruvian fare
like "outstanding seviche and fish" are the main attraction
at this candlelit, homely venue near Tower Bridge that's
also appreciated for it's "fun", "relaxed" attitude and
"very friendly" staff; takeaway is available, and there's a
cosy downstairs bar.

Fino 🅱   24 | 20 | 21 | £43 |
33 Charlotte St., W1 (Tottenham Court Rd.), 020-7813 8010;
fax 7813 8011; www.finorestaurant.com
🅴 "At last, a really good Spanish restaurant" agree admirers
of brothers Sam and Eddie Hart's "roomy yet cosy" Fitzrovian
basement; the "excellent" Iberian menu specialising in
"superb tapas" and "delightful choices of sherry" are a
"refreshing change", plus the "servers are very people
oriented"; whilst a few fume-o that Fino's "prices are a
bit steep", most insist "eating at the bar is a must try";
N.B. entrance is on Rathbone Street.

First Floor   ▽ 17 | 19 | 17 | £32 |
186 Portobello Rd., W11 (Ladbroke Grove/Notting Hill Gate),
020-7243 0072; fax 7221 9440; www.firstfloorportobello.co.uk
🅴 In a "pretty dining room" with high ceilings and large
windows overlooking Portobello Road, this "neighbourhood
stalwart" offers a "good" Modern British menu with prix
fixe options from £11; critics think it's "living on past
glories" and is "now dominated by the bar below" "for
drinks after dinner" (which is slated to undergo a major
refit at publication time).

Fish!   17 | 15 | 15 | £28 |
Cathedral St., Borough Mkt., SE1 (London Bridge),
020-7407 3803; fax 7357 8636; www.fishdiner.co.uk
🅴 "The exclamation point says it all! Fish!" – it's "fresh",
"cheap", "tasty" and "simple" and "you can choose how
it's prepared and what sauce it has on it" at this remaining
"well-located", "modern", "bright and airy" "last of a chain"
seafooder by Southwark Cathedral; still, some are no longer
hooked, deeming the concept "lacking in originality."

Fish Hoek   24 | 16 | 22 | £35 |
6-8 Elliot Rd., W4 (Turnham Green), 020-8742 0766;
fax 8742 3374
■ "Fish lovers only" need venture to Pete Gottgens'
"crowded" South African spot that's "made a difference to
eating out in Chiswick" by offering an "amazing variety" of
fin fare "cooked in inventive ways" and "presented like a
picture on a plate"; "knowledgeable servers" advise on
the more "unrecognisable" options, indeed, "you could go

again and again without having the same thing twice!";
P.S. "you'll never get in without a booking."

Fishmarket ⊠   17 14 15 £42
*Great Eastern Hotel, Liverpool St., EC2 (Liverpool St.),
020-7618 7200; fax 7618 7201; www.fish-market.co.uk*
⊿ Joining Conran Group's other restaurants Aurora and
Terminus in the Great Eastern Hotel, this "lively" Liverpool
Street venue offering "fresh" seafood from a prominent
crustacean bar and other "delicious" Modern British fare
is "perfect for a business lunch or as a place to catch up
with City friends"; still, many find tables in the horseshoe-
shaped bar next door "better than the restaurant proper."

Fish Shop on St. John St. ⊠   ▽ 19 15 16 £27
*360-362 St. John St., EC1 (Angel), 020-7837 1199; fax 7837 3399;
www.thefishshop.net*
■ The owners of the popular Upper Street Fish Shop (which
closed in 2000) have transferred their attention to this
"multilevel reincarnation" in "clean-lined" Clerkenwell
premises, offering "well-crafted" Traditional British seafood
with modern touches (it's a "lovely place to experience
expertly cooked fish 'n' chips"); the "buzzy ground floor" is
a "fun neighbourhood joint" – and much preferred to the
"more sedate basement."

FishWorks   ▽ 20 15 18 £33
*6 Turnham Green Terrace, W4 (Turnham Green), 020-8994 0086;
fax 8994 0778; www.fishworks.co.uk*
■ "If you can get past the fish in the window, it's a blast"
at this "friendly" Chiswick outpost of a four-strong West
Country–based chain, with a fishmonger's shop at the
front, and "bright, modern" restaurant at the rear serving
the "freshest catch" delivered from Cornwall daily; it's
"pricey, but worth it" and you "need to be choosy about
your table" but "you will not be disappointed."

Floriana ⊠   18 20 20 £51
*15 Beauchamp Pl., SW3 (Knightsbridge), 020-7838 1500;
fax 7584 1464; www.floriana.co.uk*
⊿ This "intimate spot" in Knightsbridge, with a "muted",
"elegant" atmosphere, "charming decor" and "attentive
staff", makes an "excellent choice for light and late meals"
from a "quality" Modern Italian menu – "but be prepared
to pay for the pleasure"; some feel it "seems to have lost
popularity" since it's pre-refurbishment heyday a few years
back, which at least means "it's easy to book."

FOLIAGE   26 23 26 £61
*Mandarin Oriental Hyde Park, 66 Knightsbridge, SW1
(Knightsbridge), 020-7235 2000; fax 7235 2001;
www.mandarinoriental.com*
■ "Perfection with every bite" swoon acolytes of the
"outstanding foodie experience" on offer from Chris Staines'

"palate-dazzling" Modern European–French menu in the "serene setting" of the Mandarin Oriental's "first-class" Knightsbridge dining room; expect "top-notch service" ("they made us feel like royalty") and a "beautiful view" of Hyde Park, especially "in autumn", plus a prix fixe lunch that may be the "best secret in town"; P.S. the "attached bar is a definite plus", attracting a "hip, noisy" crowd.

Food for Thought ⊭   22 9 12 £10
31 Neal St., WC2 (Covent Garden), 020-7836 9072

◪ One of the "most famous vegetarian restaurants in the Western world", or at least in Covent Garden, this BYO "hippie outpost", voted the *Survey's* No. 1 Bang for the Buck, has "kept its 1970s decor" and still serves "inventive" "food your veggie granny could have cooked", from its Eclectic menu; "cramped" quarters means they "pack you in like a tofu-sardine", especially during "peak hours" when there's a "rushed, but jovial" scene at the "deli-style" counter; N.B. kitchen closes at 8:30 PM.

Fortnum's Fountain ⊠   17 17 18 £25
Fortnum & Mason, 181 Piccadilly, W1 (Green Park/ Piccadilly Circus), 020-7973 4140; fax 7437 3278; www.fortnumandmason.com

◪ "There's no point shopping" in Piccadilly's Fortnum & Mason without taking an "elegant respite" at this "well-appointed room" where you're "serenaded in the old department store atmosphere"; with its "restful charm" and "attentive service (without a trace of British stiffness)", it's a place to revisit" "for a spot of tea" or a "light meal" from the all-day Traditional British menu; but the less-impressed find the fare "mediocre" and the decor "dowdy."

Four Seasons Chinese ●   24 6 11 £20
84 Queensway, W2 (Bayswater), 020-7229 4320

■ "Jeans are too formal" at this Bayswater Chinese that wins plaudits for its "unbelievably good" multiregional cooking, most notably its "famous roast duck" (a "closely guarded secret recipe") that is said to draw "people from the Far East"; the "brightly lit room" does little to dissuade loyalists, so even if you "book beforehand", join the "queue out the door" or "go at an 'off' time."

1492 ◐   20 18 17 £30
404 North End Rd., SW6 (Fulham Broadway), 020-7381 3810; www.1492restaurant.com

◪ "South America in Fulham" fawn fans who set sail for this "authentic" newcomer, an "interesting concept with a Spanish flair"; "it's a good spot to try" a wide range of "different" Latin cuisines from Argentina, Brazil and all over the continent declare discoverers; still, a few who "expected a bit more" claim "some dishes are delicious" and some are "nothing memorable."

Frederick's ●❍⊠   22 20 19 £40
106 Camden Passage, N1 (Angel), 020-7359 2888;
fax 7359 5173; www.fredericks.co.uk
■ "There's plenty to tempt" the "grown-up clientele" who've
"never been less than delighted" by the Modern British
cuisine at this "casual and classy" family-run Islingtonian
blessed with an airy rear conservatory, the feel of a "New
York art gallery" and a location convenient "after shopping
for antiques at Camden Passage"; "wine offerings work
well" with the "delish" dishes laud loyalists who also
commend "charming staff."

French Horn   24 23 24 £52
French Horn Hotel, Sonning-on-Thames, Berkshire,
01189 692204; fax 01189 442210; www.thefrenchhorn.co.uk
■ "Almost a national treasure", this "very English" family-
run hotel in a "beautiful setting" alongside the Thames
near Reading entices fans with an "imaginative yet simple
to the core" Traditional British menu, "combined with the
best service" and a 1,000-bottle strong "wine list that has
to be seen to be believed"; "come here to get away and
enjoy a meal at your own pace" – it's "worth every penny"
and "blissful for lunch on a summer's day."

French House   20 16 14 £30
49 Dean St., W1 (Piccadilly Circus/Tottenham Court Rd.),
020-7437 2477; fax 7287 9109
■ This "lovely, intimate dining room" in a historic building
in Soho "has it all: charm, good" "classic French" bistro
offerings and a "fun ground-floor pub" below where the
"boys behind the bar are a hoot"; it's "little known" – it may
even be "one of London's best-kept secrets" – indeed there's
"something that makes" insiders want to "go back."

Friends ●   17 14 14 £24
6 Hollywood Rd., SW10 (South Kensington), 020-7376 3890;
fax 7352 6368
■ Sure it's a "cheesy name" and a "little pricey for a pizza
dinner", "but we can't stay away from" this "cosy, quaint"
Chelsea haunt that has a "ski-chalet feel", "authentic
Italian food", "hearty pasta" and some of the "best thin-
crusted 'za in town" cooked in a wood-burning oven; *amici*
agree: the "friendly atmosphere" makes it the "perfect
place" "to meet friends for a casual dinner."

Frontline ⊠   – – – E
13 Norfolk Pl., W2 (Paddington), 020-7479 8960; fax 020-7479 8961;
www.frontlinerestaurant.com
TV cameraman Vaughan Smith has turned a characterful
four-story Paddington building into a restaurant-cum–
private members' club (complete with an exhibition room
and debating floor) named after his news and TV agency
for freelance reporters; the airy ground-floor eatery with

exposed bricks and maroon walls serves gutsy Modern British food with Middle Eastern and North African dishes thrown in.

Fung Shing ◖ 23 | 13 | 17 | £28 |
15 Lisle St., WC2 (Leicester Sq.), 020-7437 1539; fax 7743 0284; www.fungshing.co.uk

■ "The king of Chinatown" declare loyal subjects who pay homage to this "reliable leader's" "extensive menu" of "innovative" Mandarin dishes that offer "a chance to press your limits"; never mind the "insipid decor", the "food is wonderful enough to make you put your thick skin on and go again."

Galicia ◖ 17 | 9 | 13 | £25 |
323 Portobello Rd., W10 (Ladbroke Grove), 020-8969 3539

■ "Go with some mates" and join the "Spanish speaking customers" at this "no-nonsense" Notting Hill local spot where "you'll have plenty" of "cheap" Iberian fare "to share", including some of "the most delicious tapas and paella this side of the Channel"; sure, "service can be haphazard", and it's a "dive", even with pictures of Galicia on the wall, but it's "compensated by a soulful experience."

Gallipoli 20 | 16 | 18 | £18 |
102 Upper St., N1 (Angel), 020-7359 0630; fax 7704 0496
107 Upper St., N1 (Angel), 020-7226 5333; fax 7704 0496
120 Upper St., N1 (Angel), 020-7359 1578; fax 7704 0496

■ "Kitsch decor", "pulsing music", "fellow diners" "crowded like sardines" and "the chance to dance on chairs" are all hallmarks of this "unbelievably cheap" Turkish trio that "instantly transports you off Islington's Upper Street to the Istanbul of your imagination"; the Middle Eastern fare – "yummy mezze" and the like – is "great for large groups", and comes courtesy of "down-to-earth service"; P.S. think twice about Gallipoli-ng over "if over 25 with working ears!"

Garbo's ▽ 15 | 11 | 15 | £24 |
42 Crawford St., W1 (Baker St./Marylebone), 020-7262 6582; fax 7262 6582

◪ "You won't have to eat again until Monday" (and you don't have to be alone) to enjoy a "great Sunday lunch" from the signature Swedish smorgasbord at this Marylebone stalwart adorned with, what else, Greta Garbo pictures; it's a "funky, cosy" stop, "especially on a winter's night", plus the "homey" atmosphere "makes up for the dated decor"; N.B. there's also a weekday lunch buffet for under £10.

Gate, The ⊠ 23 | 17 | 18 | £28 |
51 Queen Caroline St., W6 (Hammersmith), 020-8748 6932; fax 8563 1719; www.gateveg.co.uk

■ "In a cheerful, airy former artists' studio in Hammersmith" this "firm favourite" "proves that vegetarian food can be as gourmet as other cuisines", offering "big portions" of "original, colourful" Modern European fare that "satisfies every" time; there's also a "lovely courtyard" for summer dining, so "try and book in advance"; P.S. many are "gutted that the Belsize Park outpost" closed down earlier this year.

GAUCHO GRILL 20 16 16 £34
19 Swallow St., W1 (Piccadilly Circus), 020-7734 4040; fax 7734 1076 ●
125-126 Chancery Ln., WC2 (Chancery Ln.), 020-7242 7727; fax 7242 7723 🚫
89 Sloane Ave., SW3 (South Kensington), 020-7584 9901; fax 7584 0045
64 Heath St., NW3 (Hampstead), 020-7431 8222; fax 7431 3714
29 Westferry Circus, E14 (Canary Wharf), 020-7987 9494; fax 7987 9292
1 Bell Inn Yard, EC3 (Bank/Monument), 020-7626 5180; fax 7626 5181 🚫
www.thegauchogrill.co.uk
◪ The "cowhide is a bit rich" and the "tongue-in-cheek decor" "may be dark, but the food is radiant" concur carnivores who "steer" over to this London chophouse chain that strikes the "right level of informality"; the "top-notch Argentinean steaks" and "an amazing wine list" "make for a great" meal "when you need your meat fix"; still, a few gaucho grousers gripe "it's not the widest of menus" and feel it's "marred by" "spotty service."

Gay Hussar 🚫 20 19 20 £36
2 Greek St., W1 (Tottenham Court Rd.), 020-7437 0973; fax 7437 4631; www.simplyrestaurants.com
■ "Take a trip back to old Budapest" at this "clubby-looking" "Soho stalwart" where "politicians who come in droves" are not only rendered in "very good caricatures on the wall" but "observed first-hand" dining on "hearty Hungarian fare"; both the "stick-to-your-ribs Eastern European" food and "extremely attentive and convivial service" solidify its status as "hidden treasure."

Geales Fish Restaurant 21 11 17 £19
2 Farmer St., W8 (Notting Hill Gate), 020-7727 7528; fax 7229 8632
◪ "Tucked away" in an "unlikely location" on a "quiet, charming street of pastel-hued houses" sits this "favourite fish 'n' chips place" where you have varieties "to choose from – imagine that!" – and the "lovely owner treats you royally"; still, the less-hooked huff it's "lost the plot" and feel it "falls down on the service side", hence they resort to the takeaway option.

George 🚫 22 21 25 £61
Private club; inquiries: 020-7491 4433
◪ A "well-run establishment where you always feel welcome", the youngest of Mark Birley's smart private

members' clubs is a "pleasant" bi-level Mayfair venue "with a sensible dress code" (i.e. not too formal) where "efficient" staff serve "high-quality" Modern European dishes with a British bent; though "overpriced" ("hope someone else is paying"), it's "inexplicably appealing", plus there's a comfy "cool bar downstairs."

Getti ⊠   16 15 16 £26
42 Marylebone High St., W1 (Baker St./Bond St.), 020-7486 3753; fax 7486 7084
16-17 Jermyn St., SW1 (Piccadilly Circus), 020-7734 7334; fax 7734 7924
■ "Friendly and unassuming", this Italian duo with spacious environs in Marylebone and St James's serves up "solid, dependable" staples that are "good for casual dining" or a "quick, tasty" bite "at a reasonable price"; get the "pasta dishes that outshine the fancier entrees" advise spaghetti lovers who also note that the Marylebone High Street site offers a "terrace for sunny days."

Gia   _ _ _ M
62-64 Fulham Rd., SW3 (South Kensington), 020-7589 2232; fax 7225 2982
On the famous old San Frediano site in South Kensington lies this latest venture from Gianni Pauro (ex-owner of Formula Veneta) with bright, glass-fronted premises, and an "interesting", seasonally changing Italian menu boasting distinct Eastern twists; the owner's "friendliness" ensures "pleasant, efficient service (most of the time)", yet a few feel "they still need to sort out the kinks."

Ginger   ▽ 16 14 13 £31
115 Westbourne Grove, W2 (Notting Hill Gate), 020-7908 1990; fax 7908 1991; www.gingerrestaurant.co.uk
◩ A "good neighbourhood" stop, "not a destination place", this colourful ("sunglasses are essential" to gingerly "make it past the screaming decor") Bayswater venue has a Bangladeshi-Indian menu that divides diners: some say the "original food" means you can "eat well", while others find the "food rather uninspiring and expensive" and give "chaotic service" a thumbs down.

Giraffe   17 14 17 £19
7 Kensington High St., W8 (High St. Kensington), 020-7938 1221; fax 7938 3330
270 Chiswick High Rd., W4 (Turnham Green), 020-8995 2100; fax 8995 4204
6-8 Blandford St., W1 (Baker St./Bond St.), 020-7935 2333; fax 7935 2334
27 Battersea Rise, SW11 (Clapham Junction/Clapham Common), 020-7223 0933; fax 7223 1037
29-31 Essex Rd., N1 (Angel), 020-7359 5999; fax 7359 6158
46 Rosslyn Hill, NW3 (Hampstead), 020-7435 0343; fax 7431 1317

(continued)
Giraffe
348 Muswell Hill Broadway, N10 (Highgate), 020-8883-4463
30 Hill St., Twickenham (Richmond), 020-8332 2646; fax 8332 9171
www.giraffe.net
■ "Kids get balloons, grown-ups get rewarded with well-executed" Eclectic dishes at this "tried-and-tested" "eco-friendly" "favourite", "one of the "better brunching chains" that's also a "fun, fast, healthy place to dine"; it's worth sticking your neck out for "imaginative" "dishes that reveal international flavours", plus "cheerful staff" including "saucy Aussies" and "world music add a nice touch"; N.B. the Muswell Hill branch opened post-*Survey*.

Glaister's Bar & Restaurant ◐ ▽ 13 15 14 £29
4 Hollywood Rd., SW10 (Earl's Court/South Kensington),
020-7352 0352; fax 7376 7341
☑ With a retractable roof, "the rear garden is a lovely place to [escape] the bustle of Chelsea" at this modest bistro with a "daily changing" Anglo-French menu; whilst some say the setting is "perfect for big groups" and "best for parties", cynics snipe it's "nothing special" and looks "a bit naff"; P.S. the Clapham branch closed earlier this year.

Glasshouse, The   25 20 21 £41
14 Station Parade, Kew (Kew Gardens), 020-8940 6777;
fax 8940 3833
■ After a "stroll in Kew Gardens", "make your way" to this "second growth of the Chez Bruce empire", now a no-smoking, recently refurbished, "striking" venue boasting "top-notch", "well-presented" Modern British food that clearly offers a "new take on old classics"; choose a wine from the "comprehensive list and the sommelier lavishes attention and advice", and when you sample the "fabulous cheeseboard, the "wonderful set lunch menu" or any "lovely meal", "service is professionally friendly."

Globe   ▽ 16 12 18 £28
100 Avenue Rd., NW3 (Swiss Cottage), 020-7722 7200;
fax 7722 2772; www.globerestaurant.co.uk
■ "An underappreciated gem" agree globe-trotters of this "airy" bi-level venue by the Hampstead Theatre – an area of Swiss Cottage "without much competition"; the "service is personal", and the Modern British "food is frequently outstanding", plus the Thursday cabaret nights also attract admirers; N.B. the Decor score may not reflect a recent revamp as well as the post-*Survey* change of the upstairs members-only bar into a private dining room.

Golden Dragon ◐   21 12 14 £22
28-29 Gerrard St., W1 (Leicester Sq.), 020-7734 2763; fax 7734 1073
■ It's "not the flashiest" of places, but this "plain-looking" Chinatown spot is an "oasis on a bustling street", where a

"good meal is guaranteed" from a "decent" multiregional menu, including "insanely good dim sum" and "delicious duck"; it's "run of the mill" as far as some sceptics are concerned, but most concede, "you get what you expect, and leave happy."

Good Earth, The   20 | 16 | 17 | £30 |

233 Brompton Rd., SW3 (Knightsbridge/South Kensington), 020-7584 3658; fax 7823 8769 ◗
143-145 The Broadway, NW7 (Mill Hill B.R.), 020-8959 7011; fax 8959 1464

■ The "smiles and service have changed", but "they've maintained excellent standards throughout the years" and "delicious, authentic tasting" Chinese "food remains" at this recently redecorated "Knightsbridge branch that's great for taking mums and aunties" and its Mill Hill sibling; you "never fail to get a good meal", plus "efficient" staff are "not overbearing"; N.B. there are also delivery-only outposts in Wimbledon, Richmond and Hampstead.

Gopal's of Soho ◗ 🖾   ▽ 21 | 11 | 17 | £20 |

12 Bateman St., W1 (Leicester Sq./Tottenham Court Rd.), 020-7434 1621; fax 7434 0840

◼ "You can taste the care" that has gone into the "enjoyable, spicy" cooking at this "traditional" Indian in a "prime [Soho] location" ("convenient for that pre-theatre tandoori"); while few "risks are taken" by the kitchen, "the flavours are incredible", enduring "satisfying results every time."

GORDON RAMSAY AT CLARIDGE'S   26 | 24 | 25 | £74 |

Claridge's Hotel, Brook St., W1 (Bond St.), 020-7499 0099; fax 7499 3099; www.gordonramsay.com

◪ "Claridge's and [Gordon] Ramsay make a dynamic duo" at this "elegant" no-smoking Mayfair dining room where the "grand", "glittering" art deco interior is only surpassed by" the "master's" "beyond delicious" New French fare, an "excellent" wine list and "service that runs like clockwork"; it's an "amazing experience from the minute you walk in", especially if you "book the chef's table for food with a [kitchen] view"; if a few snipe it's "heaven on a plate, hell on the wallet" and find staff "too cloying", most sigh, "in a word, fabulous."

GORDON RAMSAY AT 68 ROYAL HOSPITAL RD. 🖾   29 | 25 | 29 | £86 |

68 Royal Hospital Rd., SW3 (Sloane Sq.), 020-7352 4441; fax 7352 3334; www.gordonramsay.com

■ Many "swoon regularly throughout the meal" at Gordon Ramsay's "clublike", no-smoking Chelsea "tour de force", rated No. 1 in this *Survey* for Food and Service, where "extravagant creations" from a "peerless" New French menu are "as near to perfection as you're likely to find on these shores", presented by "impeccable" staff; "take the first booking available" as this "feast for the senses" is a "transcendent" "experience to savour" and the monthlong "wait worth its weight in gold"; P.S. the bargain lunch allows "you to dine like a king, but only leave half your kingdom."

Goring Dining Room 20 | 22 | 24 | £49
The Goring Hotel, 15 Beeston Pl., SW1 (Victoria), 020-7396 9000; fax 7834 4393; www.goringhotel.co.uk
■ "In a charming" hotel with "echoes of a bygone age", this "comfortable, slightly starchy" dining room near Victoria "never disappoints" for "no-nonsense" Traditional British cooking" – including perhaps "the best afternoon tea" – with "service to rival anywhere", making it a "popular rendezvous" spot for "ladies and gentlemen who 'train' up for a day's shopping"; a handful find it "stuffy", but on balance it's a "refreshing change": "not boring, the Goring!"

Gourmet Burger Kitchen – | – | – | M
44 Northcote Rd., SW11 (Clapham Junction B.R.), 020-7228 3309
131 Chiswick High Rd., W4 (Turnham Green), 020-8995 4548
50 Westbourne Grove, W2 (Bayswater), 020-7243 4344
333 Putney Bridge Rd., SW15 (Putney Bridge), 020-8789 1199
49 Fulham Broadway, SW6 (Fulham Broadway), 020-7381 4242
331 West End Ln., NW6 (West Hampstead), 020-7794 5455
www.gbkinfo.co.uk
"If you have a hankering" for a "juicy burger", "you won't be disappointed" by the gourmet options at New Zealand chef Peter Gordon's "informal", "excellent small chain" (with big ambitions) around town where "even the bun is a custom job!"; whether you "stick with the basic", "high-quality" Aberdeen-Angus beef patty, opt for toppings or order chicken, venison or lamb instead, it's "always fresh" and "perfectly cooked."

Gravetye Manor 23 | 25 | 27 | £62
Gravetye Manor Hotel, Vowels Ln., East Grinstead, West Sussex, 01342 810567; fax 01342 810080; www.gravetyemanor.co.uk
■ An "unforgettable experience" encore enthusiasts enraptured by the "hushed dining room" of this "great country house hotel" in a "magnificent" Sussex location dating back to 1598 where a "wonderful" Modern British menu using "lots of local produce and game" is on offer and service is "attentive, but relaxed"; "save for a romantic evening" is the tip from those sweet on this "magical setting", complete with open fires, a "beautiful garden" and a "terrace perfect for sipping champagne."

Great Eastern Dining Room 🗷 20 | 18 | 20 | £40
54 Great Eastern St., EC2 (Liverpool St./Old St.), 020-7613 4545; fax 7613 4137; www.greateasterndining.co.uk
◪ Part of the Will Ricker–owned group of restaurants (e&o, Cicada, et al.), this "laid-back" Hoxton haunt in a former

fabric warehouse now boasts a Pan-Asian menu with "very tasty" fusion dishes from the Far East served by "great-looking staff", plus a "fun, hip" basement bar for drinks ("litchi martinis from heaven") and dim sum; but gripers grouch that "prices have gone astronomical" advising eat here at "expense-account time."

Greek Valley ☒　　　　　▽ 17 | 13 | 21 | £19
130 Boundary Rd., NW8 (St. John's Wood/Swiss Cottage), 020-7624 3217; www.greekvalley.co.uk
■ "Not spectacular, but always enjoyable", Peter and Effie Bosnic's "friendly", family-run St. John's Wood taverna serves a never-changing menu of "cheap Greek food"; never mind the "outdated decor" as everyone "feels just at home" here, particularly on weekend evenings when the live bouzouki music enhances the "nice atmosphere."

Greenhouse, The ☒　　　　– | – | – | VE
27A Hay's Mews, W1 (Green Park), 020-7499 3331; fax 7499 5368
After taking over the site from the Capital Group last year, ambitious restaurateur Marlon Abela (who also has dining ventures in France and the U.S.), relaunched this long-established Mayfair venue, bestowing a garden-themed look upon the modern, sleek premises and installing chef Bjorn van der Horst to oversee a polished New French menu; the extraordinary, 2,000-plus strong wine list features a good sub-£40 selection as well as lots of rarities.

Green Olive, The　　　　　▽ 21 | 17 | 20 | £37
5 Warwick Pl., W9 (Warwick Ave.), 020-7289 2469; fax 7289 2463
◪ A "great neighbourhood spot" for "excellent" Italian fare this once-buzzy Maida Vale outpost of the Red Pepper Group "deserves to be more popular" say insiders who still find it "welcoming"; but sceptics skewer this Olive as "over-ambitious for its locale" and think it's a pity it's "not as good as it used to be"; N.B. a refurb is slated to be completed around press time.

Green's　　　　　　　23 | 21 | 23 | £45
36 Duke St., SW1 (Green Park/Piccadilly Circus), 020-7930 4566; fax 7930 2958; www.greens.org.uk
■ "As comfortable as a pair of [John] Lobb shoes, and as stylish", Simon Parker Bowles' "clubby" St James's "gem" awash in mahogany, leather and "old-world charm" is a "rock-steady" option for Traditional British dishes and some of the "best fish in town"; it's "still pleasing after all these years", plus there's also a "classy, less intimidating" bar to eat at that's especially "delightful if you're dining alone."

Grenadier　　　　　　　15 | 21 | 18 | £26
18 Wilton Row, SW1 (Hyde Park Corner), 020-7235 3074; fax 7235 3400
■ It's a "historic, atmospheric" "pub, not a restaurant" and it serves a "very un-Atkins"-like Traditional British menu,

nevertheless, this supposedly haunted "local tavern" "smack dab in a chic area" is "a must for Londoners and out-of-towners" who "go for the hustle-bustle" akin to a "scene out of central casting"; "if you can find it, it's the best vintage place for a banger and a pint", though many "forgo that in favour of their famous Bloody Mary's", truly a "hangover helper."

Grill Room, The   24 24 26 £60

The Dorchester, 53 Park Ln., W1 (Hyde Park Corner/Marble Arch), 020-7629 8888; fax 7317 6464; www.dorchesterhotel.com

■ "The British Empire liveth" on at this "posh" Mayfair dining room in the Dorchester hotel decorated with strong Moorish influences where the "impeccable" service is "unobtrusive" and the "beautifully done", "quintessentially" Traditional British fare from Henry Brosi is "conjured to the table as part of the show"; "go on, splurge", because this "institution" offers a "civilised" "must-have experience" ("more, please"), making it "great for the love of your life – and your parents"; N.B. jacket is preferred.

Grissini   ▽ 15 19 17 £42

Carlton Tower, 1st fl., Cadogan Pl., SW1 (Knightsbridge/ Sloane Sq.), 020-7235 1234; fax 7235 9129; www.carltontower.com

■ Bright and airy, this first-floor dining room of the Carlton Tower in Knightsbridge has a "view of Cadogan Place's garden square that's beautiful during the day", a glass canopied roof lending an alfresco ambience and a "good" Italian-Mediterranean menu that includes an "excellent Sunday brunch" with an expansive display of antipasti (kids under six go free); N.B. now closed for dinner.

Groucho Club, The 🗷   16 17 18 £46

Private club; inquiries: 020-7439 4685

◪ "If you get in, you're 'in'" (apparently), in which case, expect to find a "buzzy, bustling" atmosphere at Joel Cadbury's famous Soho private club that draws artists, writers and media types and is still a "real scene"; the "uneven" Modern British cooking may not be the prime attraction at this "hangout" but the "louche atmosphere" is "always fun" and "continues to please."

Grumbles   20 16 21 £26

35 Churton St., SW1 (Pimlico/Victoria), 020-7834 0149; fax 7834 0298

■ "Very good", "honest" Anglo-French bistro fare and "quirky but kind staff" make this "cheap and cheerful" "tiny" Pimlico "institution" a "safe haven" and an "ideal local"; "don't come for an intimate chat, as the tables are packed in", instead, come for the "great-value", "top-quality lunches" and the "relaxed", "cosy atmosphere that never lets you down."

Guinea Grill ⌧ — | — | — | E |

30 Bruton Pl., W1 (Bond St.), 020-7499 1210; www.theguinea.co.uk

"Great for Traditional British food" like steak and kidney pie and "properly grilled" meats, this "cramped", clubby "local favourite" inside the Guinea pub "right off Berkeley Square" boasts a "setting that's classic London" with walls covered with paintings and a fireplace, and service that's "friendly and helpful without being obtrusive"; it's especially popular for weekday business lunches.

Gung-Ho ● 18 | 13 | 16 | £28 |

330 West End Ln., NW6 (West Hampstead), 020-7794 1444; fax 7794 5522

◪ A "reliable, round-the-corner Chinese" with a loyal following ("I know the menu backwards and forwards"), this Hampstead local with a "funky" albeit dated decor and "quick service" cooks up "good, broad-ranging" Mandarin cuisine that "constantly delivers"; but not everyone is gung-ho – detractors are "not impressed by the food" and deem staff "uncaring."

HAKKASAN ● 25 | 26 | 18 | £49 |

8 Hanway Pl., W1 (Tottenham Court Rd.), 020-7927 7000; fax 7907 1889

◪ "It's such a scene, but that's part of the charm" of Alan Yau's "stunning" basement venue "in a back alley" off Tottenham Court Road that "challenges the concept of Chinese restaurants" with a "chic Chinoise", Christian Liagre–designed setting; it's an "exquisite" canvas for "sophisticated dim sum", "extraordinary" Cantonese cuisine "lurvely for both carni- and herbivores" and "tasty cocktails" (the two "bars are very groovy"); whilst detractors hack away at the "hipper-than-thou service" and "chaotic two-sittings" policy, most "crave going back."

Halepi 21 | 12 | 20 | £28 |

18 Leinster Terrace, W2 (Lancaster Gate/Queensway), 020-7262 1070; fax 7262 2083 ●
48-50 Belsize Ln., NW3 (Belsize Park/Swiss Cottage), 020-7431 5855; fax 7431 5844

■ Nearly "everyone's favourite Greek restaurant for good reason", these "cheery", "bustling" tavernas with "accommodating staff" by Hyde Park (an "old-fashioned" 38-year-old) and Belsize Park (the younger sib) lure punters with "authentic" "fare that's excellent for the price"; it's "not much to look at", but the "vibrant atmosphere" and "generous portions" "make for a wonderful hangout."

Harbour City ● 19 | 10 | 13 | £21 |

46 Gerrard St., W1 (Leicester Sq./Piccadilly Circus), 020-7439 7859; fax 7734 7745

◪ "A cut above the usual" assert supporters of this "classic" Chinatown haunt offering "terrific dim sum" (lunch only) and an "interesting variety of other [multiregional] dishes" in a three-level space with "brighter than average decor"; opinions are split over service with fans finding it "attentive" and others harbouring feelings about "dreadful, rude staff (some of us understand Cantonese!)"

Hard Rock Cafe ● 　　　14 | 19 | 15 | £22 |
150 Old Park Ln., W1 (Green Park/Hyde Park Corner), 020-7629 0382; fax 7629 8702; www.hardrock.com
◪ "The original and it rocks", no you "can't beat the music and atmosphere" applaud fans who "bring the kids" to this "sentimental favourite" by Hyde Park Corner for "tasty" American diner fare and a dose of "fabulous memorabilia" from the likes of Jimi, Mick and Janis; whilst taunters toss it off as the "same formula rolled out everywhere" they're overruled by crowds who cheer "it doesn't disappoint."

Harlem ● 　　　9 | 15 | 12 | £25 |
78 Westbourne Grove, W2 (Bayswater/Queensway), 020-7985 0900; www.harlemsoulfood.com
◪ Backed by esteemed rock producer Arthur Baker, this all-day Westbourne Grove newcomer serves a "simple menu" of American soul food inspired by its namesake NYC neighbourhood until 2 AM on most nights; early visitors who suggest it may be better for "drinks and the scene" in the "very cosy downstairs bar with a DJ" may welcome the arrival of new chef Fiona Ruane, formerly of Jimmy's Uptown in Manhattan; N.B. a second branch was due to open in Brixton at press time.

Harry's Bar ● 🖾 　　　23 | 23 | 24 | £64 |
Private club; inquiries: 020-7408 0844
■ "Excellent on every count", this "discreet, elegant" private club in the Mark Birley empire remains "one of Mayfair's best [dining] rooms" with "superior Italian food" that's the "closest thing to heaven (angel hair pasta straight from Gabriel's head!), a fantastic wine list" and "terrific staff" "willing to make anything one wants"; yes, the "absurd prices" leave a few aghast, but most concede this "classy joint" boasts an "unbeatable formula"; N.B. jackets and ties required, and no phones allowed.

Hartwell House 　　　– | – | – | VE |
Hartwell House, Oxford Rd., Aylesbury, Buckinghamshire, 01296 747444; fax 01296 747450; www.hartwell-house.com
"A country retreat" "to go to when you want to spoil yourself", this "very lovely" restored 17th-century hotel set in "beautiful grounds" in Buckinghamshire wins admirers' hearts with its "elegant, posh" dining room and "excellent" Modern British menu that includes "good-value" lunch "deals" (from £22); "staff are attentive but not intrusive", and the "location and decor cannot be beat", in fact, it's "wonderful for a weekend getaway"

Havelock Tavern ⊭   ▽ 21 17 13 £19
57 Masbro Rd., W14 (Olympia/Shepherd's Bush), 020-7603 5374;
fax 7602 1163; www.thehavelocktavern.co.uk
◪ With a "no-booking policy" at this "trendy" Brook Green
gastro-pub, the "competition for tables can have Darwinian
undertones", particularly for "non-locals", but selected
diners are rewarded with "imaginative" Modern British
dishes that "are always freshly cooked"; on the downside,
sceptics complain that service is oftentimes "so unfriendly
it's almost a cliché."

Hi Sushi   16 10 15 £21
16 Hampstead High St., NW3 (Hampstead), 020-7794 2828;
fax 7794 7328
40 Frith St., W1 (Leicester Sq.), 020-7734 9688; fax 7734 9882
◪ "Your legs go in the pit" at the "sunken" "communal
pod" tables of this "funky", "fun" duo in Soho (the original)
and Hampstead while your chopsticks hoist "reasonable"
Japanese food, including "fresh" fish for that sashimi and
"sushi fix"; still, a few say good-bye, not hi, declaring it's
"not that cheap and not that cheerful."

Home House ◗   18 23 23 £45
Private club; inquiries: 020-7670 2100
◪ A "real home away from home", this "luxurious, but laid-
back private club" in Marylebone boasts a "wonderful high-
ceilinged dining room" that's "improved its act" with a
"well-executed" Modern British menu, "attentive service"
and the "happening" Bison Bar downstairs; if a few find
the fare "somewhat limited" in scope, the Housebound
retort it's "imaginative", plus the "real treat is eating in the
garden in warm months."

Hoxton Apprentice   – – – M
16 Hoxton Sq., N1 (Old St.), 020-7749 2828;
www.hoxtonapprentice.com
Echoing the worthy intentions of Jamie Oliver's nearby
Fifteen and benefiting from government backing, this new
100-seat eatery in a handsome, neo-gothic Hoxton building
is a dynamic project developed by the Training for Life
charity that combines quality dining with a restaurant
training school for a select group from disadvantaged
communities; an internationally slanted Eclectic menu is
overseen by culinary doyenne Prue Leith, with each dish
offered in starter and main-sized portions; N.B. open from
11 AM straight through 11 PM.

HUNAN ⊠   26 13 20 £38
51 Pimlico Rd., SW1 (Sloane Sq.), 020-7730 5712; fax 7730 8265
■ "Go with your closest foodie friends and hours to spare"
to this "family-run" Chinese eatery on Pimlico Green where
you "put yourself in the hands of owner" Mr. Peng, and "let
him choose for you" – "every time he comes back it's a

surprise what will be on the plate"; the "dazzling array" of Chinese "delicacies" (mainly in tapas-sized portions) make it easy to "ignore" the "bland decor" so "just relax and have a delicious evening."

Hush ☒ 16 20 15 £42
8 Lancashire Ct., W1 (Bond St.), 020-7659 1500; fax 7659 1501; www.hush.co.uk

■ "No longer a secret, but still worthy", this "secluded bistro off Bond Street" comprises a "hip", "casual" ground-floor brasserie with "simple, good" fare "ideal for a mid-shopping-spree refuelling stop", and a more "romantic", "chic" – and expensive – upstairs dining room with an upscale Modern British menu for a "sexy tête-à-tête"; whilst a few fume it's "very average", supporters retort just "hush" and try the courtyard – it's a "haven in the summer."

Ifield, The ▽ 16 17 16 £22
59 Ifield Rd., SW10 (Earl's Ct.), 020-7351 4900; fax 7351 1100

■ There's "lots of atmosphere" at Ed Baines' and Jamie Poulton's "amicable" gastro-pub on the Chelsea-Fulham border with a "cosy" dining area serving "innovative" yet undemanding Modern British fare; it's the "perfect local", "even for those not into pubs, but it's just a bit smoky for eating" pout a few who are also put off when the bar is "filled to the brim with young hipsters."

Ikeda ☒ ▽ 23 10 18 £43
30 Brook St., W1 (Bond St.), 020-7629 2730; fax 8989 5857

■ Now reaching its 25th anniversary, this inconspicuous Mayfair Japanese venue offers an "excellent, traditional menu executed with precision and reliability", served by kimono-clad waitresses; but insiders confide "approach with caution" as the "expensive prices" could "burn a hole in your wallet" – this is "damned expensive fish."

Ikkyu 20 9 17 £22
67A Tottenham Court Rd., W1 (Goodge St.), 020-7636 9280; fax 7436 6169

■ "Always filled with Japanese customers and the chic slumming it", this "dingy" yet "unpretentious" underground setting on Tottenham Court Road is appreciated for its "marvellously traditional" Japanese fare, including "fresh sushi and sashimi" at "very reasonable prices"; the "set menus at lunch are a real bargain" plus there's a "wider variety" on offer for dinner.

Il Bordello – – – M
81 Wapping High St., E1 (Wapping), 020-7481 9950

"If you don't mind sitting like sardines, you'll love" this homely, industrial-style Wapping venue on the ground floor of a converted warehouse where the "excellent variety" of Traditional Italian dishes is so "worth the effort, as attested" by "packed-out" "tables and line up by the bar"; "book up early" "if more than two or in a hurry."

Il Convivio ⌧　　　　　　　21　18　19　£44
143 Ebury St., SW1 (Sloane Sq./Victoria), 020-7730 4099; fax 7730 4103; www.etruscagroup.co.uk

☑ "The chef likes to experiment with unusual combinations" at this "wonderful little Italian place near Victoria" Coach Station where "carefully executed dishes", including "melt-in-your-mouth pasta", prompt loyalists to exclaim we're "lovin' it"; still, it's "not so convincing" for a few who deem it "conservative in feel and clientele"; N.B. the rear conservatory has a retractable roof.

Il Falconiere ⌧　　　　　　▽ 16　13　20　£24
84 Old Brompton Rd., SW7 (Gloucester Rd./ South Kensington), 020-7589 2401; fax 7589 9158; www.ilfalconiere.co.uk

☑ Owned and run by the Mosquera family for over 25 years, this "friendly neighbourhood Italian" in South Kensington may look "a little tired" now, but loyal customers ("I've been visiting for 15 years") still flock here for "good quality", albeit "basic" fare, including an "excellent" £10 lunch; but for a few, the "sometimes grumpy waiters" are a cloud on the horizon.

Imperial China　　　　　　19　17　16　£24
25A Lisle St., WC2 (Leicester Sq./Piccadilly Circus), 020-7734 3388

■ A "swish new decor" – complete "with a little stream" – at this revamped and renamed eatery formerly known as China City and set in a Chinatown courtyard creates an "atmosphere more European than Chinese", but the multiregional cooking is "as good as Hong Kong's", notably the "glorious dim sum"; although it now looks "most civilised", some say "service has stayed the same": "fast, but not very friendly."

Imperial City ⌧　　　　　　18　17　16　£40
Royal Exchange, Cornhill, EC3 (Bank), 020-7626 3437; fax 7338 0125; www.orientalrestaurantgroup.co.uk

■ For "something different from the mainstream" of City dining, this "sprawling Chinese in the basement" below the Royal Exchange "is the place", with "a large menu" of "reliable" Mandarin dishes "that caters to all walks of life" and tastes (plus they also "make old favourites no longer on the menu"); but some snipe it's a "bit expensive."

INC Bar & Restaurant　　　　– – – E
7 College Approach, SE10 (Cutty Sark DLR), 020-8858 6721

Just a stone's throw from the Cutty Sark landmark, this former music hall in a Georgian Greenwich building has been transformed into a smart, multiroomed venue with two hip bars and a quirky, stylised restaurant with plasma screens displaying modern art; the Eclectic menu is dominated by grilled meats (with a wide choice of dressings) and features an abundance of bar snacks.

Incognico ● ⊘ ☒   21 | 16 | 19 | £40

117 Shaftesbury Ave., WC2 (Leicester Sq.), 020-7836 8866; fax 7240 9525; www.decarestaurant.com

■ "Perfect for the theatre crowd" chorus customers of this "jolly" "gem" in Theatreland run by Nico Ladenis' daughter Natasha that offers an "eclectic mix" of "innovative" New French dishes, including a "sensational value" set menu that's "not to be missed"; expect a "truly delightful" meal as the setting is "quiet enough to enjoy a conversation" and staff are "welcoming"; P.S. there's a "comfortable downstairs bar for pre-dinner drinks."

Indigo ●   22 | 22 | 23 | £44

One Aldwych Hotel, 1 Aldwych, WC2 (Charing Cross/ Covent Garden), 020-7300 0400; fax 7300 0401; www.onealdwych.com

◪ "One of the best hotel 'secondary' restaurants (Axis is their prime)" is the take on One Aldwych's "comfortable", "chic" balcony dining area with a "striking contemporary decor" overlooking the "amusing lobby" and "wild bar scene below"; the "inventive, quietly assertive" Modern European fare is "tasty" (albeit a few feel it's "expensive for what you get"), and "friendly service" gets brownie points: "lone women diners are treated like queens."

Inn The Park   – | – | – | M

St. James's Park, SW1 (St. James's Park), 020-7451 9999; fax (011-44-20) 7451 9998

Located at the Horse Guards Parade end of St. James's Park, and boasting scenic views of the impressive Nash-designed landscape, this lakeside cafe, recently renovated to resemble a modern log cabin, is open from 8 AM till 11 PM, and overseen by restaurateur Oliver Peyton; the seasonally changing Traditional British menu boasts more upscale options in the evening, and bookings are encouraged; N.B. parking is nonexistent.

Ishbilia ●   23 | 13 | 20 | £34

9 William St., SW1 (Knightsbridge), 020-7235 7788; fax 7235 7771; www.ishbilia.com

■ Well "located around the corner from Harvey Nicks for a post–shopping spree" meal, this Knightsbridge Lebanese looks "a bit rough", but delights fans with "refined Middle Eastern" fare that's "on a par with the best in Beirut"; if "service is pleasant" but sometimes "indifferent", never mind – it's still a "great place to go with a group" – especially for the "excellent cabaret and floor show" from belly dancers (Thursday–Saturday).

Isola ☒ 18 | 19 | 17 | £42

145 Knightsbridge, SW1 (Knightsbridge), 020-7838 1055; fax 7838 1099; www.gruppo.co.uk

◪ Oliver Peyton's "chichi" Knightsbridge venue features the Iso-Bar on the ground floor and a "sleek dining room" below spotlighting chef Marc Broadbent's "consistently delicious" Modern Italian cooking accompanied by a "superb wine list"; still, quibblers claim "it used to be glorious" and now it's "erratic" – and opinions on service are also split – "friendly, positive" vs. "downright clueless"; N.B. there's now an antipasto bar in the restaurant.

I-Thai ▽ 21 | 25 | 19 | £53

Hempel Hotel, 31-35 Craven Hill Gardens, W2 (Lancaster Gate), 020-7298 9000; fax 7402 4666; www.the-hempel.co.uk

◪ The "must-see" high-end designer hotel in Bayswater with a "fantastic", "faultless decor" ("minimalism is everything") has undergone a change of ownership (the eponymous Anouska Hempel is no longer involved), nevertheless, in the narrow, elegant dining room, the Italian-Thai fusion menu continues to impress fans who fawn "whatever you choose will" "keep you coming back"; still, a few foes fume it's "ridiculously expensive."

itsu 17 | 15 | 14 | £26

103 Wardour St., W1 (Leicester Sq./Piccadilly Circus), 020-7479 4794; fax 7479 4795

118 Draycott Ave., SW3 (South Kensington), 020-7590 2400; fax 7590 2403

Cabot Sq. E., level 2, E14 (Canary Wharf), 020-7512 5790; fax 7512 5791 ☒

www.itsu.co.uk

◪ "Blows away its peers" report supporters who roll into this Japanese conveyor belt trio in Chelsea (the original), Soho and Canary Wharf "with an air of a hip locale" for "inventive" sushi; "it's a quick in and out" – "speedy without being rushed" – plus it's "reasonably priced, if you can stop grabbing at the plates"; sure, it "doesn't cut the mustard with real aficionados", but the more tolerant shrug it's "good enough for a shopping break."

IVY, THE ◐ 23 | 20 | 22 | £48

1 West St., WC2 (Leicester Sq.), 020-7836 4751; fax 7240 9333; www.caprice-holdings.co.uk

◪ "Believe everything you've heard" about this "people-watching splurge" in Theatreland where the Modern British–European dishes are as "divine" "as the star wattage" ("wish I could sit next to Kylie or Madge"), staff are "impeccable" and the environs are "not as pretentious as you'd think"; if a few feel it's "no longer hot but smouldering" and "mobbed by the would-be-with-its", they're overruled by fans who concur it's "worth the advance planning"; P.S. best tip for a table: "dine early or late" – or be "famous."

Iznik ▽ 17 23 18 £25
*19 Highbury Park, N5 (Highbury & Islington), 020-7704 8099;
fax 7354 5697*
◪ "Like being in a Turkish bazaar" attest admirers of this
"cosy", "atmospheric" antique-filled Highbury "secret",
a "valued local" that attracts acolytes with "authentic"
Ottoman-inspired cuisine "served by a wonderful sweet
family"; still, a few feel it's "nice, but nothing exceptional."

Jade Garden ● 17 13 13 £21
*15 Wardour St., W1 (Leicester Sq./Piccadilly Circus),
020-7437 5065; fax 7429 7851*
◪ For "dim-sum fun" along with "excellent noodle dishes"
and other "inexpensive", multregional dishes, supporters
plant themselves in this "tranquil, almost Zen"-like
Chinatown venue; it's "always busy" so the staff may "rush
you a bit", but that's what makes it "good for people on the
run" or "for a post-theatre meal."

Jim Thompson's 16 20 14 £25
*8-13 Bird St., W1 (Bond St.), 020-7355 2453; fax 7499 0767
141 The Broadway, SW19 (Wimbledon), 020-8540 5540;
fax 8540 8728
408 Upper Richmond Rd., SW15 (East Putney), 020-8788 3737;
fax 8788 3738
617 King's Rd., SW6 (Fulham Broadway), 020-7731 0999;
fax 7731 2835
889 Green Lanes, N21 (Southgate/Wood Green), 020-8360 0005;
fax 8364 3006
www.jimthompsons.com*
◪ "Fun, funky" and filled with "kitschy" ornaments and
furniture, all for sale, this "colourful" Southeast Asian
chain about town named after an American adventurer
from the silk trade days "scores high with the kids", and
coupled with an "eclectic" menu, it "never fails to deliver"
for a "relaxed night out"; still, detractors deem the decor a
"bit much" and deride the food as "not very inspiring."

Jin Kichi 23 9 18 £30
73 Heath St., NW3 (Hampstead), 020-7794 6158
◼ When craving a "fix of yakitori", "fresh sushi" or
"authentic" Japanese dishes, fans head to this "secret"
Hampstead haunt; it's an "amazing" "hole-in-the-wall" with
the "genuine feel of a Tokyo basement" – which translates
to "constantly full", "often cramped and difficult to book."

Joe Allen ● 16 17 17 £30
13 Exeter St., WC2 (Covent Garden), 020-7836 0651; fax 7497 2148
◪ "If you love àpres-theatre" dining, head to this "ever-
popular" "little bit of Broadway in London" offering Eclectic-
American "comfort food" in a basement of brick archways
just off the Strand; this is where the stage "stars come out
and play", plus there's "memorabilia wherever you look" –

yes, this "long-established" "hangout" "hasn't changed over the years" and whilst some say it's "more for the buzz than the food", most agree it's "still fun to visit."

Joe's   15 | 14 | 16 | £28
126 Draycott Ave., SW3 (South Kensington), 020-7225 2217; fax 7584 1133

◪ "Rest your Jimmys" – as in Choos – "and your weary shopping feet" – "muah, muah, darling" – at this "very useful Brompton Crosser" where "Chelsea's beautiful people flock" for "great lunchtime salads" and "consistently good" Modern British fare; still, a few feel it's a "bit pompous" and "overpriced" to boot.

Joe's Restaurant Bar ⌧   19 | 18 | 19 | £25
Joseph, 16 Sloane St., SW1 (Knightsbridge), 020-7235 9869; fax 7235 3218

■ Joseph's in-store basement cafe/diner in Knightsbridge is "great fun if you're a local" or having "lunch with girlfriends" – but "good luck getting a table" because it's still "home away from home" to some "after all these years"; yes, it's "pricey, but because of its location, you turn a blind eye" and it's a "little noisy" so go for some "yadda, yadda, yadda" with a side of "excellent" Modern British cooking.

Joy King Lau ●   24 | 11 | 16 | £20
3 Leicester St., WC2 (Leicester Sq./Piccadilly Circus), 020-7437 1133; fax 7437 2629

■ "There's not much atmosphere, but then" the "masses of Chinese who congregate" at this "very busy" Chinatown venue "tucked away on a side street" come for "superior dim sum" and other "great" multiregional dishes that "make it worth a detour"; another joy to behold: the staff are "efficient" and "friendly" – yes, it's "packed full to the brim at weekends for good reason."

J. SHEEKEY ●   25 | 21 | 23 | £47
28-32 St. Martin's Ct., WC2 (Leicester Sq.), 020-7240 2565; fax 7240 8114

■ "Anyone with a love of seafood should experience" this "sophisticated" Theatreland "outfit", a "sleek sister to The Ivy" and Le Caprice with "wood-panelled rooms", a "clubby atmosphere" and a "bit of celeb-spotting for good measure"; "spankingly fresh" and "second to none", the "trademark fish dishes" "range from tastefully simple to near exotic", all toted to table by "professional staff" appreciated for "treating ordinary theatregoers the same as the stars."

Julie's   17 | 23 | 20 | £35
135 Portland Rd., W11 (Holland Park), 020-7229 8331; fax 7229 4050; www.juliesrestaurant.com

■ "So charming on the quaintest street" near Holland Park, this "intimate" restaurant-cum–wine bar is a "lovely" "hideaway" to "meet up with a friend" for a "relaxing dinner" of "imaginative" Modern British fare or for "private" liaisons with a "maze" of "comfy" rooms "to lose yourself" in, all attended to by "gorgeous servers"; P.S. "get the right table: if summer, the greenhouse area, if winter, by the fire."

Just Gladwins ⊠   – – – E

Minster Ct., 1 Mark Ln., EC3 (Bank/Monument), 020-7444 0004; fax 7444 0001; www.justgladwins.com

"The decor hides the fact you are underground so well" at Peter Gladwin's "pleasing" 10-year-old, weekday lunch-only City venue with a water sculpture that lends a "sense of calm" and "attentive service"; whilst some are just glad to have this "great place to go" come midday, the less-impressed shrug it's just "decent" Modern British "food at expense-account prices" – there's "nothing special here."

Just St. James's   14 20 16 £40

12 St. James's St., SW1 (Green Park), 020-7976 2222; fax 7976 2020; www.juststjames.com

◪ "Like eating on a permanently moored ocean liner", this "absolutely cavernous", "gorgeous" spot in an "old Barclays Bank" features a "great bar scene" and a more "peaceful" dining area with "solid" Modern European cooking; still, many feel that the "competent but ordinary food" does "not match the setting", plus "staff get lost" in "so much space"; N.B. downstairs is the lesser-known Just Oriental, a "cracking bar" with "inexpensive" snacks.

KAI MAYFAIR   27 19 22 £48

65 S. Audley St., W1 (Bond St./Marble Arch), 020-7493 8988; fax 7493 1456; www.kaimayfair.com

■ "Definitely not your plebeian Chinese dining experience", this "calm", "elegant" Mayfair venue showboats "excellent service" and "outstanding" multiregional cooking that "exceeds expectations"; if a handful huff it "doesn't knock your socks off at these prices", fans retort it's "expensive, but worth saving up for" and "even better when somebody else is paying"; P.S. the occasional "harpist is a nice touch, not over the top."

Kandoo ◑   ▽ 18 8 13 £16

458 Edgware Rd., W2 (Edgware Rd.), 020-7724 2428

■ "No-frills dining for genuine kebab lovers" is on offer at this "unusual" Edgware Road BYO venue that gets "no points for decor", but scores high praise for "splendid" Persian cuisine at "a decent price", all toted to table by "pleasant staff"; N.B. the name refers to the beehive-shaped clay bread oven in the window.

Kanteen at K-West   – – – E

K-West Hotel, Richmond Way, W14 (Shepherd's Bush), 0871-222 4044; www.k-west.co.uk

Leather seating, unusual wooden floor tiles and colourful lighting are the backdrop for the music and media crowd who gather at this new dining room inside the smart designer K-West Hotel in Shepherd's Bush for gutsy Eclectic fare; an international list from Jeroboams wine merchants starts at an eyebrow-raising £17; N.B. valet parking available.

Kastoori ‌ – | – | – | I
188 Upper Tooting Rd., SW17 (Tooting Bec/Tooting Broadway), 020-8767 7027
Even "confirmed carnivores" confide "you just don't miss the meat" at this low-key Tooting vegetarian that's been serving "authentic", "superlative" Indian dishes with East "African accents" for over 15 years, including curry dishes that are "absolute stunners"; P.S. the "awesome" offerings also include prix fixe lunch and dinner menus.

Kensington Place ● 21 | 17 | 17 | £39
201-209 Kensington Church St., W8 (Notting Hill Gate), 020-7727 3184; fax 7229 2025; www.egami.co.uk
⊠ "Dine like an 'it' girl" at this "terribly chichi" yet "friendly" Kensington "beautiful-people spot" where "you have to shout to be heard" whilst dining on Modern British fare, including "superb" seafood from the "adjoining eponymous fishmonger"; still, a few find it "moderate on all counts (except the bill)", and speculate that though it was once a "see-and-be-seen" "institution, now it's a little tired."

Kettners ● 12 | 18 | 15 | £27
29 Romilly St., W1 (Leicester Sq.), 020-7734 6112; fax 7434 1214; www.pizzaexpress.com/kettners
⊠ With its "fab", "throwback-to-a-past-era" decor, "good", "low-cost" Italian menu, "staff that know their stuff" and live pianist, this "step up from the [usual] Pizza Express experience" is "the best thing to happen" to this Soho townhouse since it was "Oscar Wilde's hangout"; whilst the less-impressed paint a different picture, pouting the "food still disappoints", even they admit the "champagne bar can be fun."

Kew Grill – | – | – | E
10B Kew Green, Kew (Kew Gardens), 020-8948 4433; www.awtonline.co.uk
Buoyed by the popularity of his Notting Grill venture, celeb chef Antony Worrall Thompson has opened a second, smaller space in homey Kew premises with leather seats, exposed-brick walls and his trademark menu of bold Traditional British fare, boasting a wide range of organic meat, fish and vegetables; the patron's wife, Jay, can often be seen lending a hand in the kitchen.

Khan's ● 18 | 9 | 12 | £17
13-15 Westbourne Grove, W2 (Bayswater/Queensway), 020-7727 5420; fax 7229 1835; www.khansrestaurant.com
⊠ The "Indian equivalent of fast food", this "ultra-casual" Bayswater eatery offers "inexpensive", "fabulous grub"

served with "conveyor belt"-like frequency by "brusque", "brisk" staff who are "part of the charm"; since the place has "gone dry" (no alcohol allowed on the premises), some argue "standards have slipped", hence "it's not as crowded as it used to be."

Khan's of Kensington ❶   19 | 10 | 15 | £22

3 Harrington Rd., SW7 (South Kensington), 020-7584 4114; fax 7581 2900

■ "Amidst all its posh neighbours" in South Kensington, this "casual", "comfortable" Indian eatery (not connected at all with the Bayswater venue) offers "a warm welcome" and an "original" menu that "has always been good"; "now that it had a face-lift" a few feel this once "stark" "student hangout" is "even better", though others fail to notice the "improvements."

Kiku   – | – | – | E

17 Half Moon St., W1 (Green Park), 020-7499 4208; fax 7409-3359; www.kikurestaurant.co.uk

"A great-value £12 set lunch" with "loads of courses served at a reasonable pace by smiling staff (who remember you from last time)" is the magnet at this simply decorated, bi-level Mayfair Japanese with a dedicated sushi counter seating 15; a handful feel the "à la carte menu" can be "expensive at dinner."

Koi   21 | 18 | 19 | £39

1E Palace Gate, W8 (Gloucester Rd./High St. Kensington), 020-7581 8778; fax 7589 2788

☑ With "delicious" fish and "good quality sushi" served by "friendly staff", this low-key, "grown-up" Kensington Japanese makes a "reliable neighbourhood" option – especially as "you can always get a table"; that said, insiders suggest you "go early since they may be out of certain dishes"; N.B. a koi-stocked interior pond adds to its appeal.

Kulu Kulu Sushi ⊠   20 | 7 | 12 | £20

76 Brewer St., W1 (Piccadilly Circus), 020-7734 7316; fax 7734 6507
51-53 Shelton St., WC2 (Covent Garden), 020 7240 5687; fax (011-44-20) 7240 5687
39 Thurloe Pl., SW7 (South Kensington), 020-7589 2225

☑ There's a "purist focus on authentic sushi rather than pretend Japanese tapas" affirm fans of this "unpretentious" "conveyor-belt" trio in Soho, Covent Garden and South Ken, where "incredibly inexpensive" prices compensate for an obvious lack of "effort on decor"; a few sceptics are "not impressed": "more about quantity than quality."

La Bouchée   21 | 16 | 16 | £30

56 Old Brompton Rd., SW7 (South Kensington), 020-7589 1929; fax 7584 8625

☑ "When Paris is too far, this bistro will tide you over" with its "homey, authentic" Gallic cooking, "great deals on little-known regional wines" and "hectic" service "without a smile – how French!"; sure, it's "cramped", yet it's "very jolly at lunchtime" when locals "go for the set meals" and it makes a "charming" setting for a "romantic" dinner.

La Brasserie   16 | 15 | 15 | £32
272 Brompton Rd., SW3 (South Kensington), 020-7581 3089; fax 7581 1435

■ "The old warhorse is seemingly on the up" agree *amis* of this "true Parisian brasserie" with a retro feel at Brompton Cross that's "authentic from the smoke-stained walls" to staff's "Gallic charm" to the "no-nonsense French menu"; it's "great for breakfast", especially "brunches on Sunday", plus there's an "awesome" set menu for lunch and dinner that focuses on different regions of France.

L'Accento Italiano ⊠   ▽ 18 | 14 | 18 | £28
16 Garway Rd., W2 (Bayswater/Queensway), 020-7243 2201; fax 7243 2201

■ A "favourite among the well-heeled Bayswater and Notting Hill crowd", this "homey neighbourhood Italian" is "welcoming to families" and applauded for its "excellent, highly reasonable set menus" (£13.50 at lunch and dinner), and even if there's "not a large" selection of dishes, some claim "the small choice suggests quality."

Ladbroke Arms ⊠   – | – | – | M
54 Ladbroke Rd., W11 (Notting Hill Gate), 020-7727 6648

"Basically a nice, traditional boozer", this "picture-perfect" Notting Hill gastro-pub with "divine", "creative" Modern European cooking "isn't over-fashioned like some"; "warm, prompt service", a "friendly owner" and an "always bustling atmosphere" where "locals mix with in-the-know celebs" lend enthusiasts even more reasons to "keep going back"; N.B. a table on the small terrace at the front is like gold dust.

La Famiglia ◑   21 | 14 | 19 | £39
7 Langton St., SW10 (Fulham Broadway/Sloane Sq.), 020-7351 0761; fax 7351 2409; www.lafamiglialondon.com

◪ All of the "shouting and bustle" may leave you "feeling exhausted", but it gives this "friendly, family-run" "small corner of Italy in" World's End "a genuine vibe"; "it's easy to see why" this "firm favourite" is "packed": the "redefined classic" Italian fare is "excellent", the "atmosphere is buzzy" (there's "always a famous face"), "staff are so much fun they make your boyfriend jealous", plus there's a "wonderful" covered garden for year-round dining.

La Fontana ◑   ▽ 20 | 12 | 22 | £42
101 Pimlico Rd., SW1 (Sloane Sq.), 020-7730 6630

■ "Well worth a visit during truffle season" assert admirers also won over by the "wonderful, warm, welcoming" atmosphere at this "understated", family-run Italian near Pimlico Green; the "great Traditional Italian dishes" are "always consistent and sometimes inspired" but be advised that when "covered with shavings" of the "sublime" tuber "watch for the bill – and try not to choke when it arrives!"

LAHORE KEBAB 25 | 5 | 13 | £14

Holiday Inn, 56 Calthorpe St., WC1 (Kings Cross), 020-7833 9787
148-150 Brent St., NW4 (Hendon Central), 020-8203 6904 ◑
2 Umberston St., E1 (Aldgate East/Whitechapel), 020-7481 9737; fax 7488 1300 ◑

◪ "Great grub" that's "amazing, fantastic, wonderful – any superlative you can think of" – prompts fans to "travel across town" to this Pakistani-Indian "must-visit" near Commercial Road; "don't wear your Sunday best", but then again, the "gaudy tables just add to the experience" of a "top-drawer curry at a good price"; but for those put off that it "looks tatty beyond the call of duty", there are now newer offshoots in a Kings Cross hotel and Hendon (BYO).

Lanes 24 | 24 | 27 | £57

Four Seasons Hotel, Hamilton Pl., W1 (Green Park/ Hyde Park Corner), 020-7499 0888; fax 7493 6629; www.fourseasons.com/london

■ "In some ways better than its more famous neighbours" say supporters of Mayfair's Four Seasons Hotel dining room boasting a "quiet elegance" and "great decor" with wood panelling, stained glass and marble details, a "chic" backdrop for "perfect service" and Bernhard Mayer's "creative" Eclectic cooking "with Asian touches"; "it's always refined with space between tables" making it "perfect for a civilised meal" and "very nice for tea."

Lanesborough Conservatory 21 | 25 | 23 | £54

The Lanesborough, 1 Lanesborough Pl., SW1 (Hyde Park Corner), 020-7333 7254; fax 7259 5606; www.lanesborough.co.uk

◪ "Lush, lavish, luxurious", the "light", "sumptuous Victorian conservatory" dining room of The Lanesborough hotel at Hyde Park Corner is "opulence itself", making it "spot on" for the "high tea one dreams of", replete with "palm trees" or for a "magical night" with "divine dining" on Eclectic fare and dancing to live jazz on weekends, capped with "class-act service"; if a few feel it's "pretty as a picture but the food is hardly worth remembering", Lanes' lovers retort "it lives up to its surroundings."

Langan's Bistro ⊠ 19 | 18 | 19 | £39

26 Devonshire St., W1 (Baker St.), 020-7935 4531; fax 7493 8309; www.langansrestaurants.com

◪ The "epitome of intimate", this "charming", "romantic" Marylebone "treasure" with "lovely art" on the walls and "sweet waiters" is a "favourite" for "reliable" French bistro "comfort food"; "contemporary without feeling pretentious", it fits the bill as a "relaxed" "neighbourhood spot" for a "friendly night out"; still, a few shrug the fare is "mediocre" and "overpriced" to boot.

LANGAN'S BRASSERIE ● ☒
`20` `18` `20` `£45`

Stratton St., W1 (Green Park), 020-7491 8822; fax 7493 8309; www.langansrestaurants.co.uk

☒ "Part of the fabric of London", Richard Shepherd's "well-trumpeted" Mayfair "standby" is "still big, noisy and going strong" after nearly 30 years laud loyalists who insist the "top-notch" Anglo-French brasserie fare is "worth its reputation and price"; "attentive service" and "friendly, unthreatening sommeliers" add to the "reliable-as-old-slippers" feel, making it a "pleasure" for the "bustling crowd"; if a few toss it off as "old hat", most retort it's "busy every day, that speaks for itself."

Lansdowne, The
`21` `15` `15` `£29`

90 Gloucester Ave., NW1 (Chalk Farm), 020-7483 0409; fax 7586 1723

■ "The menu is short but tempting" exclaim enthusiasts of the "remarkably good" Modern British dishes on offer at this "excellent gastro-pub in Primrose Hill"; the "cosy", high-ceilinged upstairs restaurant is considered "the best option", though dining in the bar "downstairs is cheaper" – just be prepared to "tolerate the smoke and noise."

La Perla Bar & Grill
`14` `13` `16` `£21`

11 Charlotte St., W1 (Tottenham Court Rd.), 020-7436 1744; fax 7436 1911
28 Maiden Ln., WC2 (Charing Cross/Covent Garden), 020-7240 7400; fax 7836 5088
803 Fulham Rd., SW6 (Parsons Green), 020-7471 4895; fax 7736 9309
www.cafepacifico-laperla.com

■ "Make a pilgrimage for a fix of real guacamole and solid enchiladas" suggest amigos of this "fun" trio of Mexican cantinas in the West End and Parsons Green; still, a few sigh it's "adequate but unexciting" ("if only the food was like the lingerie" of the same name), concurring that the "range of tequilas is the reason to come" so "order some margaritas and stay awhile."

La Piragua
▽ `14` `13` `21` `£17`

176 Upper St., N1 (Highbury & Islington), 020-7354 2843; fax 7226 5480; www.lapiragua.co.uk

■ "For a rustic but oh-so-filling meal" of "hearty food for not a lotta wonga" and some "unusual cocktails", make the trek to this "fun" South American haunt in Islington; the "small" "setting is not classy or glamourous, but hey, neither is the food" – instead it's "interesting", served in "enormous" portions, "reasonably priced" and "just nice when you need it."

La Porchetta Pizzeria   18   10   15   £16
33 Boswell St., WC1 (Holborn), 020-7242 2434
147 Stroud Green Rd., N4 (Finsbury Park), 020-7281 2892;
fax 7281 2892 ◗
141-142 Upper St., N1 (Angel/Highbury & Islington),
020-7288 2488 ◗

■ "Oddball toppings" on "enormous pizzas" ("don't think that 'one-size-only' means it's just for one!") at "incredible prices" is the "formula" at these "cheap, fast", "raucous" pizzerias in Finsbury Park, Islington and most latterly Holborn; it's "not a place to linger" over a "romantic dinner for two", but it's "brilliant for groups" and "ideal for families."

La Porte des Indes ◗   22   25   21   £39
32 Bryanston St., W1 (Marble Arch), 020-7224 0055; fax 7224 1144;
www.blueelephant.com

◪ "Diners are treated like royalty" at this "truly unusual" Indian "oasis", a sibling of The Blue Elephant near Marble Arch that's "elegant all the way around" with "marvellous", "majestic decor" that makes you "feel like you're dining in the jungle"; the "delicious, subtle" dishes are "all spot on", including the "interesting mix" of French-inspired offerings that are "clearly the big find"; if a few find it "overpriced", supporters retort "the Sunday jazz brunch is good value for the money."

La Poule au Pot   23   22   18   £44
231 Ebury St., SW1 (Sloane Sq.), 020-7730 7763; fax 7259 9651

■ "Cosy in winter, picturesque in summer when you can eat outside on lovely" Pimlico Green, this *"romantique"*, "fin de siècle" bistro, with its "rural feel" and "quaint" "nooks and crannies", is "perfect first-date material"; add in "hearty" portions of "authentic", "rustic" Gallic fare ferried by "witty servers from across the Channel", and "you'll feel you're in the French countryside"; P.S. the magnum bottles of "house wine are great value: you [only] pay for what you drink."

La Rueda ◗   15   12   13   £25
102 Wigmore St., W1 (Bond St.), 020-7486 1718;
fax 7486 1718
642 King's Rd., SW6 (Fulham Broadway), 020-7384 2684;
fax 7384 2684
66-68 Clapham High St., SW4 (Clapham North), 020-7627 2173;
fax 7627 2173
www.larueda.co.uk

◪ "Authentic tapas and a fantastic Spanish wine list", all "at a reasonable price", are the highlights of this "lively", "friendly" Iberian trio where bouts of dancing on the tables and flamenco entertainment add to the "great atmosphere"; on the downside, some find it "tacky, touristy" and "a bit too crowded and smoky at peak times" – "so thick I couldn't see my menu!"

Latium ⑤   ▽ 23 | 17 | 23 | £41

21 Berners St., W1 (Goodge St.), 020-7323 9123;
www.latiumrestaurant.com

■ "Deserves to be a success" agree admirers of chef-
patron Maurizio Morelli's yearling, a "good all-rounder"
with "caring service" in a former Fish! site near Oxford
Street; the "high-quality" Modern Italian cooking is "original
and wonderful" and it's supported by an "impressive" wine
list at "decent prices" – in short, "*molte buono.*"

LA TROMPETTE   27 | 22 | 23 | £49

5 Devonshire Rd., W4 (Turnham Green), 020-8747 1836;
fax 8995 8097

■ "To blow their *trompette*", this Chiswick "gem" under
the same ownership as Chez Bruce and The Glasshouse
is "worth the hike, and then some" chorus fans in tune with
Ollie Couillaud's "delicately flavoured" New French dishes
supported by a "well-chosen wine list" "to please all
pockets"; the "original setting" makes you feel "like you're
sitting in a perfectly upholstered, beautiful little box" –
indeed, this "outstanding" spot "easily matches anything
served in the West End"; N.B. it's nonsmoking.

La Trouvaille   23 | 19 | 22 | £37

12A Newburgh St., W1 (Oxford Circus), 020-7287 8488;
fax 7434 4170 ⑤
353 Upper St., N1 (Angel), 020-7704 8323; fax 7359 6671;
www.brasserie-trouvaille.com

■ Like a "piece of France's" "countryside" in Soho, this
"inviting" "haven" may be "hidden but worth a search" for
"creative" cuisine that "always pleases", complemented by
an "imaginative" Gallic wine list that opens "new horizons";
the "atmosphere is buzzing" thanks to the "crazy French
guys" who run the show, sealing its status as a "genuine
delight"; N.B. the lesser-known Islington sibling follows a
similar formula, with a simpler brasserie menu.

Launceston Place ◑   21 | 20 | 23 | £46

1A Launceston Pl., W8 (Gloucester Rd.), 020-7937 6912;
fax 7938 2412; www.egami.co.uk

◩ "Homey, but sophisticated" sums up the scene inside
this "charming" Kensington townhouse (affiliated with
Circus, Kensington Place, et al.) where "top-notch" Modern
British cooking is presented by "superb" staff; the "quiet"
neighbourhood offers an "escape from the hustle-bustle",
making it a "favourite" place for "your new bride" or for
"business"; still, a few feel it's "lost a bit of its vigour."

L'Aventure ⑤   23 | 19 | 19 | £45

3 Blenheim Terrace., NW8 (St. John's Wood), 020-7624 6232;
fax 7625 5548

◩ The "mouth-watering" "food is truly French and not an
imitation" at Catherine Parisot's "darling" "hideaway"

near Abbey Road that's "charming" for a "romantic" rendezvous or an alfresco meal in the "leafy garden"; if a few grouse "tables are so small one assumes their preferred clients are Beatrix Potter animals", most retort "it's less cramped in warm weather when the doors are open."

Le Boudin Blanc   21 17 17 £37
Shepherd's Mkt., 5 Trebeck St., W1 (Green Park), 020-7499 3292; fax 7495 6973; www.boudinblanc.co.uk

◪ "If you're looking for a taste of the Continent", settle into this "bustling, fun" *soeur* of La Bouchée in Shepherd's Market where the "yummy" "French favourites", "attentive service" and "hospitable", "homey" "surroundings dictate lots of red wine and rambling conversation"; it can be a "tight fit" so "be prepared to sit elbow to elbow" or opt for the "pleasant alternative" of "lovely outside" tables that make it feel "just like Paris."

Le Cafe du Jardin ●   19 18 19 £33
28 Wellington St., WC2 (Covent Garden), 020-7836 8769; fax 7836 4123; www.lecafedujardin.com

■ "Cosy", "convivial" and "convenient", this bi-level Covent Garden haunt with "very capable", "fast service" offers a "reliably good" Modern European menu that includes a "terrific prix fixe deal" for before or after the theatre or opera; the "subtle, calming atmosphere" and "people-watching" in the conservatory "can quickly make you forget the wet London winter", plus there's a live pianist nightly on the "more commodious" floor below.

Le Café du Marché ⊠   22 19 18 £42
22 Charterhouse Sq., EC1 (Barbican), 020-7608 1609; fax 7336 7459

■ The "fabulously intimate" "country French" look – "used brick, wood floors and scattered carpets" – gives this "well-kept secret" near Smithfield Market "warmth and character" that, coupled with "authentic" Gallic "bourgeois cooking" and "professional service", makes it "perfect for a romantic dinner or with close friends"; it's "not the most polished" place, but its "timeless" appeal makes "you feel like you've had an evening out, rather than just a meal."

LE CAPRICE ●   24 20 23 £49
Arlington House, Arlington St., SW1 (Green Park), 020-7629 2239; fax 7493 9040; www.caprice-holdings.co.uk

■ You "never know who you'll sit next to" at this "classy", art deco Piccadilly venue that attracts an "impressive crowd" of "famous faces" thanks to its "humming" atmosphere, "memorable" Modern British–European fare and "cordial" service that "makes every guest feel like a regular"; it's a "joyous place for a "special evening", "swell after the theatre" and "oh-so-difficult to get a table" – so remember it's also "fun to sit at the bar", and that this "perennial favourite" "lives up to its hype."

Le Cercle 🈂

| – | – | – | E |

1 Wilbraham Pl., SW1 (Sloane Sq.), 020-7901 9999;
fax 7901 9111

From the team behind Club Gascon in Smithfield comes
this stylishly informal, basement-level Sloane Square
newcomer with separate booth and banquette seating
areas for drinking and dining and continuous service from
midday through tea and dinner; head chef Thierry Beyris'
sophisticated regional French menu is offered in his
trademark tapas-style portions, and whilst reservations
are taken up till 8 PM, customers are seated on a first-
come basis in later hours; N.B. closed Mondays.

Le Colombier

| 21 | 20 | 20 | £38 |

145 Dovehouse St., SW3 (South Kensington), 020-7351 1155;
fax 7351 0077

■ "You could easily pretend" you're "on the Left Bank"
at Didier Garnier's "friendly", "well-managed" Chelsea
"gem" that attains "consistently high standards" with
"excellent" Classic French food, including a "good prix
fixe menu" and a recently expanded list of "reasonably
priced excellent wines"; it's "a fail-proof address for a date"
and "ideal for long Sunday lunches" – the "best place to
be is the terrace" – so "stop off for something special."

Le Deuxieme ◑

| 18 | 15 | 16 | £34 |

65A Long Acre, WC2 (Covent Garden), 020-7379 0033;
fax 7379 0066

◪ "Minimalist decor and low lighting set the tone" for this
"sweet little spot" in Covent Garden, *le deuxieme* venture
from the team behind Le Café du Jardin, where "tempting"
Modern British fare with an international slant is "well
presented" by "unpretentious staff"; if a few "object to the
cramped surroundings" and "formulaic" cooking, more
find it "great if you're going to the opera", with a £9.95 set
menu to boot.

Lee Ho Fook ◑

| 18 | 10 | 13 | £18 |

15-16 Gerrard St., W1 (Leicester Sq./Piccadilly Circus),
020-7494 1200; fax 7494 1700

◪ "Don't be put off by the worn decor" at this 70-year-old
"Chinatown stalwart" insist fans hooked on Fook's "tasty",
"good-value" Cantonese fare and "consistently rewarding
specials" that "make your mouth water"; whilst some say
it's still the spot "for a family meal" or a "weeknight option",
cynics snipe that it's "pleasant, but not outstanding."

LE GAVROCHE 🈂

| 27 | 25 | 27 | £82 |

43 Upper Brook St., W1 (Marble Arch), 020-7408 0881;
fax 7491 4387; www.le-gavroche.co.uk

■ "A bastion of great French cuisine", this "classy",
"comfortable", "clubby feeling" Mayfair "bunker" is
"the refuge you've been seeking" for a "sublime dining

experience", from Michel Roux's "exquisite" Classic
French menu, supported by a "memorable wine list" to
"impeccable service" with "all the bells and whistles" that
"anticipate a guest's pleasures"; bring a "wheelbarrow of
money because it's very expensive, but it's worth the price",
plus the £44 set lunch is an "absolute bargain."

LE MANOIR AUX QUAT'SAISONS　27　27　26　£88

Le Manoir aux Quat'Saisons, Church Rd., Great Milton,
Oxfordshire, 01844 278881; fax 01844 278847; www.manoir.com
■ "Chef Raymond Blanc's passion for perfection shines
through" at this "idyllic" 15th-century Cotswold manor
house with "enchanting gardens" and "charming rooms";
what elevates this "formidable establishment" to "culinary
heaven" is the "pure theatre" of "sublime" New French
cooking, an "awesome wine list" and simply "faultless
service" – indeed, it's "expensive and rightly so" as it's
"hard to better this side of paradise"; P.S. "stay the night
for maximum pampering."

Le Mercury ◑　16　15　16　£21

140A Upper St., N1 (Angel/Highbury & Islington), 020-7354 4088;
fax 7359 7186
■ "Cheerful, crowded" and "cosy", this "candlelit" Islington
New French brasserie "may be small, but it packs a romantic
wallop"; "no-nonsense food with prices at a steal" make it
"handy for the budget-conscious" (as in "good for students
to take their visiting parents") hence it "gets a bit busy" so
"reserve early" or prepare to "wait for a table."

Lemonia ◑　20　17　20　£28

89 Regent's Park Rd., NW1 (Chalk Farm), 020-7586 7454;
fax 7483 2630
■ "Neither flashy nor subtle", this "nothing-fancy" Primrose
Hill taverna "satisfies taste buds as much as your budget"
with "authentic, bargain-priced Greek food" that "never
lets you down"; the "friendly", "noisy, happy atmosphere"
makes it a "fantastic place for a family event" or a "good
place to chill" and "while away a Saturday afternoon" over
a selection of "amazing mezze"; P.S. it has a quieter "sister
opposite" called Limonia.

Le Palais du Jardin ◑　20　19　17　£38

136 Long Acre, WC2 (Leicester Sq.), 020-7379 5353;
fax 7379 1846
◪ There's "a great buzz" from a "hip, young crowd" at
this "lively" Covent Garden brasserie serving "upscale"
Modern European–Classic French fare, including an
"excellent *fruits de mer*" "platter that's a feast of Henry
VIII proportions"; still, cynical subjects lament that the
"cooking needs a lighter touch" and feel "let down by ill-
informed" "random service", opting for the "front bar that
makes a great pit stop with good people-watching."

Le Petit Max — — — E

Chatfield Rd., SW11 (Wandsworth Town), 020-7223 0999
"Presided over by" chef Max Renzland himself, this casual
yet "proper French" bistro set in a former Foxtrot Oscar
outpost, an "obscure location" by the Thames at Battersea
Reach, offers "fabulous" Gallic fare that "you'd be prepared
to pay double" for elsewhere; adding "good value for the
money", the comprehensive wine list starts at £12.50.

Le Pont de la Tour 21 21 19 £52

Butlers Wharf Bldg., 36D Shad Thames, SE1
(London Bridge/Tower Hill), 020-7403 8403; fax 7403 0267;
www.conran.com
◪ "Order a seafood selection" or any of the "marvellous"
Classic French dishes and "catch an eyeful of the world's
most famous bridge" from the "lovely" terrace of the Conran
Group's "big, brassy" Shad Thames venue, a "stunning,
spectacular spot" that "epitomises style and service"
whether "for romantic conquests, special occasions or to
impress the boss"; it's "painfully pricey" retort naysayers
who also "yawn on the food and decor", but most maintain
it's "worth crossing a river for."

L'Escargot ●🅩 22 22 19 £48

48 Greek St., W1 (Leicester Sq./Tottenham Court Rd.),
020-7437 6828; fax 7437 0790; www.whitestarline.org.uk
◪ "A grade A restaurant" maintain admirers of this Marco
Pierre White–owned venture spread across several floors of
a "classic Soho" townhouse, with "imaginative" French
cooking "well presented" by "discreet" staff; the "good-
value" set menu makes it a "perfect choice" before or
after curtain time, but for "more privacy" "book a table
upstairs" – "you'll like" the "elegant decor of the Picasso
room"; still, a minority think it "needs to try harder to
impress" and deem service "haphazard."

Le Soufflé 🅩 23 19 25 £63

Hotel Inter-Continental, 1 Hamilton Pl., W1 (Hyde Park Corner),
020-7318 8577; fax 7491 0926; www.intercontinental.com
◪ "Only the cognoscenti really know" about this "romantic"
New French "sleeper" "tucked away inside the Inter-
Continental" hotel where chef Michael Coaker prepares a
"really fine selection of dishes", including the eponymous
"superb soufflés", and "exceptional service", plus dinner-
dancing on Saturday nights add to the experience; still, a few
feel let down that the "atmosphere isn't bubbly enough."

L'Estaminet 🅩 20 17 19 £36

14 Garrick St., WC2 (Covent Garden/Leicester Sq.), 020-7379 1432;
fax 7379 1530
◼ "It doesn't get more French than this" "cute bistro" in
Covent Garden, with its "welcoming, local feel", "genuine",
"well-executed" Classic Gallic cooking (including a

"fantastic cheeseboard") and "very Continental staff", making it "good for a business lunch"; the "pre-theatre prix fixe is one of the best deals around" – *mais oui,* a "trip to Paris never cost so little."

LES TROIS GARCONS ⊠ 19 27 19 £55

1 Club Row, E1 (Liverpool St.), 020-7613 1924; fax 7613 5960; www.lestroisgarcons.com

◪ Like an "English country house on acid", the "outrageous" "visual stimulation" – complete with "cigar-smoking ape" – at this "kitschy, sparkly, sumptuous" pub conversion "off the beaten path" near Brick Lane is "unlike anything you'll ever see", making it perhaps the "least stuffiest gourmet" Gallic "establishment you'll ever eat in"; the Classic French fare may be "more hearty than exquisite", and though some say it "won't blow you away" (although the "ludicrous prices" might), it's "well worth the experience."

Le Suquet ◕ 21 17 19 £40

104 Draycott Ave., SW3 (South Kensington), 020-7581 1785; fax 7225 0838

■ "The scallops are always a delight", and so are the other "beautifully prepared fish" and shellfish dishes, all served by a "bevy of cute, young" staff "with a lovely Gallic accent" at this Brompton Cross French bistro with a "crazy, fun ambience"; "you could be in the heart of Paris", then again, it feels like you've "run away to Marseille" – either way, expect "authentic" fare and atmosphere.

L'Etranger 24 21 20 £48

36 Gloucester Rd., SW7 (Gloucester Rd.), 020-7584 1118; fax 7584 8886; www.etranger.co.uk

■ Named after Albert Camus' legendary novel, this "friendly", "modern", glass-fronted "one to follow" on Gloucester Road brings New "French cooking with Asian twists" to "an area in need of good dining"; "there are no disappointments", indeed, the "original dishes" "seem to improve and become more assured every time", plus the "brilliant wine list" boasts "outstanding" choices that are also sold at retail prices in the Vins de L'Etranger shop next door; P.S. there's also the "interesting" Opal Bar downstairs.

Levant ◕ 21 25 18 £38

Jason Ct., 76 Wigmore St., W1 (Bond St.), 020-7224 1111; fax 7486 1216; www.levantrestaurant.co.uk

■ Expect an "atmosphere straight out of *Arabian Nights*" at this "exotic" Marylebone basement with "decadent" decor where you "enjoy a true feast" of "delicious" Levantine fare (Eastern Mediterranean–North African) while "sexy belly dancers" "gyrate around you"; it's an "enchanting experience" with "welcoming service", which makes it "a must for large groups", a "great date place" and a "cool place for a cocktail."

Levantine ◐   _ _ _ M
26 London St., W2 (Paddington), 020 7262 1111; fax 7402 4039
This Middle Eastern sibling to Levant might share the same owner (Tony Kitous), but it offers a different experience altogether, with a more exotic, intimate setting – touches include unusual artefacts, incense burners, tables strewn with rose petals – and a Lebanese-focused menu made up of mezze dishes from £4.25; crudité, bread and pickles are presented on arrival, but don't expect to spend long on the wine list: there are just 10 options, all from Lebanon.

Light House   _ _ _ E
75-77 Ridgeway, SW19 (Wimbledon), 020-8944 6338; fax 8946 4440
On the edge of Wimbledon Village lies this "popular local" eatery that feels like it's "something uptown in the suburbs" thanks to a "wonderful" Eclectic menu and a global wine list; "although the combinations are different, it works" assert the enlightened who value it as much for a "quiet midweek meal" as for a "special night out."

L'Incontro ◐☒   ▽ 25 19 23 £48
87 Pimlico Rd., SW1 (Sloane Sq.), 020-7730 3663; fax 7730 5062;
www.lincontro-restaurant.com
■ "A pleasant surprise", this "refined" Pimlico eatery "with walls full of black-and-white photographs of Italy" may not have a high profile as yet, but loyalists "keep returning because when it's good, it's very good", with a "skilled chef" turning out "wonderful, but pricey" "grown-up nosh" from a Venetian menu that's "high quality without trying to be pretentious"; a "wine list balanced with affordable" selections and "welcoming staff" complete the picture.

Little Bay   17 15 17 £17
171 Farringdon, EC1 (Farringdon), 020-7278 1234; fax 7278 5368 ◐
228 Belsize Rd., NW6 (Kilburn Park), 020-7372 4699;
fax 7372 8282 ◐⇔
228 York Rd., SW11 (Clapham Junction), 020-7223 4080;
fax 020-7223-6131
■ "Unbelievable" (as in "seriously low") "prices for this sort of quality" is the rallying cry for this "laid-back" pair in Farringdon and Kilburn, with "quick", "unobtrusive staff", "ample portions" of "fab" Mediterranean fare and "decor that's unique, if a little studenty"; it's "great to have" this "unpretentious local" for those times "when one doesn't feel like eating in" agree admirers who shore up for a "casual lunch or dinner"; N.B. the Clapham branch opened post-*Survey*.

Little Italy ◐   18 14 15 £30
21 Frith St., W1 (Leicester Sq./Tottenham Court Rd.),
020-7734 4737; fax 7734 1777
■ It's like "a modern Milanese bar/trattoria transported to London" attest admirers of this Soho spot that works as a

"quick place to grab good Italian standards" during the day and morphs into a club at night; "get there late and watch it get wild" – "your meal is likely to be jostled by people dancing", but "where else can you fill up on pasta at 3 AM?"

Livebait 16 12 14 £32
21 Wellington St., WC2 (Covent Garden), 020-7836 7161; fax 7836 7141
43 The Cut, SE1 (Waterloo), 020-7928 7211; fax 7928 2279
1 Plough Pl., EC4 (Chancery Ln.), 020-7842 0510; fax 7842 0511 ◪
www.santeonline.co.uk
◪ "Don't expect a lot of frills" because the "fine", "fresh fish" gets the "simple treatment" at this "lively", "friendly" seafood trio; the "open feeling", complete with "sparkling" "black-and-white tiling reminiscent of old-time pie and eel shops", is alluring to some, albeit others feel the "stark setting" "lacks atmosphere" and assert that "inexperienced service" can let the side down; N.B. the Westbourne Grove and Watling Street outposts are now closed.

LMNT – – – M
316 Queensbridge Rd., E8 (Dalston Kingsland B.R.), 020-7249 6727; fax 7249 6538
The "surreal", "Egyptian decor is either kitsch or tacky depending on your viewpoint" at this Hackney pub that's "charming in a tongue-in-cheek way"; it's "nice for taking friends out" as the "tasty, imaginative" New French menu is "an absolute bargain", the "cocktails are marvellous" and service is "down to earth"; P.S. "check out the 'porno' toilets" – they're "outrageous."

Lobster Pot, The ◪ ▽ 18 15 17 £39
3 Kennington Ln., SE11 (Kennington), 020-7582 5556; www.lobsterpotrestaurant.co.uk
◪ "Keep it a secret" implore those smitten by this "weird and wonderful" French seafooder in Kennington where the "sounds of seagulls and foghorns" are "played lightly in the background", diners can "look out through portholes" and staff are "top of the line"; whilst most find the fare "worth the trip", a handful crab "what a disappointment."

LOCANDA LOCATELLI ◪ 25 22 21 £57
Churchill InterContinental Hotel, 8 Seymour St., W1 (Marble Arch), 020-7935 9088; fax 7935 1149; www.locandalocatelli.com
◪ "Persistence pays off if you manage to get a table" at Giorgio Locatelli's "outstanding destination" at the Churchill InterContinental Hotel near Oxford Street where "delicious, precise Northern Italian cooking" from a chef that's "on the stove more than the telly (thank goodness!)", a "huge wine list" and a "sleek" setting create "a memorable" experience; you "don't have to be a celebrity to be treated like one" making it "overall, a great place to impress

clients"; still, a few cynics cite "ridiculous prices" and huff "what's all the hype about?"

Locanda Ottoemezzo ⌀
▽ 25 | 22 | 25 | £41

2-4 Thackeray St., W8 (High St. Kensington), 020-7937 2200; fax 7313 9866

■ "Tucked away from the commotion on Ken High Street", this "laid-back" "local Italian paradise" decorated with Federico Fellini movie posters offers a seasonal menu of "divine" "rustic" dishes, "described in mouth-watering" detail by "friendly", "attentive" staff; it may be "expensive, but it's worth every penny", so "don't tell your friends" about it "or you'll never get that special table with the cushions."

Lola's
20 | 20 | 18 | £41

The Mall Bldg., 359 Upper St., N1 (Angel), 020-7359 1932; fax 7359 2209

◪ This "airy room" in a converted tram shed in Islington with "nicely spaced tables" is the "calm" canvas for "always interesting, sometimes inspired" Modern European cooking and a "good wine selection"; but dissenters declare that "service can be strained at peak times" and gripe about the "number of chefs coming and going", which recently increased with the post-*Survey* departure of Elisha Carter – and may impact the above Food rating.

Lomo ◑
▽ 18 | 12 | 16 | £24

222 Fulham Rd., SW10 (Earl's Ct./Fulham Broadway), 020-7349 8848; fax 7349 8848

◪ The "upscale tapas" is the "real thing" at this "lively", "buzzing" Fulham Road Spaniard that's "always packed with people"; if a few feel it's a "bit cramped" and a "little dated", most deem it a "good place to mix munchies with drinks" before "heading out to surrounding bars."

Lonsdale, The ◑
15 | 23 | 15 | £34

48 Lonsdale Rd., W11 (Ladbroke Grove/Notting Hill Gate), 020-7727 4080; fax 7727 4060

◪ "Wear your coolest clothes or risk feeling frumpy" at this "hip" ground-floor bar in Notting Hill that also offers grazers a "great tapas-style menu" of International-Eclectic dishes; the "crowd alone is worth coming to witness" and come they do, though more for the "outstanding cocktails and the scene" – the "food is secondary"; N.B. the members-only club Genevieve is upstairs.

L'Oranger ⌀
24 | 21 | 23 | £60

5 St. James's St., SW1 (Green Park), 020-7839 3774; fax 7839 4330; www.atozrestaurants.com

■ "Gratifying it hasn't lost its sheen" fawn fans of this "treat" in St. James's, a "serene experience" with "delightful service" and "sophisticated New French"–Med fare "executed to perfection"; the "old-world atmosphere" is "great for high-end" "power lunches when you want to impress a client" and need "a rest from cutting-edge" cuisine; a handful huff "rising prices are now stratospheric, whilst the food is merely heavenly" but most hold it aloft as "worth the price."

Lou Pescadou ●　　　– | – | – | E |
241 Old Brompton Rd., SW5 (Earl's Ct.), 020-7370 1057; fax 7244 7545
Freshly revamped, with a new glass frontage, this "reliable", nearly 20-year-old "French address" in Earl's Court is "worth rediscovering"; it's a "great informal dining experience", with a menu boasting an "excellent choice" of "outstanding seafood dishes" inspired by "the South of France" and "friendly, personal service."

Lucio　　　　　　　– | – | – | E |
257-259 Fulham Rd., SW3 (South Kensington), 020-7823 3007; fax 7823 3009
Owned by an eponymous longtime member of the San Lorenzo team, this "pleasant new venue" is located in smart U-shaped Chelsea premises that have seen several ventures come and go, the most recent being Chelsea Mandarin; the "quality Italian" menu is "reasonably priced to suit all occasions" and black-and-white photos of celebrities by celebrated snapper Terry O'Neill adorn the walls.

Lucky 7 ≠　　　　20 | 18 | 16 | £17 |
127 Westbourne Park Rd., W2 (Royal Oak/Westborne Park), 020-7727 6771; fax 7727 6798
■ "A little piece of America in Westbourne Grove", Tom Conran's "homage and celebration of the diner is a hoot" – "even if you have to share the booth with a stranger"; he "obviously researched the milieu", from the "authentically worn-around-the-edges" decor to the "proper milkshakes" and "gut-busting burgers" that "rock" – little wonder this "home away from home" is where "expats get their fix."

Luigi's of Covent Garden ●⊠　18 | 14 | 17 | £36 |
15 Tavistock St., WC2 (Covent Garden), 020-7240 1789; fax 7497 0075
◪ "It isn't classically fine dining, but one never goes wrong with" this "cosy" trattoria in Covent Garden where the "nifty crowd of theatre and opera types" "feels welcome" and the Traditional Italian menu offers "lots of choice"; if a few frown that the "food ranges between ordinary and why bother" and deem it "a relic from a bygone era", most appreciate that "they get you out in time" for the show.

Lundum's　　　　　25 | 25 | 26 | £45 |
117-119 Old Brompton Rd., SW7 (Gloucester Rd./South Kensington), 020-7373 7774; fax 7373 4472; www.lundums.com
■ "Even better after the refurbishment" and expansion is the view on this "truly Scandinavian dining experience" in

South Kensington; the "lovely, refined setting" has a "very soothing effect" attest admirers who are also lulled by the "stylish preparations" of "delicious" "Nordic delights" ("food so light I thought it would float off my plate"), the "extremely good-value Sunday brunch" smorgasbord ("as good as it gets in London") and "warm, gracious staff."

Made in Italy ●   21 15 14 £25
249 King's Rd., SW3 (Sloane Sq./South Kensington), 020-7352 1880; fax 7351 2390

◪ Perhaps "the only thing missing is a view of the Amalfi coast" at this "fun, informal" King's Road spot where "the name really means something" with "authentic" Italian cooking – notably "pizza you crave" like the "family-style three-footers to die for!" – at "sensible prices"; still, even the smitten snarl that the "food is fantastic, but you have to put up with cramped quarters and lousy service"; P.S. opt for the "lovely roof deck for summer dining."

Maggie Jones's   22 23 19 £34
6 Old Court Pl., W8 (High St. Kensington), 020-7937 6462; fax 7376 0510

■ The "rustic, antique decor" and "pleasant farmhouse" ambience make for a "romantic treat" at this "cute", "cosy" Kensington stalwart, boasting "casual service" and a "hearty, winter-warmer menu" of "satisfying" Traditional British "favourites" like "well-prepared game"; devotees deem it "a fun venue for big gatherings" or a "long Sunday lunch" helped along by "great house wines."

Maggiores   – – – E
33 King St., WC2 (Covent Garden/Leicester Sq.), 020-7379 9696

Spreading "a little bit of Mediterranean sunshine in Covent Garden", this "vibrant" "all-rounder" with an "interesting" setting and "exceptional service" "produces some very good" Franco-Italian fare accompanied by one of the "most amazing wine lists", with several at "reasonable prices"; with a "blossom"-filled conservatory boasting a "large fireplace for winter" and a retractable roof for alfresco dining, it's a "favourite lunch meet-up place", so "book ahead and dress smart."

Ma Goa   ▽ 21 11 17 £27
199 Upper Richmond Rd. W., SW14 (Barnes B.R.), 020-8876 2288
242-244 Upper Richmond Rd., SW15 (Putney B.R.), 020-8780 1767

◪ "Go with an open mind and an empty stomach" to this unassuming, "friendly" Putney eatery where the "excellent Indian" cooking is "about as far removed" from "typical curry" "as you can get" and even a "cut above the expected"; whilst doubters declare it's "overpriced" even they allow that it's "maybe worth another try"; N.B. the Sheen branch is only for takeaway.

Malabar ◐   20 | 17 | 18 | £26 |
27 Uxbridge St., W8 (Notting Hill Gate), 020-7727 8800;
www.malabar-restaurant.co.uk
■ For "inventive Indian cuisine" locals head to this "small",
"buzzing" "favourite" that still draws an "interesting Notting
Hill crowd"; "nice staff", a "relaxing" setting and Sunday
buffet lunch that allows you "to try different dishes" add to
its appeal: "superb, guys – keep going!"

Malabar Junction ◐   18 | 16 | 19 | £22 |
107 Great Russell St., WC1 (Tottenham Court Rd.), 020-7580 5230;
fax 7436 9942
◪ "Just steps from the British Museum", this "old reliable"
Bloomsbury Indian serves a "spicy, different selection of
Kerala dishes" in a "verdant, outdoorlike setting"; it's "good
after a hard day at work" or for a "quick meal", "but it's not
a destination restaurant" admit admirers; still, cynics have
a downer on fare that has "declined over the years."

Malmaison Hotel Bar & Brasserie   – | – | – | E |
Malmaison Hotel, 18-21 Charterhouse Sq., EC1 (Barbican/
Farringdon), 020-7012 3700; fax 7012 3702; www.malmaison.com
The first London hotel from Malmaison, a UK-based chain
with six properties outside the city, is housed in a redbrick
Victorian building near Smithfield Market and features a
"contemporary" French brasserie downstairs with vaulted
alcoves and an easygoing style; an "enticing" bar and bottle-
lined private dining room complete the picture.

Mandalay ⌧   24 | 7 | 25 | £17 |
444 Edgware Rd., W2 (Edgware Rd.), 020-7258 3696; fax 7258 3696
■ "By the third visit, you're one of the family" at this
"authentic", "family-run cafe" in Edgware Road with "very
friendly service" and "intriguing" "home-cooked" Burmese
food; the menu's "so cheap", it pays to "be adventurous –
it doesn't hurt if you bet wrong."

MANDARIN KITCHEN ◐   26 | 10 | 16 | £30 |
14-16 Queensway, W2 (Bayswater/Queensway), 020-7727 9012;
fax 7727 9468
■ "Don't judge this book by its cover" suggest believers
bound to "overlook the frayed surroundings" of this
Queensway Chinese, an "institution" where the "excellent
seafood" – including the "famous signature dish of lobster
noodles" – "never fails to please"; P.S. it's "always packed"
but the "very brisk service" keeps up with the "crowds."

Mandola   ▽ 20 | 15 | 11 | £23 |
139-143 Westbourne Grove, W11 (Notting Hill Gate),
020-7229 4734; www.mandolacafe.com
◪ This "welcoming", "family-owned outfit" in Westbourne
Grove makes "a fascinating experience for foodies"
"impressed" by the "interesting" Sudanese cooking – in

fact, it's a "great place to try something different"; on the downside, "don't expect your food quickly."

Mango Tree　　　　　　　22 21 19 £39

46 Grosvenor Pl., SW1 (Victoria), 020-7823 1888; fax 7838 9275;
www.mangotree.org.uk

☑ "When that Thai craving takes over", head to this "civilised" venue behind Buckingham Palace suggest admirers "transported" by the "soothing" ambience; the "huge menu" boasts a bushel full of "delights", offset by "fab" mango cocktails and staff that "work seamlessly"; if a few hedge it's "on the verge of being enjoyable" with "indifferent" service, most find a "fun-filled evening" awaits.

Manicomio　　　　　　▽ 20 18 16 £33

85 Duke of York Sq., SW3 (Sloane Sq.), 020-7730 3366;
fax 7730 3377

■ "New in the Duke of York's" barracks development, this addition to Sloane Square comprises a Modern Italian restaurant, a deli next door with a "pretty conservatory" and alfresco seating at both options; the "wonderful assault on the taste buds" centers around "great ingredients, served simply so you get the full-on impact" – so "go and be impressed"; N.B. the name translates as 'madhouse.'

Manor　　　　　　　　19 19 21 £32

6-8 All Saints Rd., W11 (Westbourne Grove), 020-7243 6363;
fax 7243 6360

☑ "Good for groups and intimate dinners" with "great" Mediterranean fare and "brilliant service", this "excellent little-known venue" near Portobello Road is only open Wednesday–Saturday evenings plus Sundays for a "lovely brunch"; "if you fancy continuing your night after your meal without having to move an inch", "yummy cocktails" await; still, a few feel it can be "hit-or-miss."

Manzi's ◗　　　　　　　18 14 18 £30

1-2 Leicester St., WC2 (Leicester Sq./Piccadilly Circus),
020-7734 0224; fax 7437 4864; www.manzis.co.uk

☑ "Year after year, you always get what you always got" at this "homey" Chinatown "find": "large portions" of "dependable seafood", "salty, long-service waiters", a location that's "convenient to theatres" and an affordable pre-theatre menu; still, a few feel this "old stalwart does not quite feel as good as it used to."

Mao Tai ◗　　　　　　　21 19 21 £36

58 New King's Rd., SW6 (Parsons Green), 020-7731 2520;
fax 7471 8992
96 Draycott Ave., SW3 (South Kensington), 020-7225 2500;
fax 7225 1965
www.maotai.co.uk

☑ A "top choice" for "very tasty", "beautifully presented" Chinese food, this "smart"-looking duo in Parsons Green (the 20-year-old original) and Brompton Cross (the "fancier address") with "unusually friendly service" "meets all your needs, whether taking the whole family for a feast or that last-minute romantic escape" or "takeaway that's not your standard fare"; still, a handful balk that it's "overpriced for what you get."

Mark's Club ⊠ | 24 | 24 | 28 | £72 |
Private club; inquiries: 020-7499 2936
■ "Old-world charm at its most charming" is on the menu at Mark Birley's "very grown-up" Mayfair private dining club in a "gorgeous Regency townhouse", an "expensive, but worth it" "buzzy", "plush experience" where members "savour" "impeccable" Traditional British fare "served by aproned ladies" and most agree "every restaurant should have a manager like Bruno" Rotti; N.B. jacket and tie required and no phones allowed.

Maroush ● | 21 | 12 | 16 | £25 |
21 Edgware Rd., W2 (Marble Arch), 020-7723 0773; fax 7723 3161
68 Edgware Rd., W2 (Marble Arch), 020-7224 9339; fax 7723 3161
4 Vere St., W1 (Bond St.), 020-7493 5050; fax 7723 3161
62 Seymour St., W1 (Marble Arch), 020-7724 5024; fax 7723 3161
123 Connaught St., W1 (Marble Arch), 020-7262 0222
38 Beauchamp Pl., SW3 (Knightsbridge), 020-7581 5434;
fax 7723 3161
www.maroush.com
■ "When you want a Middle Eastern feast" "at 2 AM on the way home from dancing" or an "antidote to retail exhaustion", this "legend" around the West End is the "perfect spot"; the "decor is nothing special", but the "atmosphere is lively", "staff make you feel like visiting sheiks" and the "solid" Lebanese fare "satisfies taste buds."

Masala Zone | 18 | 16 | 16 | £18 |
9 Marshall St., W1 (Oxford Circus/Piccadilly Circus),
020-7287 9966; fax 7287 8555
80 Upper St., N1 (Angel), 020-7359 3399; fax 7359 6560
www.realindianfood.com
■ "At the vanguard" of the "fast-food-plus scene", the Chutney Mary and Veeraswamy group's "funky, cool" Soho "pit stop for a dose of good curry" and younger "inviting" Islington sibling "aim to be trendy but authentic" with "remarkable" tribal murals on the wall and "quick meals" of "modern", "tasty", even "healthy" "Indian food with a difference"; it's "good for a lunchtime dash" and "ideally located after a day's shopping."

Mash ⊠ | 13 | 14 | 16 | £28 |
19-21 Great Portland St., W1 (Oxford Circus), 020-7637 5555;
fax 7637 7333
◩ Oliver Peyton's "modern, bright" all-day eatery near Oxford Street offers an "interesting menu" of Modern

European fare including "gourmet pizzas" and a "good Caesar salad", making it "great for a meal with friends to get in the mood for a night on the town"; if a few feel the food is "nothing to write home about", the beer from the "on-site microbrewery is worth sampling."

Matsuri ⌧　　　　22　14　19　£49
71 High Holborn, WC1 (Holborn), 020-7430 1970; fax 7430 1971
15 Bury St., SW1 (Green Park), 020-7839 1101;
fax 7930 7010
www.matsuri-restaurant.com
◪ "The real deal for Asian cuisine" declare devotees who descend on this St. James's venue and "new Holborn" premises for "crowd-pleasing teppanyaki", "sublime sashimi" and "very fresh sushi"; whilst it's a "good place for business", it has "little atmosphere" for "romantic dinners" and unless you order the "pre-theatre bargain [£15] menu", prices can be "sky high."

Mediterraneo ●　　　21　15　18　£32
37 Kensington Park Rd., W11 (Ladbroke Grove), 020-7792 3131;
fax 7229 7980
■ "Too bad there aren't more" "original finds" like Osteria Basilico's "lively" sister sigh the smitten who "after a few hours at the Portobello Market repair here" to this trattoria that "takes you to any corner of Italy" via "terrific" cooking that "won't break the bank", an "informally inviting setting" and "genuine staff"; it's a "favourite for a tête-à-tête with friends or family dinners", plus the "late-night hours are particularly nice."

Mela ●　　　19　14　17　£27
152-156 Shaftesbury Ave., WC2 (Leicester Sq.), 020-7836 8635;
fax 7379 0527; www.melarestaurant.co.uk
◪ A "real treat", this "bright", casual Indian eatery near Cambridge Circus "stands out"; there's "none of the attitude of its posher competitors", instead, staff are "courteous and attentive" and the "diverse" regional Indian menu offers "interesting" dishes "with a twist", including "fabulous vegetarian options", plus a "great pre-theatre" menu for under £10; still, a few feel the fare is "bland" and "takes ages" to arrive.

Melati ●　　　▽　17　8　14　£20
21 Great Windmill St., W1 (Piccadilly Circus), 020-7437 2745;
fax 7734 6964
◪ "Duck down a narrow street and upstairs to this delightful" Soho "standby" for "generous servings" of "affordable", "different, healthy" Indonesian-Malaysian cooking and "individual service"; despite a recent redo, the "basic decor" "isn't much" to look at and the "seats are more uncomfortable than McDonald's!", still, some say the "food makes up for the space."

Memories of China　　　22 ⏐ 16 ⏐ 19 ⏐ £37 ⏐
353 Kensington High St., W8 (High St. Kensington), 020-7603 6951; fax 7603 0848
65-69 Ebury St., SW1 (Victoria), 020-7730 7734; fax 7730 2992 ◑
www.atozrestaurants.com
☑ "For a good Chinese nosh-up", devotees value this "venerable, venerated" pair in Belgravia (the 25-year-old original) and Kensington, with "friendly service" and "first-rate", "fresh" multiregional fare "one can always count on" – even if "you do pay for it"; a few, however, harbour "memories" of "bland" cuisine.

Memories of India　　　17 ⏐ 12 ⏐ 18 ⏐ £22 ⏐
18 Gloucester Rd., SW7 (Gloucester Rd.), 020-7581 3734; fax 7589 6450
160-162 Thornbury Rd., Osterley (Osterley), 020-8847 1548 ◑
■ "An Indian stalwart", this unprepossessing Gloucester Road spot is "convenient" for nearby museums and "child-friendly" to boot; "attentive staff" serve a "wide range" of "favourites" that are "cheap, considering the area" – in brief, "good" recollections all around; N.B. the little-known Osterley sibling generates little comment.

Meson Don Felipe ⌧　　　20 ⏐ 15 ⏐ 14 ⏐ £27 ⏐
53 The Cut, SE1 (Southwark/Waterloo), 020-7928 3237; fax 7736 9857; www.mesondonfelipe.co.uk
☑ "Authentic" and "hectic", this Southwark "institution" "has a real Spanish feel to it" and "always amuses" with "fantastic tapas and wine" – "though the real novelty is the chap on a platform playing flamenco guitar"; it's "not for those who need a lot of personal space" as "you'll be packed in like a sardine, but the food is worth the squeeze."

Metrogusto　　　23 ⏐ 20 ⏐ 22 ⏐ £38 ⏐
11-13 Theberton St., N1 (Angel/Highbury), 020-7226 9400; fax 7226 9400; www.metrogusto.co.uk
■ "Imagination and an eye for colour characterise the food and decor" at this "lovely" "local" that started out in Battersea and is now "one of the best Italians in Islington"; the "inventive cooking" reveals a "modern twist" with "influences from northern provinces" and the "quirky" "art on the walls" adds "interest", whilst "knowledgeable staff" and a "great wine list" also get the thumbs up.

Mildreds ⌧⌿　　　19 ⏐ 12 ⏐ 14 ⏐ £17 ⏐
45 Lexington St., W1 (Oxford Circus), 020-7439 2392; fax 7494 1634; www.mildreds.co.uk
☑ "Very inventive, indeed" is the take on this "popular" Soho eatery considered "a better class of veggie restaurant" by "young professionals, theatregoers" and others who just appreciate its "constantly changing", "extensive menu" of "excellent" "grub" at "great prices"; whilst some find it "nice and bright", a handful sigh it "could be more cheerful."

Mimmo d'Ischia ●⊠   21 ‖ 16 ‖ 21 ‖ £41

61 Elizabeth St., SW1 (Sloane Sq./Victoria), 020-7730 5406;
www.mimmodischia.co.uk

■ Owner "Mimmo makes you feel right at home" at this
"good, old-fashioned", 36-year-old Belgravia Italian
that, despite its "dated formula", remains a "sentimental
favourite"; the "enormous portions" of "very tasty" food
and staff that "attend to your every need swiftly and
unobtrusively" add to the "festive dining experience" –
with "celebrity spotting" the icing on the cake.

Mint Leaf ⊠   22 ‖ 24 ‖ 18 ‖ £49

Corner of Haymarket & Suffolk Pl., SW1 (Piccadilly Circus),
020-7930 9020; fax 7930 6205; www.mintleafrestaurant.com

■ "A feast for the eyes", the "chic, sharp interior" of this
"trendy" Indian "must-try" set in a former banking hall
near Trafalgar Square makes "beautiful" use of partitions
to conceal its vast size; Leaf lovers lavish praise on the
"brilliant" dishes, "friendly service" and the "unpretentious
yet cool atmosphere"; but cynics cite "top dollar" prices
for "portions that are good if you are a model", deeming
the "cool" bar the "best part."

MIRABELLE ●   23 ‖ 22 ‖ 22 ‖ £55

56 Curzon St., W1 (Green Park), 020-7499 4636; fax 7499 5449;
www.whitestarline.org.uk

■ "Very posh for lots of dosh", yes, the "whole package
works" at Marco Pierre White's "underground delight" in
an "elegant Mayfair basement" with "delicious, refined"
Classic French fare that takes a "lighter, more modern
approach" and "impeccable service", plus "fantastic
outside tables" (they're back) and a "twinkling", "disco"
Mirabelle "mirror ball" in the "spacious bar" providing
"glamourous moments"; but a few lash out that it's "terri-
belle" – "too highbrow" and "behind the curve" – but even
they concede the £19.95 set "lunch is a steal."

Mitsukoshi   22 ‖ 12 ‖ 21 ‖ £38

14-20 Lower Regent St., SW1 (Piccadilly Circus), 020-7930 0317;
fax 7839 1167; www.mitsukoshi-restaurant.co.uk

■ Expect "authentic food from a Japanese point of view" at
this "nondescript basement setting" in an Asian department
store near Piccadilly Circus that offers a "nice departure",
with "super-fresh sushi", "traditional bento varieties",
shabu-shabu and sukiyaki, made with natural and organic
ingredients; "visit at lunchtime" is the tip as it's "better
value than the ultra-expensive dinner" at "Tokyo prices."

Miyama   21 ‖ 15 ‖ 21 ‖ £38

38 Clarges St., W1 (Green Park), 020-7499 2443; fax 7493 1573

■ "Sublime sashimi", "wonderful sushi" and "friendly
service" are all on offer at this bright, albeit a "bit dated"
looking venue in a Mayfair townhouse; even if the menu

"comes at a price", the £12 "lunch is unbelievable value";
N.B. the teppanyaki offer has been discontinued.

Mju ⊠   20   17   20   £48
Millennium Knightsbridge Hotel, 17 Sloane St., SW1
(Knightsbridge), 020-7201 6330; fax 7201 6302
■ "Hidden away" in the Millennium Knightsbridge Hotel,
this "understated" first-floor dining room and bar is a
"surprising find" fawn fans who fall for the "succulent"
Pacific Rim fare, an "interesting fusion blend" that's
"as good as it gets", though a few feel "prices are high",
especially for "miniscule portions"; the "tasting menu paired
with perfect wines selected by the sommelier" also elicits
"bravos"; N.B. chef Paul Peters departed at press time.

Momo   18   24   18   £44
25 Heddon St., W1 (Piccadilly Circus), 020-7434 4040;
fax 7287 0404 ◗
Selfridges Department Store, 2nd fl., 400 Oxford St., W1
(Bond St.), 020-7318 3620; fax 7318 3228
www.momoresto.com
■ "Ambience is everything" at this "exotic" Moroccan
"kasbah" near Regent Street that's "an experience for all
five senses"; the "hopping" atmosphere, "heady incense",
world music, "tasty tagines" and "delicious" North African
dishes "transport you" to the "souks of Marrakesh" – it's
enough to "make you feel like an Arabian princess"; below is
a "loungey private club" and next door is the tearoom that
feels like a "glamourous bazaar"; N.B. the Selfridges in-
store outpost includes a restaurant and patisserie.

Mon Plaisir ⊠   18   17   16   £34
21 Monmouth St., WC2 (Covent Garden/Leicester Sq.),
020-7836 7243; fax 7240 4774
■ "You could be across the Channel" muse supporters
pleased by this 63-year-old "perennial favourite" with
"class and flair", where "utterly reliable, genuine French
fare at a reasonable price" is served in a "densely packed"
warren of rooms; it's "charming in its way, particularly the
service", plus the "pre-theatre dinner is a great bargain";
if a few feel it's a "time warp" "resting on its laurels", most
amis agree it's "still a lovely place to go."

MONSIEUR MAX   26   18   24   £53
133 High St., Hampton Hill (Fulwell B.R.), 020-8979 5546;
fax 8979 3747
◪ "It's a bit of a hike from the city", but this "hidden jewel"
in Hampton Hill "charms" those who make the trek with
"generous portions" of "interesting, inventive" French bistro
cooking and "excellent", "attentive service"; whilst some
find the decor "classy" and conducive to "feeling as if you're
in France", the less-enamoured deem it "old-fashioned"
and "quibble" about this BYO's "steep corkage charges."

Monte's ⌧   21 | 20 | 24 | £41
164 Sloane St., SW1 (Knightsbridge), 020-7245 0896;
fax 7235 3456; www.montes.co.uk
☑ He may have moved on from this "posh" private club in Knightsbridge a few years ago, nevertheless, "Jamie Oliver has left his mark" on the "tasty", "top-quality" Italian-Med menu; the "elegant" first-floor dining room boasts "well-spaced tables" so you can "still hear and talk", making it "ideal for business", plus there's also an "elegant" bar above and a basement nightclub; still, a few feel "it's lost its magic"; P.S. "you can go for lunch without being a member."

Montpeliano ◑   17 | 16 | 18 | £43
13 Montpelier St., SW7 (Knightsbridge), 020-7589 0032
☑ Why this "colourful" "'70s throwback reels them in come boom or bust" is a matter of debate: loyalists love the "jovial" attitude ("by your third visit staff make you feel like family") and "well-turned-out Italian staples", finding it "a cute place to get a decent bite after shopping" in Knightsbridge; but it's a "bit tired" according to detractors who are also put off by service that can be "better if you know somebody."

Monza ◑   19 | 16 | 21 | £34
6 Yeoman's Row, SW3 (Knightsbridge/South Kensington),
020-7591 0210
■ "Intimate, with a regional feel" and a "motor-racing theme" that pays "tribute to Formula 1", this "lovely Knightsbridge Italian" is a "real treat with imaginative food", "warm service" and a "festive ambience"; even fans who find it "fun" to gear up at this "energetic" "weekend starting point before a night out" admit it's a "happy although" "conversation-forbidding place" on Fridays and Saturdays, and "smoky too – yet, "it does have its charm."

Morgan M   24 | 15 | 20 | £45
489 Liverpool Rd., N7 (Highbury & Islington), 020-7609 3560;
fax 8292 5699
☑ A "corner of upmarket Paris in the most unlikely location" near Highbury Corner, this "unpretentious", "simply decorated" spot is "more about the food", with eponymous Morgan Meunier offering "interesting, but not too way out" New French fare, plus an "innovative" degustation menu; the "knowledgeable sommelier" gets a thumbs up, though staff are sometimes "slow"; N.B. a chef's table near the kitchen was introduced post-*Survey*.

MORO ⌧   24 | 17 | 19 | £37
34-36 Exmouth Mkt., EC1 (Angel/Farringdon), 020-7833 8336;
fax 7833 9338
■ It's "always fiendishly difficult to get a table" at this "simply marvellous" Exmouth Market venue where fans are "seduced by the possibilities", from the "bar snacks that taste particularly Moorish when nibbled with a nutty

sherry" to the "gutsy" Spanish–North African–Eastern
Mediterranean dishes that use a "creative mix of spices"
to "stunning" effect; the "convivial" "atmosphere still hits
all the right spots" – "yes, it really lives up to the hype" –
and may even be "better now that it's less trendy."

Morton's   –   –   –   VE
Private club; inquiries: 020-7518 2982
One of London's more recognised restaurant names returns
to its original Berkeley Square townhouse with Marlon
Abela, the city's latest whirlwind restaurateur, at the helm;
the swish, high-octane private club reflects the owner's
emphasis on all things epicurean, from the comfy dining
room with a refined New French menu (featuring subtle
Asian influences) to the striking modern art and armies of
staff; there's also a slick bar open till 3 AM and a private
dining room with a view of the 3,000-bin strong wine cellar.

Moshi Moshi Sushi   16   9   12   £23
Waitrose, Canada Pl., E14 (Canary Wharf), 020-7512 9201;
fax 7512 9685
7-8 Limeburner Ln., Ludgate Circus, EC4 (St. Paul's/Thames City),
020-7248 1808; fax 7248 1807 ⊠
24 Upper Level, Liverpool St. Station, Broadgate, EC2
(Liverpool St.), 020-7247 3227; fax 7247 3227 ⊠
www.moshimoshi.co.uk
◪ "Great for folks with an urge to browse and pick" from
the sushi conveyor belt, and "cheap enough to go anytime",
this "cheerful" Japanese chain, with weekday-only City
branches, including a "remarkably transformed" Liverpool
Street site and a Ludgate Circus stop, plus a venue in a
Canary Wharf supermarket ("makes shopping less of a
chore"), offers "good cuts of fresh fish" and "fun, quick"
fare; but if you "bring your appetite", take along "your wallet,
because one plate ends up being a stack."

MOSIMANN'S ⊠   27   26   27   £61
Private club; inquiries: 020-7235 9625
■ Inside the Belfry, a Belgravia "church-turned-restaurant"
built in 1830, with a "bright, open" dining room and several
"classy" rooms, "awesome" chef, Anton Mosimann
conjures up a "simply divine" Eclectic menu of "subtle
food that makes a change from in-your-face cooking";
"outstanding service" and an "exceptional wine list" add
to the appeal of this "unique" private club that "sticks
rigidly to the jacket and tie policy."

Motcombs   18   18   19   £38
26 Motcomb St., SW1 (Knightsbridge/Sloane Sq.), 020-7235 6382;
fax 7245 6351; www.motcombs.co.uk
◪ "Better than your normal neighbourhood" spot, this 36-
year-old Belgravia "institution" comprises an "intimate"
restaurant downstairs with "nice artwork" on the walls

and a "decent" Eclectic menu, plus a "wonderful wine bar" on the ground floor with pavement dining, a "buzzing" perch from which to "watch the beautiful people" walk by; but a disgruntled few gripe it "should be renamed grotcombs."

Mr. Chow ◐   21 | 19 | 20 | £48 |
151 Knightsbridge, SW1 (Knightsbridge), 020-7589 7347; fax 7584 5780; www.mrchow.com

◪ The "old formula stills works" declare loyalists of this "fashionable" Knightsbridge Asian stalwart that still attracts a "chic", "interesting crowd of fashionistas and theatre types mixed in with regular folk", with "simply sublime", "beautifully presented Chinese cuisine" and a "European atmosphere"; still, a vociferous minority balk that "you can feed a village in China for the price of an appetizer", adding "Chow, Chow, not now."

Mr. Kong ◐   25 | 11 | 18 | £23 |
21 Lisle St., WC2 (Leicester Sq.), 020-7437 7341

■ "What would we do without Mr. Kong?" ponder the appreciative who "just dive in and enjoy" the "high-standard" Cantonese cuisine at "reasonable prices" at this 20-year-old Chinatown haunt that "looks like a dive from the outside, but almost feels like Shanghai when you're" seated; staff are "friendly and fast" and what's more, it keeps "mercifully late hours" (till 2.45 AM most nights) providing the "answer" "so you don't have to go for a Big Mac."

Mᴠʜ   – | – | – | VE |
5 White Hart Ln., SW13 (Barnes Bridge B.R.), 020-8392 1111; fax 8878 1616

"Dining here is certainly an experience", especially "for foodies" encore enthusiasts of Michael von Hruschka's "tremendously inventive" Eclectic cooking, "meticulously prepared" with "unique French-Asian" touches and presented in an "interestingly decorated" bi-level space in Barnes; the "bizarre" concept is divided into 'heaven', with an angel sculpture presiding over the white dining room, and 'hell', a red-coloured "top-floor bar with couches, a fireplace and distinctive art" on the walls.

Nahm   23 | 20 | 21 | £64 |
Halkin Hotel, 5 Halkin St., SW1 (Hyde Park Corner), 020-7333 1234; fax 7333 1100; www.halkin.co.uk

◪ Australian chef David Thompson offers "high-class, nouveau Thai for the adventurous who aren't sticklers for authenticity" at this "Zen-like" "spot of tranquillity" in Belgravia's Halkin Hotel where "attention is given to the slightest detail"; the "mind-blowing combinations" "assault your mouth with strange and wonderful flavours", creating a "taste experience" that's "out of the ordinary"; but non-believers find the menu "ridiculously inflexible" and "too pricey."

Naked Turtle ◕ ▽ 17 18 23 £31
505 Upper Richmond Rd. W., SW14 (Richmond), 020-8878 1995; fax 8392 1388

■ "Great jazz" every night along with performances from the "famous singing staff" create a "lively", "excellent atmosphere" at this "amazing little local gem" in East Sheen with "warm, friendly" service where adventurous game lovers seek shelter, hunting down a "diverse" Eclectic menu that includes "unusual" fare like signature platters of kangaroo, crocodile and ostrich.

Nam Long-Le Shaker ◑ 🗷 17 15 16 £36
159 Old Brompton Rd., SW5 (Gloucester Rd./South Kensington), 020-7373 1926; fax 7373 6043

■ An "excellent and potent" cocktail selection, particularly the "great flaming Ferrari" is the lure at this "cosy but still buzzy" South Ken stalwart with a "vibrant atmosphere" that also happens to offer a "fun, funky menu" of Vietnamese fare, making it a "perfect neighbourhood" "hangout"; still, it's more of a "bar with food", so most suggest you stick to the "fantastic" drinks.

Nathalie – – – E
3 Milner St., SW3 (Sloane Sq./South Kensington), 020-7581 2848

A "great neighbourhood find", this Chelsea newcomer boasts an "inventive" New French menu from chef Stephane Galibert incorporating organic ingredients and it bears the name of the infant daughter of owner Eric Chatroux, ex-manager from La Tante Claire, and his wife; the smitten sigh that the "variety of dishes really complement each other" and the "express lunch" menu for £14.50 offers "excellent value", concurring "I'm now a regular!"

Nautilus Fish 🗷 ▽ 23 7 17 £18
27-29 Fortune Green Rd., NW6 (West Hampstead), 020-7435 2532

■ Since it "doesn't offer the most elegant of surroundings", this "very friendly" 30-year-old "local" seafooder in West Hampstead may be "better with mates than with a date"; aficionados agree that the "simple" menu is the lure, particularly the "excellent fish 'n' chips" made with "crispy batter" that's also "great for takeaway."

Neal Street Restaurant 🗷 23 17 20 £41
26 Neal St., WC2 (Covent Garden), 020-7836 8368; fax 7240 3964

◪ "The mushroom-enhanced" Italian "cuisine is out of this world" – especially when "truffles are in season" – and it's "served with passion" fawn funghi fans who find Antonio Carluccio's "modern, clean-cut" yet "homey" "Covent Garden hideaway" "wonderful for after the theatre" or before; it's "utterly delicious, but it's also pricey" say quibblers who also quip "it would be cheaper to fly to Pisa" for a meal.

New Culture Revolution | 17 | 12 | 14 | £15 |

157-159 Notting Hill Gate, W11 (Ladbroke Grove/Latimer Rd.),
020-7313 9688
75 Southampton Row, WC1 (Holborn), 020-7436 9706
305 King's Rd., SW3 (Sloane Sq.), 020-7352 9281
42 Duncan St., N1 (Angel), 020-7833 9083
43 Parkway, NW1 (Camden Town), 020-7267 2700
www.newculturerevolution.co.uk

☑ "With basic rooms adorned with Chairman Mao sayings" and "funkily dressed staff", this "easy noodle house" chain may not be "for lingering", but it's "great" for a "pre-cinema meal"; the Culture clan clamours for "hearty soups", "tasty dumplings" and "cheap" Mandarin eats that "make you feel healthy"; still, the unconverted snipe "it looks cooler from the outside" and believe it's "better for takeaway."

New World ◑ | 16 | 9 | 13 | £17 |

1 Gerrard Pl., W1 (Leicester Sq.), 020-7434 2508; fax 7287 8994

☑ "Trolleys just roll past crammed with tempting goodies" – yes, "it's hard to say no to anything" at this "old-school" "dim-sum haven" in Chinatown; go for the "great brunch" (it's "worth" the "wait during peak hours"), "not the à la carte menu", overlook the "run-down decor" and "barely adequate service" and "you will be happy."

Nicole's ☒ | 19 | 16 | 17 | £38 |

Nicole Farhi, 158 New Bond St., W1 (Bond St./Green Park),
020-7499 8408; fax 7409 0381; www.nicolefarhi.com

☑ "After a hard day" of browsing on Bond Street "when the Manolos are digging into your heels", step into this "ladies-that-shop favourite" below Nicole Farhi's boutique for a "special lunch" from a Modern European–Med menu "pitched just right"; "even if it's pricey, the air kisses flying left and right and celeb spotting make it worthwhile"; N.B. it's also open for weekday dinner.

noble rot. ☒ | 18 | 18 | 16 | £47 |

3-5 Mill St., W1 (Oxford Circus), 020-7629 8877; fax 7629 8878;
www.noblerot.com

☑ "Very chic with friendly staff" – a "rare combination" – Soren Jessen's "fun", glass-fronted ground-floor Mayfair eatery with "imaginative" Modern European fare is "a must for wine lovers and connoisseurs" thanks to an impressive selection of bins (the name refers to the mould that causes grapes to shrivel), and "if you're in the mood" for a "lively" night, there's a "Moroccan"-style private club downstairs; still, a few feel "it's not as good as it once was."

NOBU | 27 | 21 | 21 | £64 |

Metropolitan Hotel, 19 Old Park Ln., W1 (Hyde Park Corner),
020-7447 4747; fax 7447 4749

■ There are "not enough superlatives to describe" this "buzzing" first-floor "culinary summit" inside Park Lane's

Metropolitan Hotel, which retains its coveted mantle as this *Survey*'s Most Popular haunt; the "hypnotic" Japanese–South American fusion dishes are "so divine you want to genuflect at the true mastery of it all" – this is where you'll find "some of the sexiest" "tidbits"; "celeb sightings abound" so "dress to kill" ("dig out that Armani suit"), just "be prepared to melt your credit cards" and remember the "staff mantra seems to be 'I'm too sexy for this job.'"

Noor Jahan ❶　　　　　　20 | 13 | 17 | £28

26 Sussex Pl., W2 (Lancaster Gate), 020-7402 2332; www.noorjahan2.co.uk
2A Bina Gardens, SW5 (South Kensington), 020-7373 6522
☑ "Great Indian food without fanfare" is the appeal of this "crowded" 42-year-old South Kensington eatery and new, "nice Lancaster Gate stopover" sib where dishes are "speedily prepared" and "charmingly served"; whilst some shrug they "wouldn't go out of the way to get here", most feel it fits the bill as a "dependable" option.

North Sea ☒　　　　　　– | – | – | M

7-8 Leigh St., WC1 (Kings Cross), 020-7387 5892; www.northseafish.com
Place your order for "glorious fish 'n' chips", "pick your beer" and then "settle down for a tasty treat" at this Traditional British seafooder housed on two floors in "modest" premises near Russell Square; the "warm staff make you feel like you live here", and whilst "there isn't a huge selection", the fare is "fresh" and "reasonably priced", making it a "great hangout" for "lots of students" and bargain-seekers; N.B. takeaway is also an option.

Noto ☒　　　　　　18 | 5 | 14 | £18

2-3 Bassishaw Highwalk, EC2 (Bank/Moorgate), 020-7256 9433; fax 7588 5656; www.noto.co.uk
■ "The genuine article, judging by the number of Japanese" "businessmen queuing for a seat" encore enthusiasts who seek out this "hard to locate", "low-key, traditional", "crowded" City "canteen" behind the Guild Hall for "tasty", "authentic" sushi and Asian fare; sure, it gets "crowded at lunch", but "service is super quick" and take note: "dinner is more relaxed."

Notting Grill　　　　　　24 | 19 | 18 | £40

123A Clarendon Rd., W11 (Ladbroke Grove/Holland Park), 020-7229 1500; fax 7229 8889; www.nottinggrill.com
☑ Antony Worrall Thompson's "superb homage to meat" is a "relaxed, informal" Notting Hill grill and bar with "exposed bricks" and an open kitchen so "you can see AWT" at work; the celebrity chef "gets hold of some great organic reared" beef, with a different "well-sourced" breed featured monthly, and his Traditional British fare makes "excellent use of herbs and spices"; there'd be "nothing to complain

about, were it not for the prices"; N.B. the first-floor space
is nonsmoking.

Notting Hill Brasserie   22   23   21   £43
92 Kensington Pl., W11 (Notting Hill Gate), 020-7229 4481;
fax 7221 1246
■ "Everything a neighbourhood brasserie should be", this
"atmospheric" "classic all-rounder" in Notting Hill delights
diners with "delicious" Modern European fare and a "cosy,
elegant, yet not at all stuffy" setting comprised of a "sleek
bar with more rustic", "candlelit" dining rooms; the live jazz
"really cooks" and "staff are attentive", making it "perfect"
"for a first date: success guaranteed!"

Noura ◗   25   20   21   £36
16 Hobart Pl., SW1 (Victoria), 020-7235 9444; fax 7235 9244;
www.noura-brasseries.co.uk
■ Combines "exquisite Lebanese" cuisine revealing
"homemade flair" "with a chic London atmosphere" and
"unbeatable service" applaud admirers who agree it's
"always a treat to dine" at this "modern" venue near Victoria
Station; "quality ingredients and fine preparation are
evident" in the mezze and other "favourites", and whilst
it's "not cheap, it's worth it", especially "for large groups";
P.S. there's also "excellent delivery service", plus there's a
Paris branch too.

Novelli in the City ⊠   –   –   –   E
15 Abchurch Ln., EC4 (Monument), 020-7717 0088
Two years after closing Maison Novelli, Jean-Cristophe
Novelli returns to the kitchen of this traditional private
club near Monument offering French-accented Modern
European fare in a plush revamped room that befits his
classy menu; meals are served throughout the day to
members but only available to nonmembers on weekday
evenings; N.B. the heartthrob chef also remains behind
the stove at Auberge du Lac in Hertfordshire.

number 10   –   –   –   E
10 Golborne Rd., W10 (Westbourne Park), 020-8969 8922
In addition to housing a private members' lounge, this quirky
all-day newcomer near Westbourne Park offers live music
from eclectic instrumental soloists who perform in the airy,
white-walled first-floor dining room whilst customers dine
on Modern European cooking from young chef Julien
Maisonneuve; by contrast, the ground floor is home to a hip
bar with thumping music and occasional performances,
where snacks are served all day.

Nyonya   19   14   19   £18
2A Kensington Park Rd., W11 (Notting Hill Gate), 020-7243 1800;
www.nyonya.co.uk
◪ A "modern setting" with bench-style seating and
"particularly fine service" on a busy Notting Hill junction

is the canvas for "unusual", "authentically prepared" Malaysian-Chinese" "treats" from a husband-wife team from Singapore brought over by the Como hotel group; it's "not a place to linger" but it is "great for a quickie bowl of noodles" and other "inexpensive" dishes, plus there's another "small" room with more "comfortable" chairs.

Oak, The · 16 19 15 £25
137 Westbourne Park Rd., W2 (Westbourne Park), 020-7221 3355
◪ Expect "delicious wood-fired pizzas", "fab" Italian dishes and a "good vibe" at this "bustling" "converted pub" in "a mixed stretch of Westbourne Grove"; still, a few wonder why the food is "so pricey" and find it "disappointing"; P.S. "the "very sophisticated members-only" club upstairs is a "great place to go with friends away from home" yet still "gives the feeling of an intimate dinner party."

Odette's · 23 19 19 £43
130 Regent's Park Rd., NW1 (Chalk Farm), 020-7586 5486; fax 7580 0508
◪ The ownership of this "quaint" Primrose Hill "bijou spot from a time gone by changed hands last year and the chefs'" "magic" New French–Modern European fare has "flourished"; the subtly refurbished, "charming" velvet-and-gilt "interior with mirrors everywhere" "makes you feel posh" and is "great for a romantic" "tête-à-tête", especially the "intimate downstairs" wine bar; still, a few feel the food is just "deeply ok" and deem "service utterly indifferent."

Odin's ☒ · 20 22 22 £47
27 Devonshire St., W1 (Baker St.), 020-7935 7296; fax 7493 8309; www.langansrestaurants.co.uk
◪ "Simply a classic", this "friendly" Marylebone stalwart is "still going strong" after nearly 40 years, offering "superb" Anglo-French dishes in an "arty, homelike" setting adorned with the works of David Hockney and Patrick Procktor; "diligent staff" and a "relaxed atmosphere" make it "excellent for a power lunch or romantic dinner"; still, a few feel it "can be hit-or-miss."

Oliveto · 21 15 16 £29
49 Elizabeth St., SW1 (Sloane Sq./Victoria), 020-7730 0074
■ With a "Mediterranean atmosphere", this "casual" Belgravia Italian looks "a bit like a good quality canteen", but the "honestly priced", "rustic" Sardinian cooking and "tasty pizzas straight from the wood-burning oven" ensure it's "always crammed"; it's a "good stopover at lunch or dinner", plus one diner who "sat next to Madonna and Guy" reveals there's even the occasional celeb sighting.

Olivo · 22 14 19 £35
21 Eccleston St., SW1 (Victoria), 020-7730 2505
◪ "Steady as she goes", Oliveto's "reliable" older Italian sibling behind Victoria" Station is "always busy" on account

of a "well-crafted", "high-end" menu of "imaginatively prepared Sardinian food" and an "eclectic wine list"; even if some feel the "decor's tired" and staff are better to "local regulars", the "laid-back" atmosphere makes amends.

1 Lombard Street ⑤   18 19 17 £49

1 Lombard St., EC3 (Bank), 020-7929 6611; fax 7929 6622; www.1lombardstreet.com

◪ By day, Soren Jessen's venue opposite the Bank of England is "a lively City power lunch spot" where long-standing chef Herbert Berger's "interesting combinations" of New French cooking are "served serenely", whilst by night it has a "great vibe for post-work drinks" and a "quiet environment" for dinner; still, detractors deem it "expense-account-driven" ("the full monty may bankrupt you") and too "loud when busy."

1 Lombard Street Brasserie ⑤   18 19 18 £35

1 Lombard St., EC3 (Bank), 020-7929 6611; fax 7929 6622; www.1lombardstreet.com

◪ "If you don't mind a room full of bankers", "fun times" await at the "friendly", "unpretentious", more "relaxed" part of Soren Jessen's restaurant-cum-bar/brasserie opposite the Bank of England; it's an "enjoyable" option for a "quick" meal from a Modern European menu and a "few pounds less than" the main restaurant; but a few fume when it's "full you have to shout to be heard", especially if "sitting near the central bar area."

One-O-One   25 18 21 £57

Sheraton Park Tower, 101 William St., SW1 (Knightsbridge), 020-7290 7101; fax 7235 6196

◪ "This welcoming seafood restaurant" with a constantly changing art exhibition within Knightsbridge's Sheraton Park Tower is "very 'in' with serious eaters" attracted by Pascal Proyart's "original", albeit "pricey" New French menu boasting "sublime combinations" and presented by "congenial, solicitous" staff; but dissenters snipe that "such great food should have a room to match" instead of "slightly dodgy decor."

Opera   19 16 16 £23

68 Heath St., NW3 (Hampstead), 020-7794 6666

◪ Fans sing the praises of this former pub-turned-Chinese spot with a "Hampstead Village feeling"; the "good-value, authentic mostly Cantonese" fare, including "excellent dim sum", is served in a "warm, comfortable" 1960s-inspired setting that's "quite quiet and smart"; but a few find the "food only average" and gripe service can be "rude."

Oriel   13 15 13 £27

51 Sloane Sq., SW1 (Sloane Sq.), 020-7730 2804; fax 7730 7966

◪ "A place to be seen at the start or end of a hectic day", this "bustling" "Sloane Square icon" is a "haven for the harried shopper", a "rendezvous" point for a "young, hip" crowd and a "breakfast staple"; whilst loyalists insist the Modern European "brasserie-type" menu "tends to positively surprise", most find that "serious appetites can do better"; still, it's "worth it" just to experience that "street-cafe-in-Paris" feel on a "sunny day."

Oriental, The ☒

| 24 | 23 | 25 | £58 |

The Dorchester, 53 Park Ln., W1 (Hyde Park Corner/Marble Arch), 020-7317 6328; fax 7317 6464; www.dorchesterhotel.com

◪ "Almost flawless all-round", this "sumptuous" spot within Mayfair's famous Dorchester hotel is one of the "most creative of the high-end Chinese restaurants" thanks to Kenneth Poon's "exquisite", *très cher* cuisine; "there's a lot to love here", from the "elegantly prepared" food to the "decadently exotic decor"; still, a few fume that it's "wonderful, but you pay for it", with "stratospheric prices" for "tiny portions"; P.S. the trio of "private rooms are a must" for a "special occasion."

Original Tagine

| 20 | 13 | 17 | £24 |

7A Dorset St., W1 (Baker St.), 020-7935 1545; www.originaltagines.com

■ "A tiny treasure of a place" near Baker Street, this "small", "sweet", "unpretentious" North African venue is "very pleasant" for "delicious", "inexpensive" Moroccan fare, including, as "the name implies", its namesake "tagines, cooked to perfection"; with "little pillows on the chairs" and "friendly service", it's a "great pick" "for a low-key romantic dinner."

ORRERY

| 26 | 22 | 23 | £56 |

55 Marylebone High St., W1 (Baker St./Regent's Park), 020-7616 8000; fax 7616 8080; www.orrery.co.uk

■ "Bring the Birkin bag full of loot – you're gonna need it" at this "visually stunning and deliciously varied", "slick, professional" Marylebone eatery considered the "best Conran restaurant" to many; acolytes give "a massive thumbs up" to Andre Garrett's "inventive", "delectable" New French cooking that's "fabulous by any measure", and conclude that whilst this "class act" is a "complete indulgence", it's a "great experience."

Orso ◉

| 19 | 16 | 17 | £37 |

27 Wellington St., WC2 (Covent Garden), 020-7240 5269; fax 7497 2148

◪ Expect to be "bowled over by big, gutsy flavours", "well-trained staff" and a "relaxed ambience" applaud admirers of this Tuscan sibling of the Manhattan mainstay in Covent Garden that "draws a theatrical crowd" to its "tucked away subterranean" setting; the "distinctive", "straightforward specialties" and "constantly changing menu" make it "difficult to decide what to eat"; still, a few knockers wonder "why come to London for New York Italian" when it's "not anywhere as good."

Osia ⌂ | 21 | 18 | 20 | £44 |

11 Haymarket, SW1 (Piccadilly Circus), 020-7976 1313;
www.osiarestaurant.com

■ Australian chef—"fantastic host" Scott Webster brings a "breath of fresh air" to Haymarket with this "first-rate import", a "hip spot to enjoy delicious Down Under fare" and a unique selection from the New World wine list; the "adventurous" "combinations and textures" make use of "little known seasonings" whilst revealing his "good sense of flavours", and it's "all very delicious"; P.S. "check out the trendy" leather-walled Long Bar in an adjacent room.

OSLO COURT ⌂ | 25 | 14 | 26 | £47 |

Charlbert St., Prince Albert Rd., NW8 (St. John's Wood),
020-7722 8795

■ "Go in hungry and leave Atkins behind" at this "charming time capsule" in St. John's Wood, "which is forever" "in the 1970s", serving "huge portions" of "simply cooked", "wonderful" Classic French fare from an "extensive menu packed with favourites"; this "oldie but goodie" is "great for celebrations" or "for that cross-generational family get-together" as "nothing is too much trouble" for "excellent staff" that "make you feel loved."

Osteria Antica Bologna   ▽ | 22 | 15 | 19 | £27 |

23 Northcote Rd., SW11 (Clapham Junction B.R.), 020-7978 4771;
fax 7978 4771; www.osteria.co.uk

▣ The "old-fashioned" wood panelling makes you feel "like you're inside a wine barrel" and the Bologna "mural is twee", but it just adds to the novelty of this "down-to-earth" Battersea trattoria with regional "rustic Italian cooking" and "friendly service"; it's "not exactly a destination", but "it's still a fave some 15 years after opening."

Osteria Basilico | 24 | 17 | 20 | £29 |

29 Kensington Park Rd., W11 (Ladbroke Grove), 020-7727 9957;
fax 7229 7980

■ "Don't even think of coming" to this "convivial", "earthy", "bustling", bi-level Notting Hill trattoria "without booking a table or you will be looked upon with pity by the other diners enjoying wonderfully delicious" Italian dishes and "excellent" "pizza that's among the best in town"; "downstairs is cosy" with "very small tables" so you "have to breathe in turns with the person sitting behind you" – still, you may find yourself "seated next to a movie star."

OXO TOWER | 22 | 25 | 21 | £52 |

Oxo Tower Wharf, Barge House St, SE1 (Blackfriars/Waterloo),
020-7803 3888; fax 7803 3838; www.harveynichols.com

▣ With "incredible views up and down the Thames" and "exceptional service", this "simply stunning setting" on the top floor of a South Bank landmark building is "a must for power business" meals and a "special" "night on the town", especially on a "balmy summer's evening"; supporters say that the "edgy" Eclectic Asian-influenced cooking has "improved" of late, still, a few find it "more scene and be seen than serious restaurant"; P.S. it's handy for "the Tate Modern."

Oxo Tower Brasserie   21 25 17 £42
Oxo Tower Wharf, Barge House St., SE1 (Blackfriars/Waterloo), 020-7803 3888; fax 7803 3838; www.harveynichols.com
■ Expect an "unsurpassed" "panorama that makes a meal all the more enjoyable" and "creative" Med–Pacific Rim fare that's "not too shabby either" at this "bright, clean-lined" glass-fronted brasserie that's "convenient for a business lunch south of the river", a "great hangout" and offers "better value than its bigger brother next door"; there's also a "happening", "stylish bar" for "under 30s – over 30s bring earplugs" – and a "sunny terrace."

Ozer Restaurant & Bar ●   20 18 18 £27
5 Langham Pl., W1 (Oxford Circus), 020-7323 0505; fax 7323 0111
■ The "cheesy interior" (ersatz opulence) of this "energetic" Modern Ottoman restaurant owned by the Sofra group near Regent Street "belies a very good" Turkish menu – perhaps "better than what you can get in Istanbul" – including "delicious grilled" meats, "nice little mezze" plates offering a "panoply of flavours" and an "extremely good-value" £8 set lunch; expect a "warm welcome" after "threading your way through the popular bar to the restaurant."

Pacific Oriental ☒   11 14 15 £33
1 Bishopsgate, EC2 (Bank), 020-7621 9988; fax 7929 7227; www.orientalrestaurantgroup.co.uk
☑ "Unusual" Pacific Rim offerings and "great-value lunch boxes" draw some to this "striking" bi-level Bishopsgate "fusion of choice" with a six-meter-high waterfall; if detractors suggest the fare has "slipped", others think the brasserie/bar downstairs makes a "great after-work location" especially on Thursday and Friday disco nights.

Painted Heron, The   23 18 19 £32
112 Cheyne Walk, SW10 (Sloane Sq.), 020-7351 5232 ☒ 205 Kennington Ln., SE11 (Kennington), 020-7793 8313 www.thepaintedheron.com
■ Offering "a refreshing change to flock, flounce and frills", the "cool, uncluttered surroundings" and nice garden of this "quiet", "civilised" Chelsea riversider in the former Busabong Tree space form the backdrop for a "challenging, interesting" Indian menu that's "not afraid to break out of the mould" – and offers "good value" to boot; N.B. a second branch opened post-*Survey* in Kennington.

Palmerston, The 🖄   – – – E
91 Lordship Ln., SE22 (East Dulwich B.R.), 020-8693 1629
Jamie Younger, a former head chef from Bibendum, makes
his proprietorial debut at this revamped pub in East Dulwich
(previously called The Lord Palmerston), which has retained
its handsome panelling as well as most of its original
features; the sophisticated, weekly changing Modern
British menu aims to be a notch above the gastro-pub
norm, and an eclectic wine list starts at a creditable £11;
N.B. the rear dining area is no-smoking.

Paolo 🖄   – – – E
16 Percy St., W1 (Tottenham Court Rd.), 020-7637 9900;
www.paolorestaurants.com
An "excellent addition" to the hinterland around Tottenham
Court Road, this "terrific" spot simply decorated with
marble and wood is quietly ploughing its own furrow, with
"helpful, friendly service" and a "contemporary" menu of
"fresh, light" Italian fare made with seasonal ingredients;
"nothing special", shrug a minority.

Parsee 🖄   ∇ 21 4 18 £28
34 Highgate Hill, N19 (Archway), 020-7272 9091;
www.theparsee.co.uk
🖄 "Discover a palette of new flavours" at this "cheerful"
"Indian restaurant with a difference" in Highgate where
chef Cyrus Todiwala of Café Spice Namaste fame offers his
"truly different", "top-class Parsee food" – an "innovative"
blend of Persian and Gujarat recipes – along with "great
chutneys" in a "contemporary" photo-decorated space;
whilst a few feel that the "decor is a bit bland", par-takers
report it's "not your usual curry house."

Pasha ●   19 14 17 £29
301 Upper St., N1 (Angel/Highbury & Islington), 020-7226 1454;
fax 7226 1617
🖄 "For Turkish food, you can't go wrong" at this "standby"
for Islingtonians, with "careful service", "reasonable wine
prices" and a "quality" menu that features a "long list of
well-made mezze"; it's more "swish" and "comfortable"
after a redo last year, but they still "cram people in"; N.B. it
has no connection with the same-named venture in SW7.

Pasha ●   19 25 18 £37
1 Gloucester Rd., SW7 (Gloucester Rd.), 020-7589 7969;
www.pasha-restaurant.co.uk
🖄 The "magnificent Moroccan" "fantasyland" setting at
this "intimate" South Kensington venue "sets the mood right
off the bat" for "enjoyable" North African cuisine that's
"thoughtful, delicate" and a "great option for something a
bit different"; but sceptics sigh that it "promises more than it
delivers" – wish "the food lived up to the setting" – and
"recommend deep pockets" for "when the bill appears."

Passione ⊠
22 | 14 | 19 | £46

10 Charlotte St., W1 (Goodge St.), 020-7636 2833; fax 7636 2889;
www.passione.co.uk

☑ "Tasty food served and prepared with true *passione*"
that "shows on the plate" draws admirers to this "busy",
"excellent Italian" in Fitzrovia; "listen to the waiter's
recommendations" because chef Gennaro Contaldo – "a
dab hand with mushrooms" – produces "wonderful dishes"
and "flawless desserts"; still, a handful harrumph "they've
raised their prices too much to accompany their success."

Patara
24 | 17 | 19 | £33

3-7 Maddox St., W1 (Oxford Circus), 020-7499 6008; fax 7499 6007
181 Fulham Rd., SW3 (South Kensington), 020-7351 5692;
fax 7351 5692
9 Beauchamp Pl., SW3 (Knightsbridge/South Kensington),
020-7581 8820; fax 7581 2155

■ "Small, but perfectly formed portions" of "exquisite Thai
cuisine" that "always delights" are the main attraction at
this "contemporary"-looking "jewel" of a trio with "discreet,
efficient service" and "well-situated" branches around
Mayfair and South Ken; the "fresh and fragrant" dishes are
"interesting" and "gentle on the taste buds", plus there's
also an "excellent set lunch menu."

Patisserie Valerie
19 | 13 | 14 | £16

27 Kensington Church St., W8 (High St. Kensington),
020-7937 9574; fax 7937 9574
105 Marylebone High St., W1 (Baker St./Bond St.), 020-7935 6240;
fax 7734 6133
44 Old Compton St., W1 (Leicester Sq.), 020-7437 3466;
fax 7935 6543
8 Russell St., WC2 (Covent Garden), 020-7240 0064; fax 7240 0064
Duke of York Sq., Kings Rd., SW3 (Sloane Sq.),
020-7730 7094; fax 7730 7094
215 Brompton Rd., SW3 (Knightsbridge), 020-7823 9971;
fax 7589 4993
17 Motcomb St., SW1 (Knightsbridge), 020-7245 6161;
fax 7245 6161
www.patisserie-valerie.co.uk

■ "Considered a legend" – especially the nearly 80-year-old
Soho and Knightsbridge venues with their "old charms" –
these "crowded" "Parisian escapes" about town "let you
linger" over "tempting treats", "divine cakes" and "hot
savouries" from an all-day bistro menu in a "wonderfully
battered French setting"; if a few feel "service varies from
friendly to sour", most shrug it's a "gratifying pit stop."

Patterson's ⊠
∇ 23 | 18 | 21 | £41

4 Mill St., W1 (Oxford Circus), 020-7499 1308;
www.pattersonsrestaurant.com

☑ Though open since 2003, Raymond Patterson's "friendly",
family-run affair – supported by his wife and children – in

modern Mayfair premises is still an "undiscovered gem", but
a "splendid" New French menu indicates they are "trying
hard" and "will no longer be a secret"; whilst some find
service "attentive", a few feel it's "very slow at lunchtime",
but a "good-value set menu" helps compensate.

Pearl – | – | – | VE |

Renaissance Chancery Court Hotel, 252 High Holborn,
WC1 (Holborn), 020-7829 7000; fax 7829-9889;
www.pearl-restaurant.com
The smart Renaissance Chancery Court Hotel in Holborn
has revamped the space that was once the headquarters
of Pearl Assurance building and more recently the QC
restaurant into an opulent dining room with a pearlescent
and walnut theme throughout the lavish design; classically
trained chef Jun Tanaka remains in situ from the dining
room's previous incarnation offering high-end New French
fare with innovative twists, supported by an impressive wine
list with over 30 options by the glass.

Pellicano 20 | 17 | 17 | £36 |

19-21 Elystan St., SW3 (South Kensington), 020-7589 3718;
fax 7584 1789
■ "Relaxed" and "reliable", this Sardinian spot with
Mediterranean-style decor near Chelsea Green offers an
"excellent" Italian menu of "simple, clean flavours" and a
"small, well-priced wine list"; acolytes adore the "cosy
neighbourhood ambience", and all agree it's "lovely in
summertime with outside tables" on the pavement.

People's Palace 19 | 20 | 16 | £36 |

Royal Festival Hall, level 3, South Bank Ctr., SE1 (Charing Cross/
Waterloo), 020-7928 9999; fax 7928 2355;
www.peoplespalace.co.uk
☑ Loyalists find the "river view through the floor-to-ceiling
windows dazzling" at this "vast rectangular" space with
a "retro-chic sensibility" within the South Bank's Royal
Festival Hall – "what a glorious building!" – plus the "nice"
Modern British–European menu makes a "fine choice for
a pre-concert meal" ("dessert at intermission is a highlight");
but the disenchanted declare the "prices aren't exactly
the people's", "servers are haughty" and feel the fare
"comes in second to the splendid" sights.

Pepper Tree 20 | 12 | 15 | £15 |

537-539 Garratt Ln., SW18 (Earlsfield B.R.), 020-8879 3599;
fax 8879 7341
19 Clapham Common Southside, SW4 (Clapham Common),
020-7622 1758; fax 7720 7531
■ The "mess hall–style decor" and communal tables
"dissuade lingering" at this "eat-and-go" duo with branches
in Clapham and Earlsfield, nevertheless it makes a "cheap
and cheerful" option for "tasty", "traditional Thai curries"

"before a night out"; they don't take reservations and "can get very packed", but "queues go down quickly"; N.B. the Clapham branch now has a "no-smoking policy."

Pescatori ⌧   20 | 16 | 18 | £36

11 Dover St., W1 (Green Park), 020-7493 2652; fax 7499 3180
57 Charlotte St., W1 (Goodge St.), 020-7580 3289; fax 7580 0539
www.pescatori.co.uk

■ "General revelry" prevails at this "delightfully Italian" duo in Mayfair and Fitzrovia (a 45-year-old stalwart) that's "lively for lunch", "welcoming" for dinner and a "regular haunt" for locals who laud the "impeccably fresh", "well-executed" "simple fish dishes" and wine list that's a "treat"; the servers are "so nice" – "just eat what they tell you" – it's sure to be "tasty."

PÉTRUS ⌧   27 | 24 | 26 | £80

Berkeley Hotel, Wilton Pl., SW1 (Hyde Park Corner),
020-7235 1200; www.petrus-restaurant.com

■ "Living up to its lofty reputation", this Gordon Ramsay/Marcus Wareing–owned no-smoking venue in the Berkeley Hotel is "seriously sexy" (the "purple decor inspires purple prose") and a "joy to behold"; it's a "fine dining experience", from Wareing's "extraordinarily excellent, extraordinarily expensive" New French cuisine to the "formidable wine list" to "non-stuffy service", led by "seasoned manager Jean Philippe" Susilovic; although a few "preferred St. James's Street", most agree "the new location created a burst of enthusiasm in the kitchen."

PIED À TERRE ⌧   29 | 21 | 25 | £64

34 Charlotte St., W1 (Goodge St.), 020-7636 1178; fax 7916 1171;
www.pied.a.terre.co.uk

■ "An all-around winner", this New French "favourite" in Fitzrovia with a "sleek", "cool interior" and "unpretentious yet professional" service is one of the "best of the Charlotte Street foodie explosion"; "every mouthful" of chef Shane Osborn's "amazing", "cutting-edge" creations is a "taste sensation" and the "wines are super", and while it all "comes with" an "expensive" price tag, most find it "pretty reasonable for high-end" dining – with some "great lunchtime deals" too.

PIZZA EXPRESS   16 | 13 | 15 | £17

137 Notting Hill Gate, W11 (Notting Hill Gate), 020-7229 6000 ◗
35 Earl's Court Rd., W8 (Earl's Ct.), 020-7937 0761 ◗
29 Wardour St., W1 (Leicester Sq./Piccadilly Circus),
020-7437 7215; fax 7494 2582 ◗
9-12 Bow St., WC2 (Covent Garden), 020-7240 3443;
fax 7497 0131 ◗
46-54 Battersea Bridge Rd., SW11 (Earl's Ct./Sloane Sq.),
020-7924 2774 ◗

(continued)

(continued)
PIZZA EXPRESS
363 Fulham Rd., SW10 (Fulham Broadway/South Kensington),
020-7352 5300 ◐
895-896 Fulham Rd., SW6 (Parsons Green), 020-7731 3117;
fax 7371 7884 ◐
The Pheasantry, 152-154 King's Rd., SW3 (Sloane Sq.),
020-7351 5031; fax 7349 9844 ◐
7 Beauchamp Pl., SW3 (Knightsbridge), 020-7589 2355;
fax 7589 5159 ◐
125 Alban Gate, London Wall, EC2 (Moorgate/St. Paul's),
020-7600 8880; fax 7600 8128
www.pizzaexpress.com
Additional locations throughout London
■ "Always dependable, rarely exciting, but enjoyable
nonetheless", this "monument of London" pizzerias "still
sets the standard" with a "straightforward Italian" menu
majoring on "wonderful thin-crust pizzas you'll crave" with
"just the right amount" of "inventive toppings" "(didn't
drown, didn't skimp)"; "great for a quick", "no-hassle meal"
and "light on the wallet", it's a "square deal" all around.

Pizza Metro   24 | 9 | 18 | £23
64 Battersea Rise, SW11 (Clapham Common/
Clapham Junction B.R.), 020-7228 3812; fax 7738 0987
◪ "It really does feel like a quick visit to Italy" at this "noisy,
fun, cheap" and "cramped" Battersea Italian where "staff
are crazy (in a good way!)" and "authentic" cooking ensures
it "gets extremely busy at the weekend"; but "after a change
of ownership" in 2003, a few find the pizzas from the wood-
burning oven "are not as exceptional as they used to be."

Pizza on the Park ◐   17 | 14 | 16 | £23
11 Knightsbridge, SW1 (Hyde Park Corner), 020-7235 5273;
fax 7235 6853; www.pizzaonthepark.co.uk
■ "See the latest in jazz while enjoying" a "crispy pizza"
"on the side" – or "simple, solid" Italian fare – at this "feel-
good", "hip" sibling of Pizza Express "pleasantly positioned
at Hyde Park Corner" and "romantic enough for a date";
"sit by the window" of the "airy" dining room and "watch
the parade of passersby" – or head to the Music Room
downstairs for nightly live performances; P.S. "teens love it."

Pizza Pomodoro ◐   15 | 11 | 12 | £21
51 Beauchamp Pl., SW3 (Knightsbridge), 020-7589 1278;
fax 7247 4001
7-8 Bishopsgate Churchyard, EC2 (Liverpool St.), 020-7920 9207;
fax 7920 9206 ⊠
www.pomodoro.co.uk
◪ "Popular amongst the twentysomethings" and "university
students" "who make it a regular hangout" (and "adults who
refuse to grow up"), these "lively" pizzerias in Knightsbridge
and the City offer "good simple fare that won't blow the

budget" – but it's the "lively music [and dancing] every night" and the "bizarre decor" that gives this duo "character."

PJ's Bar & Grill ●　　　　　　　**18**　**18**　**16**　**£29**

52 Fulham Rd., SW3 (South Kensington), 020-7581 0025;
fax 7584 0820
30 Wellington St., WC2 (Covent Garden), 020-7240 7529;
fax 7836 3426

■ "Packed with every age", this "see-and-be-seen" American-style diner "well located" on Fulham Road is a "weekend brunch favourite", especially for the "expat community in Chelsea", with "wonderfully reliable" fare, and also features a "popular rendezvous" bar where the "cocktails are excellent" and "if you come alone, you won't be for long"; P.S. the semi-related Covent Garden branch shares one owner and has a more "clubby atmosphere."

Planet Hollywood ●　　　　　　　**11**　**15**　**13**　**£22**

13 Coventry St., W1 (Leicester Sq./Piccadilly Circus),
020-7437 7639; fax 7734 0835; www.planethollywood.com

☑ "There's a ton to do and see" at this "fun" outpost of the international chain with "plenty of [movie] memorabilia to peruse while you wait" for your "regular American food"; whilst some buffs find it "fine" "for a quick burger with the kids", the less forgiving give it a thumbs down, declaring it's "good if you're 15" – "might as well eat one of their T-shirts!"

Plateau　　　　　　　　　　　**20**　**23**　**20**　**£48**

Canada Pl., Canada Sq., E14 (Canary Wharf), 020-7715 7100;
www.conran.com

■ Bringing "well-combined" New French "flavours" and a "wonderful" "style to Canary Wharf", this "bright" glass-fronted, rooftop Conran yearling boasts a "steel and chrome interior that fits in well with the skyscraper panorama" over Canada Square Park; the fine dining area offers a "pricey", "interesting menu and high comfort factor", whilst the more "relaxed", "buzzy" bar/grill serves brasserie-style fare; still, a few feel it needs to "buck up its ideas and execution."

Poissonnerie de l'Avenue ●☒　　**23**　**17**　**20**　**£46**

82 Sloane Ave., SW3 (South Kensington), 020-7589 2457;
fax 7581 3360

■ Expect "nicely dressed clientele" at this "intimate", "popular" Brompton Cross seafooder with "quality" Classic French fare that's "cooked to perfection" and "quite expensive, but worth it"; even those hardly smitten by the "old-fashioned" atmosphere concede it's "like a good old friend who always wears the same ball gown."

Polygon Bar & Grill　　　　　　**–**　**–**　**–**　**E**

4 The Polygon, Clapham Old Town, SW4 (Clapham Common),
020-7622 1199; fax 7622 1166; www.thepolygon.co.uk

"Too good for Clapham" fawn fans of this bar/restaurant that reveals many sides, from an "excellent" Pacific Rim–

Modern British menu to "a bit of good English attitude from staff"; still, it doesn't shape up that way for a few who find the menu "a fusion too far" and "overpriced" – though perhaps not a comment levelled at the £12.50 'early-bird' menu.

Pomegranates ● 🖪   – | – | – | VE
94 Grosvenor Rd., SW1 (Pimlico), 020-7828 6560; fax 7828 2037
It's "not hugely exciting", yet this 30-year-old stalwart, located down a flight of stairs by the Thames in Pimlico, and run by Patrick Gwynne Jones, remains "a favourite" for a few who applaud the "interesting" Eclectic menu and "terrific service"; but it doesn't hold the same appeal to others who say it's "overpriced" and "living on past glory."

Poons   17 | 11 | 14 | £21
Whiteley's Shopping Ctr., 151 Queensway, W2 (Bayswater/ Queensway), 020-7792 2884; fax 8458 0968
27 Lisle St., WC2 (Leicester Sq.), 020-7437 4549 ●
4 Leicester St., WC2 (Leicester Sq.), 020-7437 1528; fax 7437 2903 ●
Royal National Hotel, 50 Woburn Pl., WC1 (Euston/Russell Sq.), 020-7580 1188; fax 8458 0968 ●
◪ "Still a good bet for reliable, if not lip-smacking dining", this "busy" "long-established chain" in the West End and Bayswater lures loyalists with "keenly priced" Cantonese fare and "very fast service" ("good before movies"); but foes feel it's "past its prime" and find the fare "uninspiring."

Pope's Eye 🖪 ⊅   ▽ 21 | 9 | 20 | £34
108 Blythe Rd., W14 (Olympia), 020-7610 4578; fax 7376 7210
277 Upper Richmond Rd., SW15 (East Putney), 020-8788 7733
■ "If you like steak, you'll love" these "dimly lit", "cramped" bistros in Olympia and Putney, but "don't go expecting a huge choice" as the "plain, simple" menu sticks to the "basics"; "an excellent wine list" at "great prices" and "relaxed service" complete the picture; P.S. "forget your plastic, they only accept cash."

Porters ●   16 | 15 | 18 | £21
17 Henrietta St., WC2 (Covent Garden), 020-7836 6466; fax 7379 4296; www.porters.uk.com
◪ "Specialising in British savoury pies" and Traditional British fare, this "charming" 25-year-old "fave" in Covent Garden owned by the Earl of Bradford "meets expectations" for "reasonably priced" "grub"; it's a "good choice for families with teenagers in tow" plus "reliable for after the theatre"; still, a few feel it "needs to be better to compete."

Portrait   17 | 22 | 16 | £28
The National Portrait Gallery, 3rd fl., 2 St. Martin's Pl., WC2 (Charing Cross/Leicester Sq.), 020-7312 2490; fax 7925 0244; www.searcys.co.uk
◪ "Wow your overseas friends" with an "incomparable view" "over the rooftops down towards Trafalgar Square"

from this "buzzing" venue in the National Portrait Gallery, a "perfect place to regroup after touring" the exhibits; the Modern British menu (from caterers Searcy's) is "pleasing" in some eyes, and merely "so-so" and "overpriced" in others, while "weak service" is an occasional bug-bear; N.B. open for dinner on Thursdays and Fridays.

Potemkin ⌖   ▽ 21 | 18 | 19 | £37 |

144 Clerkenwell Rd., EC1 (Farringdon), 020-7278 6661; fax 7278 5551; www.potemkin.co.uk

■ "The caviar options tantalise" and so does the "first-class" "Russian food like my mother made" at this "fun", dapper bi-level restaurant/bar in Clerkenwell run by "feisty owner Elena" Getman and named after Catherine the Great's legendary lover; it's the "real McCoy", plus it also serves an "interesting range of vodkas."

Prince Bonaparte   15 | 11 | 11 | £20 |

80 Chepstow Rd., W2 (Bayswater/Notting Hill Gate), 020-7313 9491; fax 7792 0911

☑ "If you're lucky enough to get a table" (no reservations taken) at this "crowded", "down-to-earth" Notting Hill gastro-pub, expect "unpretentious, solid" Modern British fare alongside "a lively bar scene" "for the younger set"; yet it's "nothing special" to quibblers who quip "a waiter would be a novelty."

Princess Garden ◑   22 | 21 | 23 | £44 |

8-10 N. Audley St., W1 (Bond St.), 020-7493 3223; fax 7629 3130; www.princessgardenofmayfair.com

■ "High-class" Chinese fare "with a quality twist" draws loyal subjects to this twentysomething Mayfair stalwart that recently underwent a "really lovely renovation" ("they spent a fortune"); the crowning touch: "helpful, polite staff" and "very nice private rooms."

Prism ⌖   ▽ 20 | 20 | 21 | £43 |

147 Leadenhall St., EC3 (Bank/Monument), 020-7256 3888; fax 7256 3883; www.harveynichols.com

☑ You'll find a "stylish City lot" at this "beautiful" Harvey Nichols—owned venue, an old banking hall near the Lloyd's of London building with a mezzanine level and an "upscale" Modern British menu that's "great for a business lunch" exult the enlightened; but dissenters say the "standard fare lacks originality" and warn, it "can be noisy in the day, lonely at night."

Providores, The/Tapa Room   21 | 17 | 17 | £36 |

109 Marylebone High St., W1 (Baker St./Bond St.), 020-7935 6175; fax 7935 6877; www.theprovidores.co.uk

☑ "An explosion of flavours" from chef Peter Gordon's "genuinely innovative" Eclectic menu "with a Down Under twist" is the culinary hook at this "buzzy" Marylebone venue with two options: a "casual" first-floor dining room ("reserve ahead") boasting a "wine list to take notice of" and a "lively" ground-floor Tapa Room where you sit "cheek by cheek at communal tables" and "have little nibbles" or a "delicious brunch"; still, a few gripe about "overly complex cuisine" and "slow service."

Pug　　　　　　　14 | 15 | 14 | £31

66-68 Chiswick High Rd., W4 (Stamford Brook/Turnham Green), 020-8987 9988; fax 8987 9911

◪ To the faithful, this "hip" Chiswick haunt with leather banquettes and green walls is a "versatile venue for any occasion", with a "surprisingly good" Modern British menu, "excellent bar" and "great outside space" that's "ideal in summer"; but bashers bark this "sparse" space is "without a mission: whatever charm it once had is well gone."

Putney Bridge　　　　22 | 24 | 19 | £50

1 Embankment, Lower Richmond Rd., SW15 (Putney Bridge), 020-8780 1811; fax 8780 1211; www.putneybridgerestaurant.com

◪ "The residents of Putney are so lucky" sigh those smitten by this "sexy" "funky-shaped" local with "lovely views" of the Thames where Anthony Demetre's "creative" New French cooking is on offer along with a "great wine list"; it's "expensive, but worth it for a treat" – particularly for "champagne evenings and new lovers" – plus the "bargain set lunch" (£18.50) is "much more accessible"; still, a few feel "service varies" from "impeccable" to "distracted."

Quadrato　　　　　　23 | 22 | 23 | £43

Four Seasons Hotel Canary Wharf, 46 Westferry Circus, E14 (Canary Wharf), 020-7510 1999; fax 7510 1998; www.fourseasons.com

◪ "All the big bankers" of Canary Wharf frequent this "formal, yet comfortable" dining room inside this "discreet" Four Seasons outpost where "supreme" Northern Italian dishes, "impeccable service" and a "lovely" outside terrace are the hallmarks; but a minority find it "mostly suitable for those on expense accounts" and whisper that it can be "as quiet as a library"; P.S. the £29.50 "Sunday brunch is a magnificent feast."

Quaglino's ◖　　　　　18 | 22 | 17 | £43

16 Bury St., SW1 (Green Park), 020-7930 6767; fax 7839 2866; www.quaglinos.co.uk

◪ "Upbeat, upscale and uptown" with a "dramatic staircase" "to enter by", the Conran Group's "awesome space" in St. James's is "still going strong", offering "artfully presented", seafood-focussed Modern European fare and a "great little jazz combo in the bar"; still, wallet-watchers suggest a visit "if your rich uncle feels like treating", while a handful are "put off" by "haphazard service" and some of the "crowd": "Essex on the strut!"

Quality Chop House ●　　17　13　13　£34

94 Farringdon Rd., EC1 (Farringdon), 020-7837 5093; fax 7833 8748

▣ "One of London's most original restaurants", this "bohemian" Farringdon venue with "homey atmosphere" serves "solid", "extremely credible versions" of British-French "comfort food" with a "small, well-chosen wine list"; but it's the famous "pewlike benches" that splinter votes: traditionalists insist "to change them would be sacrilege" whilst knockers note they're "painfully hard."

Quilon ●🛇　　24　18　23　£38

Crowne Plaza London St. James, 41 Buckingham Gate, SW1 (St. Jame's Park/Victoria), 020-7821 1899; fax 7828 5802; www.thequilonrestaurant.com

◨ The "light" West Coastal cuisine of India with "fresh flavours in unusual combinations" is the draw at this "somewhat exotic" Bombay Brasserie sibling done up with murals of Kerala in the Crowne Plaza London St. James near Buckingham Palace; "good service" means dishes are "cooked to taste: if you don't want spicy, it won't be"; but a few are less endeared by "small portions" and a "hotel atmosphere."

QUIRINALE 🛇　　26　23　26　£41

1 Great Peter St., SW1 (Westminster), 020-7222 7080; fax 7233 3080

■ "So light and bright, you'd hardly know you were dining in a basement" at this Westminster "standout" where Stefano Savio's "fantastic" Modern Italian menu offers "straightforward dishes [with] a complex taste"; "attentive service" and "good politician spotting" prompt diners to declare "definitely will return"; N.B. the name refers to Piazza del Quirinale, the presidential palace in Rome.

Quod ●🛇　　16　16　15　£28

57 Haymarket, SW1 (Piccadilly Circus), 020-7925 1234; fax 7839 4545; www.quod.co.uk

◨ "High-quality ingredients and simple preparations" go into the "delicious" Modern Anglo–Italian meals at this "very cool spot" with "warm service" in Haymarket decorated with the owner's "fab art"; the "huge" quarters and "buzzy" vibe make a "great meeting place" for a "casual lunch" or "before clubbing", and though the "food isn't amazing", the "menu is varied", "reliable" and "inexpensive"; still, a few feel "service can be a let-down."

Quo Vadis 🛇　　20　19　15　£46

26-29 Dean St., W1 (Leicester Sq./Tottenham Court Rd.), 020-7437 9585; fax 7736 7593; www.whitestarline.org.uk

◨ "A refuge from the busy Soho streets" that "fits the mood perfectly", this "still pretty hip" Marco Pierre White establishment pleases supporters with Italian cooking that's a "treat" and "interesting" "art adorning the walls";

but "disappointed" quibblers quip "with the waiters, it's not so much 'whither goest thou?', as 'where art thou?'"

Racine   23 17 21 £39
239 Brompton Rd., SW3 (South Kensington), 020-7584 4477; fax 7584 4900

■ "Trendy and old-fashioned at the same time", this "divine" "find" in Knightsbridge "feels like France and tastes like France"; "diners are packed in a convivial fashion" for Henry Harris' "refreshingly different", "high-end bistro fare" that delivers "a lot of punch for the pound" (including early-bird specials), plus "charming staff" make "you feel you're getting special attention" without "being over-catered to" – in sum, it's a "winner" that "matches expectations."

Rainforest Cafe   12 21 14 £24
20-24 Shaftesbury Ave., W1 (Piccadilly Circus), 020-7434 3111; fax 7434 3222; www.rainforestcafe.com

◪ "Behold" the "striking" jungle-themed behemoth in Piccadilly that's a "surefire hit with kids" where "helpful" servers dole out "simple" "American burger fare" whilst a "full-volume tropical storm" blows by; still, there's "lots going on" ("nobody can hear the children if they get fussy"), so "ask the ape to shut up", overlook the "uninspired food" and just "grin and bear it: it will make the little ones happy."

Randall & Aubin   18 14 15 £33
14-16 Brewer St., W1 (Piccadilly Circus), 020-7287 4447; fax 7287 4488
329-331 Fulham Rd., SW10 (Fulham Broadway/ South Kensington), 020-7823 3515; fax 7823 3991 ●

◪ "It's so much fun" at this "retro", "hip" Soho spot in a converted butcher's shop with "relaxed service" where "you share communal counter tops that barely fit your plates" of "fab fish" and "yummy" Eclectic fare and overlook the "uncomfortable seats"; the Fulham Road sib where chef-patron Ed Baines prepares seafood-biased, "tasty" brasserie fare is "fun for a local night out."

Rani   – – – M
7 Long Ln., N3 (Finchley Central), 020-8349 4386; fax 8349 4386; www.rani.uk.com

"Hard to beat for value and quality", this little-known, family-run vegetarian Indian "gem" is "worth the trip" to Finchley for "fresh, homey Gujarati cooking"; wallet-watchers opt for the prix fixe dinner for £28 or the £9.90 pre-theatre "buffet option that solves the problem of choice as you can see what they have."

Ransome's Dock   ▽ 17 14 18 £40
35-37 Park Gate Rd., SW11 (Sloane Sq./South Kensington), 020-7223 1611; fax 7924 2614; www.ransomesdock.co.uk

◪ With Modern British–Eclectic fare that makes "innovative use of British produce", some of the "best bin ends" and outside seating by a "scenic" Battersea dock, respected chef Martin Lam's "reliable local" set in an old ice factory with "feel-good ambience" "hits the right buttons"; still, a few feel the international wine list is "better than the food" advising "drink well and it will be wonderful."

Raoul's   17   13   14   £20

13 Clifton Rd., W9 (Warwick Ave.), 020-7289 7313; fax 7266 4752
◪ "You'll see many regular faces" at this "cosy", "good-value local cafe" and patisserie in Maida Vale with a "commanding presence in the neighbourhood" and an Eclectic menu of "fresh, imaginatively prepared" dishes; whilst some say there's "there's no better place to stumble into for weekend breakfast, brunch" or an "informal dinner", a few feel it "lacks variety" for "proper meals"; P.S. the "deli across the street offers gourmet groceries."

Rasa   24   16   21   £28

6 Dering St., W1 (Bond St./Oxford Circus), 020-7629 1346; fax 7637 0224
5 Charlotte St., W1 (Tottenham Court Rd.), 020-7637 0222; fax 7637 0224
55 Stoke Newington Church St., N16 (Stoke Newington B.R.), 020-7249 0344; fax 7637 0224
56 Stoke Newington Church St., N16 (Stoke Newington B.R.), 020-7249 1340; fax 7637 0224
www.rasarestaurants.com
■ "If you think you know Indian, the Keralan cuisine" at this family-run quartet "will show the error of your ways"; "each bite is heaven", so "go with a crowd to sample" all the vegetarian dishes boasting "subtle spicing" and "complex flavours"; "any location is worth visiting" – each has an "intimate feel", "like dining in the owner's home", and "fabulous service" – but "cost differs according to branch"; N.B. Charlotte Street offers seafood too.

Rasoi Vineet Bhatia   –   –   –   VE

10 Lincoln St., SW3 (Sloane Sq.), 020-7225-1881; fax 7581-0220
Revered chef Vineet Bhatia, who made his name at Zaika, acts as chef-patron at this classy, no-smoking Chelsea newcomer (in the former English Garden space) decorated with interesting Indian artefacts, plus he's drafted in Mrs Bhatia as front of house and a sommelier from Browns Hotel; the sophisticated Indian menu is a notch or two higher from his previous ventures and includes a nine-course tasting menu; N.B. 'rasoi' means kitchen in Indian.

Ravi Shankar   ▽ 20   13   17   £15

133-135 Drummond St., NW1 (Euston), 020-7388 6458; fax 7388 2494
422 St. John St., EC1 (Angel), 020-7833 5849
◪ "Consistent for many, many years", this "dirt-cheap but flavourful Indian vegetarian hole-in-the-wall" in Euston

and its BYO sibling on St. John Street offer "authentic", "flavourful" Southern Indian food that's "a nice change from the usual *tikka masala*"; the "lunch buffet is an irresistible deal", plus it's "great for a late-night vindaloo"; still, some snipe it's "overrated."

Real Greek, The ⊠   20 17 15 £33

15 Hoxton Mkt., N1 (Old St.), 020-7739 8212; fax 7739 4910
140-142 St. John St., EC1 (Farringdon), 020-7253 7234;
fax 7253 7235
www.therealgreek.co.uk

☑ "What every Greek restaurant should be like, but never is" declare disciples of Theodore Kyriakou's "lovely" Hoxton haunt where service can be a "bit patchy" but "hearty" Hellenic fare and an "excellent wine list" compensate; "small bites" are served next door at the "funky" attached Mezedopolio mezze/wine bar in a former Christian mission hall, whilst the "cracking souvlaki joint" in Clerkenwell offers a "great escape" "after work."

Rebato's ⊠   – – – M

169 S. Lambeth Rd., SW8 (Stockwell), 020-7735 6388;
www.rebatos.com

Offering a "little bit of Spain in London", this modestly attired Iberian features a cosy bar at the front serving "tasty tapas" and for "sit-down dinners", a large, "pleasant atrium dining room" with "finer food than you'd expect on South Lambeth Road"; "friendly, helpful service" earns another round of *olés*.

Red Fort ⊠   24 21 21 £38

77 Dean St., W1 (Oxford Circus/Tottenham Court Rd.),
020-7437 2525; fax 7434 0721; www.redfort.co.uk

■ "Delicious" Central Indian fare with "inventive variations", and a "luscious", "sensual environment" that "works for formal and informal gatherings" (or as a "great seduction spot") coupled with "excellent service" make for a "truly superb dining experience" at Amin Ali's "vibrant" "Soho institution"; sure, it's "expensive, but you get what you pay for", plus the set menu for lunch offers an "incredible meal for so little money"; P.S. "start your evening" at Akbar, the "fantastic cocktail bar in the basement."

Redmonds   – – – E

170 Upper Richmond Rd. W., SW14 (Mortlake B.R.),
020-8878 1922; fax 8878 1133

One of "the best in this part of London" rejoice admirers of Redmond Haywood's unassuming, glass-fronted spot in an East Sheen shopping parade where a "top-notch" Modern British menu includes "succulent, scintillating", "adventurous dishes" at "affordable prices"; the chef-patron's wife, Pippa, oversees "warm, friendly" staff that "make you feel you're not in stuffy and formal ol' England."

Red Pepper
20 11 14 £28

8 Formosa St., W9 (Warwick Ave.), 020-7266 2708; fax 7266 5522
◪ There's "always a buzz" at the Red Pepper Group's "little Italian joint" in Maida Vale with an "interesting, varied" menu dominated by "very good pizza" and pasta; for those who feel the "service could be better" and find the bi-level space "a bit squashed" ("have to sit upstairs") and "lacking charm", they "also do takeaway pizza."

Red Room at Waterstones, The ⊠
∇ 15 13 16 £27

Waterstones, downstairs, 203-206 Piccadilly, W1 (Piccadilly Circus), 020-7851 2464; fax 7851 2469; www.searcys.co.uk
■ A "nice bookworm refuge", this brightly lit basement eatery with red leather banquettes in the Waterstones' store in Piccadilly makes a "tranquil spot" for "great" Modern European fare from caterers Searcy's, served from 10 AM; N.B. the comfy Studio Lounge on the fifth floor serves snacks.

Refettorio
– – – E

Crowne Plaza, 19 New Bridge St., EC4 (Blackfriars), 020-7438 8052
With high-profile chef Giorgio Locatelli as a consultant, it's little surprise that this new Crowne Plaza hotel dining room in Blackfriars offers upscale regional Italian fare, including a fine selection of beautifully displayed antipasti; the L-shaped space features chunky wooden tables, some of which are refectory-style for sharing, and there's a worthy wine list starting at £13; N.B. at press time it was scheduled to open for dinner on Saturdays.

Restaurant 7
18 20 16 £24

(fka Café 7)
Tate Modern, Bankside, SE1 (Blackfriars/London Bridge), 020-7401 5020; www.tate.org.uk/modern
◪ "It's all about the view and what a view it is" from this "delightful retreat from the crowds" on the seventh floor of the Tate Modern next to the Thames on the South Bank; whilst most "don't expect the best food in London", this "very good little cafe" offers a "healthy" Modern British menu that's "more adequate than some of the questionable art in the galleries below."

Reubens
13 8 12 £21

79 Baker St., W1 (Baker St.), 020-7486 0035; fax 7486 7079
◪ "Like a slice of NYC, right down to the mustard", this "neon-lit" Jewish Marylebone cafe is divided into a downstairs restaurant that's "perfect" for those who come round for "a quick kosher salt beef" and a "street level deli that has cheaper options"; still, detractors declare that "if you're expecting good, *hamishe* food" remember that "it wouldn't get any nice comments from a New Yorker."

Rhodes Twenty Four ⊠   ▽ 21 | 21 | 21 | £49

Tower 42, 24th fl., 25 Old Broad St., EC2 (Bank St./Liverpool St.), 020-7877 7703; fax 7877 7788; www.rhodes24.co.uk

■ Following the closure of his eponymous eateries in Pimlico and Holborn, Gary Rhodes has resurfaced at this "winner" on the 24th floor of the City's tallest skyscraper, offering "fantastic views" across town, along with Modern British fare that's "delicious without being overly complicated"; tall prices and a subdued air make it "suitable for business", plus there's a "cocktail bar on the 42nd [floor] to complete the evening"; N.B. closed weekends.

Rib Room & Oyster Bar   22 | 20 | 20 | £59

Carlton Tower, 2 Cadogan Pl., SW1 (Knightsbridge/Sloane Sq.), 020-7858 7053; fax 7823 1708; www.carltontower.com

◨ "If you like meat", steer over to this "clubby" dining room with "attentive service" within the Carlton Tower hotel in Knightsbridge, now owned by Jumeira International; the Traditional British menu is a "treat", boasting one of the "best ribs of beef in town" and "delicious steaks", plus it's "fun to eat at the oyster bar"; still, a few find "prices as awe inspiring as the chops."

Riccardo's ◗   19 | 11 | 16 | £31

126 Fulham Rd., SW3 (Gloucester Rd./South Kensington), 020-7370 6656; fax 7373 0604

■ The "ultimate *rustica*" "haunt", this "casual", "crowded" Chelsea trattoria is "laid-back and fun", whether you "share the starter-sized plates" of "fresh, delicious" Italian fare "around the table with your friends" or gather the "family" for a "relatively cheap" meal ("unheard of for the area"); the "no-frills" premises may "look like a breakfast room in a tourist hotel", nevertheless, the "gazebo part in the front" is "fabulous on summer evenings."

Richard Corrigan at   24 | 20 | 22 | £63
Lindsay House ⊠

21 Romilly St., W1 (Leicester Sq./Piccadilly Circus), 020-7439 0450; fax 7437 7349; www.lindsayhouse.co.uk

◨ "One of Soho's culinary high spots", this "beautiful Georgian" townhouse with a warren of "characterful, charming" dining areas is the canvas for chef-patron Richard Corrigan's "robust but refined" Modern British–Irish cooking revealing "intense flavours" matched with an "excellent wine list"; "eager-to-please staff" make you "feel like one of the family", and the "overall experience is delightful"; still, a handful huff at "outrageous prices" and "lugubrious service", retorting "not impressed."

Richoux   14 | 14 | 14 | £22

172 Piccadilly, W1 (Green Park/Piccadilly Circus), 020-7493 2204; fax 7495 6658
41A S. Audley St., W1 (Bond St.), 020-7629 5228; fax 7491 0825

(continued)
Richoux
86 Brompton Rd., SW3 (Knightsbridge), 020-7584 8300;
fax 7589 8547
3 Circus Rd., NW8 (St. John's Wood), 020-7483 4001;
fax 7483 3810
www.richoux.co.uk
☑ "Cheap and cheerful", these "old-fashioned tearooms" in the West End and St. John's Wood with a "nice Edwardian atmosphere" make "great pit stops" for lunch, breakfast, "lovely pastries" or "just a light bite" of "basic" British fare on "those nights when you're too tired to cook"; if a few scoff it's "stuffy" and "touristy", most retort it's an "oasis" to "rest your feet" from "shopping mania."

RITZ, THE 23 | 28 | 26 | £58 |
Ritz Hotel, 150 Piccadilly, W1 (Green Park), 020-7300 2370;
fax 7907 2681; www.theritzlondon.com
■ Retaining its crown as No. 1 for Decor in the *Survey,* this "sumptuous space" in the "legendary" Ritz Hotel by Green Park is so "grand" "you expect the Queen to walk in at any moment"; from the "divine" Classic French–Traditional British cooking to the "romantic" Louis XIII-style setting to the "zillion waiters in tails" that make you "feel pampered", it "never fails to ignite the passions"; it's "oh-so-expensive", but for a "splurge", "what could be better?", plus tea in the Palm Court is "one of life's pleasures"; N.B. a post-*Survey* change of chef may impact the above Food score.

Riva 21 | 12 | 19 | £45 |
169 Church Rd., SW13 (Hammersmith), 020-8748 0434;
fax 8748 0434
☑ "Remains an object lesson in not judging a book by its cover" confide acolytes who look beyond the "eminently" "uninspiring decor" of Andrea Riva's "cosy" "long-standing favourite" and focus on the "inventive" Italian cooking that's "worth the drive" over the Thames to Barnes; "completing the setup": "enthusiastic (but unflash) staff" that make you "feel so comfortable it's like breakfast in bed"; still, cynics snipe it's "so-so for the price" and "needs renovation."

RIVER CAFE 26 | 21 | 22 | £56 |
Thames Wharf, Rainville Rd., W6 (Hammersmith), 020-7386 4200;
fax 7386 4201; www.rivercafe.co.uk
☑ "Worth the effort to find" in residential Hammersmith, this "lively" Modern Italian icon with "amiable" service, "no-frills" decor and a "lovely" terrace "overlooking the Thames" is "driven by a passion for quality" and "still the high cathedral of the best possible ingredients, cooked in the simplest", most "mouth-watering" way; but some bridle at the "ridiculous price tag" and dislike being "up against the clock" due to local "laws that require you to leave by 11 PM", suggesting "have lunch at a slower pace instead."

River Spice ◑　　　– – – M

83-85 Wapping Ln., E1 (Wapping), 020-7488 4051

Hampshire restaurateur Forid Miah makes her London debut with this colourful, modern destination where young chef Babul Kamali's varied, unusual Indian-dominated menu with Thai and European twists takes centre stage; plus points include a speedy 20-minute lunch comprising a large mixed platter for under £6, and a wide-ranging wine list that starts at £10.

Rivington Grill Bar Deli　　∇ 21 19 19 £37

28-30 Rivington St., EC2 (Old St.), 020-7729 7053; fax 7729 7086; www.rivingtongrill.co.uk

■ "A cool space, but not a cold one", this "laid-back" venture with a "cosy leather bar" in a "smart", "stylish" converted warehouse off Old Street serves "adventurous" British "comfort food with a twist" from "a flexible menu that suits every budget"; whether you "go *à deux*, with friends or even family members, you're made to feel at ease", thanks to "self-confident management" and "professional service"; N.B. there's also a deli for takeout.

Rocket　　　17 16 14 £25

4-6 Lancashire Ct., W1 (Bond St.), 020-7629 2889; fax 7629 2881 🖂

Putney Wharf, Brewhouse St., SW15 (East Putney), 020-8789 7875; fax 8789 7876

■ "Notoriously difficult to find", this "straightforward eatery buried in a Mayfair" backstreet and younger Putney riverside sib have a "lively, "relaxed vibe", attracting a "young, hip crowd" with "absolutely massive, freshly made", "cracking pizzas", "affordable" Italian-Med fare, plus, "as you would expect, plenty of rocket salad"; service ranges from "cheerful" to "abysmal", but mainly when "it's full."

Rodizio Rico ◑　　18 11 15 £28

111 Westbourne Grove, W2 (Bayswater/Notting Hill Gate), 020-7792 4035; fax 7243 1401

■ The "nearest thing to a real Brazilian experience" in London, this "unique", "informal" "meat-lovers' mecca" in Bayswater offers a "good attempt at a traditional churrascaria", where the grilled sausage, chicken and beef "keep coming until one can eat no more"; it's "great fun for big parties", and without question, "committed carnivores" "won't leave hungry."

Rosmarino　　　20 17 16 £42

1 Blenheim Terrace, NW8 (St. John's Wood), 020-7328 5014; fax 7625 2639

⊿ "We're lucky to have it in our neighbourhood" laud St. John's Wood locals who head to this "charming little place" with a "romantic ambience" and conservatory for "fabulous" Modern Italian cooking; if a few feel the "great

terrace makes up for any shortcomings", detractors declare
it's "too pricey for what it is"; N.B. new owners known as
The Kitchen Club took it over at publication time, which
may impact the above ratings.

ROUSSILLON ☒   27 | 22 | 25 | £58 |

16 St. Barnabas St., SW1 (Sloane Sq./Victoria), 020-7730 5550;
fax 7824 8617

■ "Not for those looking for a phony power scene" but for
anyone seeking an "exquisitely crafted dinner in the modern
French manner", this "well-kept secret" with "charming
service" on a "quiet Pimlico side street" feels like the "dining
room of your posh aunt"; chef Alex Gauthier "accepts that
vegetarians can be lovers of great cuisine", plus the non-
veggie offerings are "equally outstanding", especially
accompanied by the "exciting wine list"; it's "excellent for
business or pleasure, but quality comes with a price."

Rowley's ◗   17 | 19 | 16 | £35 |

113 Jermyn St., SW1 (Piccadilly Circus), 020-7930 2707;
fax 7839 4240; www.rowleys.co.uk

◪ The "house specialty steak, with endless frites" is the
draw on the Traditional British menu at this St. James's
"faithful", which recently underwent a revamp; whilst there's
still "nothing fancy" about this remodelled old butchers'
shop, it's "good for a change of pace"; still, a few deem the
menu "limited" and service "inattentive."

ROYAL CHINA   23 | 13 | 14 | £27 |

13 Queensway, W2 (Queensway), 020-7221 2535; fax 7792 5752
24-26 Baker St., W1 (Baker St.), 020-7487 4688; fax 7935 7893
68 Queen's Grove, NW8 (St. John's Wood), 020-7586 4280;
fax 7722 4750
30 Westferry Circus, E14 (Canary Wharf), 020-7719 0888;
fax 7719 0889

◪ "Witness weekend queues no matter the weather" so
"reservations are a must at this hopping Chinese" quartet
where, in some locations, "Sinophiles" turn a blind eye to
the "1970s-Beijing-disco" decor and "brusque" servers
and focus on the "divine dim sum", plus "specials worth
trying"; the Canary Wharf branch has a "fantastic riverside
location with outdoor dining" that "compensates" for any
shortcomings, whilst the Baker Street site recently moved
to smarter premises down the street.

Royal Exchange   ▽ 19 | 26 | 19 | £32 |
Grand Café & Bar ☒

The Royal Exchange, The Courtyard, EC3 (Bank), 020-7618 2480;
fax 7618 2490; www.conran.com

◪ "Conveniently located" in a "cool", huge atrium that
recently housed the Financial Futures Exchange, this all-
day Conran Group "oasis" is one to bank on as a "luxury
lunchtime meeting place" thanks to its "light" Modern

European menu of cold dishes (seafood, salads, et al.); still, a few find it a "bit isolated" and "limited" in scope; P.S. there's also a comfy bar on the mezzanine level that "was brilliant until everyone else discovered it."

R.S.J. 🗷   19   12   16   £33

33 Coin St., SE1 (Waterloo), 020-7928 4554; fax 7401 2455; www.rsj.uk.com

■ An "excellent, Loire-inspired wine list" "allied to quality cooking" and an "unfailingly worthwhile set menu" (from £15.95) are the pleasure beacons at this low-key Waterloo brasserie "staple", a "terrific spot" for "post–National Theatre dining"; whilst the modest "decor is the lesser attractive aspect", most agree that the "good" Modern British "food saves the day."

Rudland Stubbs 🗷   –   –   –   E

35-37 Green Hill Rents, Cowcross St., EC1 (Farringdon), 020-7253 0148; fax 7490 2650

"Fantastic fish 'n' chips" and "really fresh", "tasty" fin fare with "great sauces" lure loyalists to this understated, traditional seafooder set in a former sausage factory on the edge of the Smithfield Market; still, some shrug it's "ok, but nothing great" whilst those with vision feel it has "potential", insisting a "bolt of electricity and enthusiasm could take it to another level."

RULES ◗   22   25   22   £45

35 Maiden Ln., WC2 (Covent Garden), 020-7836 5314; fax 7497 1081; www.rules.co.uk

▨ "For those who think" "truly authentic" "Traditional British food is dull, think again" is the rallying cry for this "quaint", "clubby" Covent Garden "grande dame of English cuisine" (est. 1798) with an "old London" feel and "unique menu" specialising in "sumptuous game dishes"; even if a handful rule it out as a "clichéd" "tourist trap", the majority proclaim you "feel like you're dining with Dickens."

Saigon ◗🗷   ▽ 19   15   18   £24

45 Frith St., W1 (Leicester Sq./Piccadilly Circus), 020-7437 7109; fax 7734 1668

▨ "Somehow the tourists never make it to this" modest-looking "consistently outstanding" Soho "gem" where the Vietnamese cooking is "excellent" (aromatic crispy duck and BBQ beef are signature dishes) and "service is genuine, if a bit rough sometimes"; but detractors declare "decor must be updated soon."

Sakura   –   –   –   E

9 Hanover St., W1 (Oxford Circus), 020-7629 2961

"You feel like you are sitting in a busy Tokyo restaurant" at this "no-nonsense", "casual" spot near Oxford Street that "has been there for many years" and still offers "excellent sushi and sashimi", plus a "very wide range" of "genuine", "delicious" Asian specialties; they take "no reservations", so "expect to queue at peak times" with "Japanese, local and tourist" customers.

Sale e Pepe ●☑   20   15   20   £41
9-15 Pavilion Rd., SW1 (Knightsbridge), 020-7235 0098; fax 7225 1210

■ Now into its fourth decade, this "lively" Knightsbridge "institution" is known for its "singing", "clowning waiters", "festive atmosphere" and "solid" cooking that "satisfies tummies"; whilst the disenchanted find it "a bit crammed" and "noisy" ("don't come here for a quiet dinner"), most agree "its sunnyness brightens any London day."

Salisbury Tavern, The   ▽ 21   18   19   £29
21 Sherbrooke Rd., SW6 (Fulham Broadway/Parsons Green), 020-7381 4005; fax 7381 1002

☑ "One step further than a gastro-pub", this "smart" Admiral Codrington sib in Fulham has a "dining area separated from the pub (so it's not as noisy)" where a "frequently changing" and "reasonably priced", "manna-from-heaven" menu of "very good" Modern European fare is supported by a "very comprehensive wine selection"; but others concede it's "not bad" but a bit "bland."

Salloos ●☑   25   15   20   £40
62-64 Kinnerton St., SW1 (Hyde Park Corner/Knightsbridge), 020-7235 4444

■ The setting of this Knightsbridge "time capsule" "in a cosy mews location" might appear "somewhat dismal", but reassurers report that "the food is fresher than the look"; in fact, most maintain that the "extensive menu" of "delightful", "different" "Indo-Pakistani" cooking "never disappoints" (although a handful find it "too expensive for what it is") and salloot "service that's cheerful enough."

Salusbury Pub & Dining Room   ▽ 15   12   16   £25
50-52 Salusbury Rd., NW6 (Queen's Park), 020-7328 3286

☑ Located in Queens Park ("an improving area"), this "laid-back, chilled" gastro-pub with a "separate dining area" "full of trendy people" divides diners – some find the Modern Italian cooking to be "interesting", whilst others find it "pricey" and "a bit hit-or-miss"; similarly, surveyors say "staff range from attentive to different"; P.S. it can get "very crowded and smoky in the pub."

Sambuca ●☑   –   –   –   E
62 Lower Sloane St., SW1 (Sloane Sq.), 020-7730 6571; fax 7225 1210

"Predictable but reassuring" sums up the appeal of Sale e Pepe's "quintessentially Italian" 31-year-old sibling near Sloane Square; acolytes are sweet on the "great fare", "friendly service" and "very pleasant" atmosphere on busy evenings; but the less-ardent sigh "it could be better."

San Lorenzo ●⊠≠　　　19　18　19　£54
22 Beauchamp Pl., SW3 (Knightsbridge), 020-7584 1074; fax 7584 1142

◪ "The beautiful people" head to this "glamourous scene" in Knightsbridge (which "became well-known because of Princess Di") where there are "celebrity sightings almost daily" and "solid" Traditional Italian cooking is served with "panache"; if a few feel it's "living on past glories" and bridle at "hefty bills", most maintain there's really only "one downside – they don't take credit cards."

San Lorenzo Fuoriporta　　　▽　24　21　21　£37
38 Wimbledon Hill Rd., SW19 (Wimbledon), 020-8946 8463; fax 8947 9810

◪ "Nicely situated" at the bottom of Wimbledon Hill, this "lovely" sibling of the Knightsbridge San Lorenzo (run by the sons of owners Mara and Lorenzo Berni) lures loyalists with an "affordable", "authentic" Traditional Italian menu and "well-priced wine list"; snipers say it's "not particularly inspiring", but that doesn't deter "all the stars from coming here during Wimbledon [tennis] fortnight."

Santa Fe　　　　　　17　14　16　£23
75 Upper St., N1 (Angel), 020-7288 2288; fax 7288 2287; www.santafe.co.uk

◪ There's a "roaring, lively crowd" at this "fun, happening", "always-packed" Islingtonian restaurant/bar (with six siblings outside London); though its "take on Southwestern cuisine" might be a tad "faux" for some sticklers who claim it's "a far cry from Mexican", most amigos maintain that it "has definitely improved."

Santa Lucia ●　　　　▽　19　11　12　£32
2 Hollywood Rd., SW10 (South Kensington), 020-7352 8484; fax 7351 2390

◪ "Quieter than its sister, Made in Italy", and "owned by the same family", this one-year-old Chelsea trattoria in "tight quarters" boasts a wood-burning oven that produces "good" Southern Italian fare and "pizzas that taste the way they should"; still, sceptics cite "patchy service" and are puzzled by a "limiting menu that's prix fixe only", from £16.50 for three courses.

Santini　　　　　　21　18　20　£52
29 Ebury St., SW1 (Victoria), 020-7730 4094; fax 7730 0544; www.santini-restaurant.com

■ Although "there are cheaper Italians in the area", this "grown-up" eatery near Victoria Station is a "special place", conjuring up an "upscale" Venetian-inflected menu and "expansive wine list", all delivered by "dedicated staff"; last year's "refurb" passed with little comment, but the expanded "outdoor terrace is great for summer evenings"; P.S. there's a "good lunch deal" for £16.50.

SARKHEL'S   26 | 13 | 21 | £30

*197-199 Replingham Rd., SW18 (Southfields), 020-8870 1483;
fax 8874 6603; www.sarkhels.com*

■ "Out of the way but worth the schlep" is the consensus
on Udit Sarkhel's "friendly", down-to-earth Southfields
venue; with an "outstanding" Indian menu offering "exciting
variations", as well as "faded decor" that adds to its charm,
it gets "extremely busy" – so "book ahead"; N.B. Calcutta
Notebook, a cosy sibling serving Bengali fare, recently
opened next door.

Sartoria ◐   19 | 19 | 19 | £50

*20 Savile Row, W1 (Oxford Circus/Piccadilly Circus),
020-7534 7000; fax 7534 7070; www.conran.com*

☑ "Fashionable in an understated way", this "nice" spot
from [the] Conran Group near Regent Street is "comfy" with
a "stylish" sartorial theme and an "interesting", "reliable"
Modern Italian menu that's "pricey, but a good treat";
doubters declare it's "nothing to rave about" and "lacks
atmosphere", but to many it's a "proper restaurant" with
the added appeal of "live jazz" at the bar on weekends.

Satsuma   18 | 13 | 14 | £21

*56 Wardour St., W1 (Leicester Sq./Piccadilly Circus),
020-7437 8338; fax 7437 3389*

■ This "clean", minimalist Soho "gem" with "communal
tables" and a "buzzy" feel attracts a "hip" crowd wanting
"a quick bite" of "fab noodles, sushi" and other "tasty"
Japanese fare "at reasonable prices"; even if some find the
"staff not too friendly", at least they "do a good job moving
people through"; P.S. "they have wonderful bento boxes."

SAVOY GRILL   24 | 24 | 24 | £58

*Savoy Hotel, The Strand, WC2 (Covent Garden/Embankment),
020-7420 2065, 020-7592 1600; fax 7592 1601;
www.savoy-group.com*

☑ After a major "modernisation" of this famous "institution"
in the Strand's Savoy Hotel, fans applaud its "classy",
"civilised" setting ("feels like a '50s movie"), "seamless
service" and "classic yet innovative" Modern British menu
that "achieves the kind of quality" expected from chef-of-
the-moment Marcus Wareing; whilst "some think it's
stuffy", "pricey" and "needs a little more savoy *faire*",
most appreciate that it "oozes power"; P.S. it's also "great for
pre-theatre" and a no-smoking venue.

Scalini ◐   23 | 18 | 19 | £47

*1-3 Walton St., SW3 (Knightsbridge/South Kensington),
020-7225 2301; fax 7225 3953*

☑ With "classic" Italian dishes served by "engaging staff",
this "bustling, fun" Chelsea trattoria "has been consistently
excellent for years"; it's still a "great place to spend time
with friends of colleagues", even if a handful have a downer

on the "deafening decibels", "cramped" seating and "stuck-in-the-'80s decor."

Scotts 🦓   21 | 20 | 20 | £51
20 Mount St., W1 (Bond St./Green Park), 020-7629 5248; fax 7499 8246; www.scottsrestaurant.co.uk
☑ Offering "leisurely dining in hushed surroundings", this Mayfair "solid performer" with a Traditional British menu from Michael MacEnearney caters for "seafood lovers" with "beautiful fish straight from the sea"; a few gripe that it's "past its glory", but most acknowledge this "swanky" spot is "still trying hard" – after 154 years.

Seashell 🦓   18 | 8 | 11 | £20
49-51 Lisson Grove, NW1 (Marylebone), 020-7224 9000; fax 7724 9071; www.seashellrestaurant.co.uk
☑ "Huge portions" of "classic fish 'n' chips" (with "delicious mushy peas as a side") are what reel in fans to this "casual seafood hangout" in Marylebone; still, some foes snipe that it "has lost its edge over the years", whilst others cite decor that "needs sprucing up" as proof that "it's better to takeaway" – just "ask the cabbies lining up outside."

Seraphin Rest. & Wine Bar   – | – | – | E
341 Upper St., N1 (Angel), 020-7359 7374; fax 7359 7380
In bright corner premises formerly occupied by a branch of Sofra and close to Islington's Business Design Centre, this funky yearling with hip-looking staff, sleek booths and atmospheric lighting delivers an upscale Modern European menu overseen by a former chef from Gordon Ramsay's Claridge's venture; the Jade bar upstairs attracts a cool crowd, and at press time, plans were underway to unveil a large rear patio opening onto Camden Passage market.

Shepherd's 🦓   17 | 17 | 18 | £36
Marsham Ct., Marsham St., SW1 (Pimlico/St. James's Park), 020-7834 9552; fax 7233 6047; www.langansrestaurants.co.uk
☑ Many "MPs" of the nearby Houses of Parliament come to Richard Shepherd's Westminster stalwart for "comfort dining" upon "classical" "Traditional" British fare with modern touches in a "consciously clubby" room with enough "space for good conversation"; still, some stray from the flock, lamenting "the quality of food and service."

Shumi 🦓   17 | 17 | 16 | £45
23 St. James's St., SW1 (Green Park), 020-7747 9380; fax 7747 9389; www.shumi-london.com
☑ The Modern Italian cuisine is "pretty good once you get down to eating" agree admirers of this "bright", first-floor St. James's spot (formerly Che) that was once a bank and now boasts a "cool South Beach decor" and a "lovely", "trendy" bar; although some nonbelievers find the selection "weird", supporters say it adds up to a "nice meal", plus a recently opened chef's dining room overlooking the kitchen adds to

its appeal; N.B. the Japanese-influenced menu was dropped post-*Survey* which may impact the above Food score.

Signor Sassi ●☑　　21　16　21　£42
14 Knightsbridge Green, SW1 (Knightsbridge), 020-7584 2277; fax 7225 3953

■ There's "a lot of hustle and bustle" at this "upbeat" Italian (now into its third decade) in a "handy" Knightsbridge location where "attentive service" and "wonderful food" from a "diverse menu" make for "a fun" experience; a few find "it a little hectic at times" and "expensive", but "if you are in the mood" for a "lively" meal, it "will not disappoint."

Signor Zilli ●☑　　21　12　17　£35
41 Dean St., W1 (Leicester Sq./Tottenham Court Rd.), 020-7734 3924; fax 7734 8156; www.zilliado.com

■ Celebrity chef Aldo Zilli's original Soho trattoria remains a "favourite" of those who appreciate its "cosy atmosphere", "friendly service" and "amazing homemade pasta" from a midpriced Traditional Italian menu, along with "fun" "pavement tables in summer"; N.B. they've also opened a deli down the street.

Silks & Spice　　　19　15　17　£25
95 Chiswick High Rd., W4 (Turnham Green), 020-8995 7991; fax 8994 7773
Temple Ct., 11 Queen Victoria St., EC4 (Bank/Mansion House), 020-7248 7878; fax 7248 9595 ☑

◪ Fans "choose from an enormous selection" of "fresh", "authentic" Thai-Malaysian at this "great Asian" duo, whether at the "reliable, cosy" Chiswick original, the "noisy, crowded" City sibling or via the latter's "fantastic takeaway menu"; critics counter that the "food is perfectly acceptable without being inspired" but it's "now far surpassed by other" options.

Simply Nico　　　17　13　17　£35
12 Sloane Sq., SW1 (Sloane Sq.), 020-7896 9909; fax 7896 9908
48A Rochester Row, SW1 (St. James's Park/Victoria), 020-7630 8061; fax 7828 8541 ☑
www.simplynico.co.uk

◪ These "dependable" Sloane Square and Victoria spots have "good, old-fashioned French" bistro menus that *amis* agree are "perfectly acceptable", as well as "polite" staff providing "discreet service"; some concede they're "ok if you're restricted to the area", adding that the name (after former chef-owner Nico Ladenis) "makes expectations run higher than delivery can meet."

Simpson's-in-The-Strand　　　19　22　21　£45
100 The Strand, WC2 (Charing Cross), 020-7836 9112; fax 7836 1381; www.the-savoy-group.com

◪ "When in the mood for Traditional British fare" and a "great Dickensian atmosphere", this "splendid", 177-year-old Strand dining room (part of the Savoy Group) offers "a trip to the way England used to be", with "charming, old-fashioned" service and "massive silver trolleys" for "roast beef carved at your table"; critics charge it's a "shadow of its former glory"; N.B. upstairs is a quieter dining room with a lighter set menu from £15.50.

Singapore Garden
19 | 12 | 17 | £29

83/83A Fairfax Rd., NW6 (Swiss Cottage), 020-7328 5314; fax 7624 0656

◪ Fans of this Singaporean-Malaysian spot "a little off the beaten track" in Swiss Cottage are willing to overlook its "cramped", "tacky" setting thanks to its "very good" dishes, including "great satay and fresh fish"; a few warn that it "can be noisy" and say the "bill often comes as a shock", but in the main most appreciate this "nice little place" with "friendly staff."

Singapura ⊠
14 | 12 | 15 | £29

1-2 Limeburner Ln., EC4 (Blackfriars/St. Paul's), 020-7329 1133; fax 7236 1805
78-79 Leadenhall St., EC3 (Aldgate/Tower Hill), 020-7929 0089; fax 7621 0366
31 Broadgate Circle, EC2 (Liverpool St.), 020-7256 5045; fax 7256 5044
www.singapura-restaurants.co.uk

◪ Devotees of this modern City trio consider them "fine for business lunches" thanks to "nice" Southeast Asian cuisine and "efficient" service; still, the disenchanted retort "quality has gone down" of late and the "menu needs revamping"; either way, most sing their praises as "group friendly" and flexible for parties.

Sir Charles Napier
23 | 22 | 19 | £47

Spriggs Alley, Chinnor, Oxfordshire, 01494 483011; fax 01494 485311; www.sircharlesnapier.co.uk

◪ This "fascinating", "atmospheric" 18th-century inn situated in the Chiltern Hills is "great for a lazy Sunday lunch", with an "excellent" Modern British menu "long on yummy things", and an "eclectic wine list"; yes, it is "expensive", but keep in mind that "you're paying for the country location"; P.S. in good weather, don't miss alfresco dining upon the "fantastic lawn."

Six-13 ⊠
▽ 20 | 18 | 18 | £47

19 Wigmore St., W1 (Bond St./Oxford Circus), 020-7629 6133; fax 7629 6135; www.six13.com

■ "Delicious, especially for a kosher restaurant" is how aficionados sum up the "properly presented" (albeit "expensive") Modern European dishes at this "delightful" Marylebone spot; N.B. the smart, elegant premises are only open Monday–Thursday, but are available for private hire at the weekend.

Sketch ☒   – – – VE

9 Conduit St., W1 (Oxford Circus), 0870-777 4488;
fax 0870-777 4400; www.sketch.uk.com

"Over-ambition makes for a lot of fun" at this "cool" venue
off Regent Street that's "pure theatre"; the upstairs Lecture
Room "is a foodies' nirvana" where Pierre Gagnaire
"pampers" acolytes with New French cooking; in the "chic
Gallery" below, where brasserie fare is served to a "rock-
star crowd" and video art is projected on a wall, it's as if
"you're on the catwalk" – or in the "pod-shaped loos", like
you've entered "*A Clockwork Orange*"; N.B. there's also the
Parlour for breakfast, lunch and tea, plus a members bar.

Smiths of Smithfield –   20 17 16 £33
Dining Room ☒

67-77 Charterhouse St., EC1 (Barbican/Farringdon),
020-7251 7950; fax 7236 0488; www.smithsofsmithfield.co.uk

■ Located "between the bare-bones ground-floor [bar]
and the posh top-floor" restaurant of the "multi-tiered
Smithfield emporium" is this "fun outpost", an "informal
venue for uncomplicated" Modern British "comfort food";
even if "service can be patchy", most report that they "have
never been disappointed" by this "meat-eaters' heaven."

Smiths of Smithfield – Top Floor   23 20 20 £49

67-77 Charterhouse St., EC1 (Barbican/Farringdon),
020-7251 7950; fax 7236 0488; www.smithsofsmithfield.co.uk

◪ "In the middle of the [Smithfield] meatpacking district",
this "wonderfully airy top-floor eating space" with "stunning
rooftop views" is "ideal for a special" occasion, offering
a "quality", "accomplished" Traditional British menu,
including a "bountiful bonanza of beef"; a handful bemoan
"indifferent service" and "expense-account prices", but
most are moo-ved by this "simple formula, done well."

Smollensky's American   16 15 15 £31
Bar & Grill

Bradmore House, Queen Caroline St., W6 (Hammersmith),
020-8741 8124; fax 8741 5695 ☒
105 The Strand, WC2 (Charing Cross/Covent Garden),
020-7497 2101; fax 7836 3270
1 Nash Ct., E14 (Canary Wharf), 020-7719 0101; fax 7719 0060 ☒
Hermitage Wharf, 22 Wapping High St., E1 (Tower Bridge/
Wapping High St.), 020-7680 1818; fax 7680 1787
62 Carter Ln., EC4 (St. Paul's), 020-7248 4220; fax 7248 4221 ☒
www.smollenskys.co.uk

◪ "Good if you want a bit of North American fare", this
quintet around town serves "large portions" of "solid",
"standard" staples ("hamburgers are a standout") in
"noisy, fun" settings that are "great for family dining" or an
"after-work" bite; still, many feel "service needs to be
perked up"; P.S. the Strand original has "live music" every
night (and kids entertainment at weekends).

Snows on the Green   19 | 16 | 15 | £32

*166 Shepherd's Bush Rd., W6 (Hammersmith), 020-7603 2142;
fax 7602 7553*

■ Sebastian Snow's "swish eatery on lovely Brook Green"
"deserves to do better than it does", thanks to a "romantic
ambience" and "fabulous, interesting" Modern British fare
that's "excellent for the price"; still, others who give it the
cold shoulder, convinced the "sometimes shoddy service
lets it down", quip that it's "more like slows on the green!"

Sofra   18 | 13 | 17 | £22

*18 Shepherd St., W1 (Green Park), 020-7493 3320;
fax 7499 8282* ☻
*1 St. Christopher's Pl., W1 (Bond St.), 020-7224 4080;
fax 7224 0022* ☻
*36 Tavistock St., WC2 (Covent Garden), 020-7240 3773;
fax 7836 6633* ☻
*11 Circus Rd., NW8 (St. John's Wood), 020-7586 9889;
fax 7586 8778*
21 Exmouth Mkt., EC1 (Angel/Farringdon), 020-7833 1111

■ "Authentic", "inexpensive Turkish food in copious
quantities" served by "accommodating", "ultra-fast" staff
accounts for why this "convivial" five-strong chain around
town is "very popular", especially "with the lunch crowd";
whilst a minority find it "lacking spice and pizzazz", most
"just love" the "great experience" ("we even packed a
picnic for our flight home!").

Soho House ☻   16 | 18 | 16 | £37

Private club; inquiries: 020-7734 5188

◪ Enjoy "wonderful, easy Modern British dining with stars"
from "stage and screen" at this "characterful" Soho private
club ("if you're in, you're 'in'") that has "spawned varied
offshoots" in London, New York and Somerset; there are a
few gripes – "variable cooking", "pouting members" – but
most agree "the overall experience is better than the sum
of its parts"; P.S. it's a "perfect location for a party."

Soho Spice ☻   20 | 13 | 13 | £23

*124-126 Wardour St., W1 (Tottenham Court Rd.), 020-7434 0808;
fax 7434 0799; www.sohospice.co.uk*

◪ Offering "creative", "memorable" Indian "food that's
not afraid to be spicy", this "modern" Soho spot with an
"energetic vibe" is "still popular" for an "upmarket curry"
at "affordable prices" – notwithstanding the "nonexistent
service" and the wait for tables ("be patient"); N.B. at press
time it was acquired by the Mela Group, which plans to
refurbish and revise the menu.

Solly's   18 | 14 | 15 | £25

148A Golders Green Rd., NW11 (Golders Green), 020-8455 2121

■ "Good for entertaining kosher guests", this "spacious",
bi-level Golders Green eatery with a "truly original setting"

serves "delicious" fare from a "cheap, no-frills" Middle Eastern menu; still, detractors who claim it's "nothing special" confide it's "better for a takeaway schwarma than a full meal."

Song Que Café | 19 | 7 | 15 | £18 |
134 Kingsland Rd., E2 (Old St.), 020-7613 3222
■ With "a multitude of delicious dishes for under a fiver", this "outstanding Vietnamese"-Chinese venue in a "less than salubrious" part of Shoreditch is a "first choice" of many; true, the "weird decor" "isn't the greatest", but "once you get into the pho, you forget everything else"; P.S. with "all the hype it has received", it's "always busy", so "bookings are now advisable."

Sonny's | ▽ 20 | 16 | 16 | £36 |
94 Church Rd., SW13 (Barnes Bridge B.R.), 020-8748 0393; fax 8748 2698
■ "Worth the trip from town" attest admirers of Rebecca Mascarenhas' "terrific spot" where an "interesting" Modern British menu "sometimes misses the mark but more often hits straight and true"; though the "cosy setting" is usually quite "pleasant", it "can be warm" for tables situated near the striking "open fireplace" designed by Bruce McLean.

Sophie's Steakhouse & Bar ◐ | 20 | 16 | 17 | £29 |
311-313 Fulham Rd., SW10 (South Kensington), 020-7352 0088; fax 7349 9776; www.sophiessteakhouse.com
◪ "Finally, a decent place in Chelsea to enjoy comfort food" – that's the word on this "relaxed", "buzzy" American steakhouse with a "lovely range of favourites on the menu (not just steaks)"; it's a "nice meeting place for a thirtysomething crowd", plus it's especially "convenient after the cinema" opposite, but "be warned" that they take "no reservations [so] you may need to wait a long time."

Souk ◐ | – | – | – | M |
27 Litchfield St., WC2 (Leicester Sq.), 020-7240 1796; fax 7240 3382; www.soukrestaurant.net
It's "like walking into another world" at this Moroccan-inspired venue near Leicester Square with "great" North African cooking ("stuff you can't cook at home") and a "fabulous atmosphere" that's "best when it's busy"; although somewhat "spotty service" gets the thumbs down from a few, it nevertheless fits the bill "for a night out of food and clubbing in a single venue."

Spago ◐⌷ | 19 | 12 | 15 | £26 |
6 Glendower Pl., SW7 (South Kensington), 020-7225 2407
◪ "Unpretentious and casual", this South Ken haunt with a modest entrance serves "good" pizzas and other Traditional specialties from The Boot, all at "very reasonable prices"; still, detractors have a downer on the "basic decor" and

"sparse wine offerings" and "unexceptional" fare; P.S. it's "lively any night that Italian football" is screened.

Spiga   19 | 15 | 16 | £28

84-86 Wardour St., W1 (Leicester Sq./Piccadilly Circus), 020-7734 3444; fax 7734 3332; www.atozrestaurants.com

■ "Fun" and "friendly", this spot in Soho is "excellent for simple [Modern] Italian food", including wood-fired pizzas, at "decent prices", making it a "dependable" option for "pre- or post-cinema intake" or a "reliably great place to take the kids"; P.S. they "don't kick you out if you linger over that last glass" – and there's a "good wine list" too.

Spighetta   20 | 14 | 18 | £26

43 Blandford St., W1 (Baker St.), 020-7486 7340; fax 7486 7340 www.atozrestaurants.com

■ Despite its affiliation with the A-Z Group (Aubergine, et al.) and its seven years as a "neighbourhood" spot, few "know about this best-kept secret" for "reliable" Modern Italian fare and "crispy pizzas" set in a Med-style Marylebone basement; the "excellent" dishes are served in a "family atmosphere", completing the "informal" experience.

Spoon+ ◗   20 | 24 | 18 | £56

Sanderson Hotel, 50 Berners St., W1 (Goodge St./Oxford Circus), 020-7300 1444; fax 7300 5540; www.chinagrillmgt.com/spoon/

◩ "Perfect for jet-setters" and "*Sex and the City* girls", "this "chic", "minimalist" spin-off of Alain Ducasse's Parisian concept in Ian Schrager's Sanderson Hotel showcases this celebrated chef's "prowess" with an Eclectic "combination menu that's still a novelty"; it's "brilliant to eat outside under the stars" and "great for people-watching", so "go to be seen"; but detractors declare "it requires a PhD" to order and find it difficult to fork out for such "pricey" fare, suggesting "stick to" the "more impressive bar."

SQUARE, THE   27 | 22 | 25 | £73

6-10 Bruton St., W1 (Bond St./Green Park), 020-7495 7100; fax 7495 7150; www.squarerestaurant.com

■ "This hot pistol is at the top" of its game gush gastronomes of chef/co-owner Philip Howard's "discreet" Mayfair venture that's "in a class by itself" with "orchestrated service" and "impeccable" New French "food for discerning grown-ups" that "hits a high note", accompanied by a "fabulous wine list"; the "open", "modern" art–bedecked, "tastefully decorated" room is "perfect for a celebration" and a "favourite" for a "power lunch", and whilst the experience is "pricey, it's worth every penny."

Sri Nam ⊠   19 | 14 | 15 | £25

10 Cabot Sq., E14 (Canary Wharf), 020-7715 9515; www.orientalrestaurantgroup.co.uk

◩ Formerly a branch of Yellow River Cafe, and retaining the involvement of "celebrity chef Ken Hom", this spacious, bi-level Canary Wharf venue kitted out with bright lanterns offers a "good-quality" Thai-Malay menu boasting a "mishmash of Asian" and vegetarian offerings; "fast-paced service" means it's "not a place to linger", but it's "great for lunch" or a "quick bite after work" (there's a "miraculous exodus after happy hour!").

Sri Siam City ⊠   19   15   16   £29
85 London Wall, EC2 (Liverpool St.), 020-7628 5772; fax 7628 3395;
www.orientalrestaurantgroup.co.uk
☑ Offering "a touch of the Orient in the City", the "pleasant surroundings" and "spicy, authentic" cooking of this basement Thai make it "a good standby for lunch" or after "late nights at the office", although a few feel the "service leaves something to be desired"; P.S. the underground "location renders your mobile useless – a plus or minus depending on the day!"

Sri Thai Soho   18   13   16   £28
16 Old Compton St., W1 (Leicester Sq./Tottenham Court Rd.),
020-7434 3544; fax 7287 1311;
www.orientalrestaurantgroup.co.uk
◪ Diners are divided over this "Soho Thai": disciples claim the "sexy setting", "upscale service" and "good choice" of "fine", "succulent servings" "never disappoint", whilst non-believers insist it "used to be better" and is "high priced for what it is" in an area "spoiled for choice"; either way, it's "always busy, but you never have to wait long to get a seat."

Star of India ◓   23   17   20   £33
154 Old Brompton Rd., SW5 (Gloucester Rd./
South Kensington), 020-7373 2901; fax 7373 5664
◪ "What a star" insist those over the moon about this "high-energy" South Kensington Indian eatery where seasonally changing "hearty", "interesting food" and "lovely service" have "never not met expectations"; if a minority are crestfallen by the "curious" layout and feel it's "lost the plot", the majority retort it's a "dependable" "neighbourhood standby" and perhaps the "best in this neck of the woods."

Sticky Fingers   14   15   13   £24
1A Phillimore Gardens, W8 (High St. Kensington),
020-7938 5338; fax 7937 0145; www.stickyfingers.co.uk
◪ "You can get satisfaction" at this "family-friendly" Kensington venue where "youngsters of all ages" devour "good ol' American cheeseburgers" and "reliable" diner fare; the "Rolling Stones memorabilia makes this teenage food worthwhile" (plus, you never know when Bill Wyman will bop by) and it's all served with a "spot of rock 'n' roll music to boot"; on the flip side, disappointed detractors tut it's "too tacky."

ST. JOHN ⊠　　　　　　　25 | 17 | 22 | £40

26 St. John St., EC1 (Farringdon), 020-7251 0848; fax 7251 4090;
www.stjohnrestaurant.com

■ "Eat things you didn't know existed" and "everything else you wouldn't eat as a kid" at this "great experience for passionate meat eaters" in a "stark", "quirky" old Smithfield smokehouse where chef Fergus Henderson ("a titan!") conjures up "hearty" Modern British fare that's "challenging for sophisticated gourmands"; from the "satisfyingly large portions" and "wonderful staff" to the "convivial atmosphere it's "fabulous in virtually every respect."

ST. JOHN BREAD & WINE　　　23 | 16 | 20 | £28

94-96 Commercial St., E1 (Liverpool St.), 020-7247 8724;
fax 7247 8924; www.stjohnbreadandwine.com

■ "Brave St. John expand their breathtaking concept" with this "buzzing", "relaxed" all-day Shoreditch "treasure", which boasts a full working bakery for "wonderful bread" and an "inventive", "bistro-style" Modern British menu that's "friendly for offal-fiends and offal-don'ts" and "always has something interesting to try"; "we need more of these" is the plea from disciples.

Strada　　　　　　　　19 | 14 | 17 | £21

15-16 New Burlington St., W1 (Oxford Circus), 020-7287 5967;
fax 7287 6074

Market Pl. 9-10, W1 (Oxford Circus), 020-7580 4644;
fax 7580 7877

6 Great Queen St., WC2 (Holborn), 020-7405 6293;
fax 7405 6284

91 Wimbledon High St., SW19 (Wimbledon),
020-8946 4363

11-13 Battersea Rise, SW11 (Clapham Junction), 020-7801 0794;
fax 7801 0754

175 New King's Rd., SW6 (Parsons Green), 020-7731 6404;
fax 7731 1431

237 Earl's Court Rd., SW5 (Earl's Court), 020-7835 1180;
fax 7835 2093

102-104 Clapham High St., SW4 (Clapham North), 020-7627 4847;
fax 7720 2153

105-106 Upper St., N1 (Angel), 020-7226 9742;
fax 7226 9187

8-10 Exmouth Mkt., EC1 (Farringdon), 020-7278 0800;
fax 7278 6901

www.strada.co.uk

Additional locations throughout London

■ "Functional but fun", this "mildly crowded and thoroughly enjoyable" "welcome chain" around town proves "time and time again they are dependable" for "tasty", "properly cooked" Italian fare – most notably "decent wood-fired pizzas" with "thin bases" – that's "easy on the purse strings"; it's a "winning formula" that "caters well for large groups" ("great for a birthday"), plus "helpful staff" are "very child-friendly."

Stratford's
▽ 22 | 18 | 18 | £35

7 Stratford Rd., W8 (High St. Kensington), 020-7937 6388; fax 7938 3435

◨ In "bright", "boutique"-sized premises with a Gallic feel in a quiet Kensington street, this "tasteful restaurant" "always produces excellent" French seafood dishes; still, there's a bit of stratification amongst surveyors: for many this decade-old spot remains a "favourite", whilst a handful feel it "lacks atmosphere" and can be let down by "intrusive service."

Sugar Club
24 | 19 | 22 | £46

21 Warwick St., W1 (Piccadilly Circus), 020-7437 7776; fax 7437 7778; www.thesugarclub.co.uk

■ "Oz lives" at this "sweet" Soho spot that "entrances" enthusiasts with "adventurous" Pacific Rim–Eclectic meals, a "soothing" "environment" and "accommodating service"; the "explosion of flavours" "still astound" with "wildly exotic ingredients" that provide "pleasure with every bite" matched with a "well-priced wine list"; if a few feel it's "lost some of its sparkle", Sugar fiends feel now that the "'in' crowd have moved on, this is the time to enjoy it."

SUGAR HUT ●
22 | 26 | 18 | £38

374 North End Rd., SW6 (Fulham Broadway), 020-7386 8950; fax 7386 8428; www.sugarhutfulham.com

■ "You must ring the doorbell to get in to" this "opulent setting", "one of the swankier places in Fulham" enhanced by Asian and Moroccan artefacts; the "atmospheric Oriental" surroundings are a canvas for an "excellent" Thai menu with dishes served all at once instead of in courses; expect a "surprising crowd of beautiful people and rednecks", especially in the "trendy", "clubby" bar.

Sugar Reef ● 🚱
13 | 14 | 11 | £33

41-44 Great Windmill St., W1 (Piccadilly Circus), 020-7851 0800; fax 7851 0807; www.sugarreef.net

◨ This "funky, chilled-out" multilevel bar/restaurant/nightclub near Piccadilly Circus serves Modern European fare that some claim "lives up to interesting" expectations, but others decry as "basic" and "overpriced", concluding "food is definitely an afterthought" here; P.S. the "music is so loud only sign language will work in the downstairs bar."

Sumosan ●
24 | 21 | 21 | £53

26 Albemarle St., W1 (Green Park), 020-7495 5999; fax 7355 1247; www.sumosan.com

◨ "If you're fed up waiting to get into trendy Japanese restaurants, try this" family-owned Mayfair spot where a "chic" setting with lots of "pretty people" combined with Bubker Belkhit's "innovative", "exquisite" fare – like "melt-in-your-mouth sushi", "exquisite" cooked dishes and "fantastic desserts" – make it a "good alternative"; but cynics snipe it's a "blonde-wood imitation of Nobu and not worth the expense"; P.S. the "buzzy" J Bar downstairs with a DJ Thursday–Saturday offers another string to its bow.

Sweetings 🗷　　　　　　　24　16　19　£35
39 Queen Victoria St., EC4 (Mansion House), 020-7248 3062
■ With its "clubby atmosphere" and look "of a captain's table on a fishing boat", this "legendary" weekday lunch-only "City bastion of Traditional British seafood" is a "unique" environment, which, coupled with "uncomplicated fish at its freshest best" and "understated service", ensures it gets "sensationally crowded" – so "get there early to avoid a wait" as they don't take bookings; P.S. "no hot drinks" are served – a quirk since "the start of time."

Taman gang 🗷　　　　　19　21　16　£54
141 Park Ln., W1 (Marble Arch), 020-7518 3160; fax 7518 3161
◪ "The mood is sexy" at this "subterranean", "Zen-like space" in Mayfair with Balinese-inspired decor where "models and famous girls" congregate for Hiroki Takemura's (ex Nobu and Zuma) "high-end, well-prepared [Southeast] Asian" cooking at "expense-account prices"; snipers aim their fire at "erratic service" and "indifferent food", but at least the "great cocktails" "hit their target."

TAMARIND ●　　　　　　25　20　22　£46
20 Queen St., W1 (Green Park), 020-7629 3561; fax 7499 5034; www.tamarindrestaurant.com
■ "Many rupees are required, nevertheless you want to order everything" at this "classy", "fab" Mayfair basement where "helpful staff" serve "gourmet Indian in grown-up surroundings"; chef Alfred Prasad, who took over when Atul Kochhar left to open Benares, prepares "finely judged dishes" of "seriously delicious" fare with "bright, clear flavours" – "mild enough not to frighten, authentic enough to feel exotic" – and "each bite is a taste treat"; if a few feel it's "overpriced", most retort it's "a real winner."

Tampopo　　　　　　　▽ 17　16　16　£21
140 Fulham Rd., SW10 (South Kensington), 020-7370 5355
◪ "Ideal pre- or post-cinema", this "trendy" Pan-Asian spot, named after the cult 1980s Japanese film about a noodle restaurant, is set in former Wok Wok premises on the Fulham Road and offers a cheap, "varied menu" where "hot, flavourful meals are served in a flash"; still, the unconverted believe "service needs brushing up – the growing pains of a new establishment, no doubt."

Tas ●　　　　　　　　20　16　17　£20
20 New Globe Walk, SE1 (London Bridge), 020-7928 3300; fax 7261 1166
33 The Cut, SE1 (Southwark), 020-7928 1444; fax 7633 9686

(continued)
Tas
72 Borough High St., SE1 (London Bridge), 020-7403 7200;
fax 7403 7022
www.tasrestaurant.com
■ "Offering something for everyone", this "jolly" Turkish trio
in "simple, modern" premises near Waterloo and the South
Bank serves "fantastic food" with "knockout flavours" –
"equal parts authentic and inventive" – at "amazing prices";
the "friendly" atmosphere is "great for family gatherings",
a "relaxed, unfancy meal" "prior to a performance" at the
Old Vic or a "quick bite for lunch."

Tate Gallery Restaurant   18   20   17   £28
Tate Britain, Millbank, SW1 (Pimlico), 020-7887 8825;
fax 7887 8902; www.tate.org.uk
◪ "After touring the gallery, relax and refresh" in this "fab
place" inside the Tate Britain on Millbank boasting a "lovely
mural" (created by Rex Whistler in 1925) and a "light", but
"satisfying" Modern British menu, supported by a "well-
chosen wine list" with "unbelievable prices"; staff are
"amazingly good-tempered" given the "endless, heaving
queue" at busy times.

Tatsuso ⊠   25   16   24   £62
32 Broadgate Circle, EC1 (Liverpool St.), 020-7638 5863;
fax 7638 5864
◪ "You get both teppanyaki and sushi at this wonderful" bi-
level Broadgate eatery where an "impressively expansive"
Japanese menu of "amazing food" is on offer and "faultless
staff" are appreciated for doing "all they can to make dining
pleasurable"; but it's "strictly business only" thanks to
"pocket-melting" prices, so "go with an expense account –
yours or someone else's."

TECA ⊠   22   21   19   £51
54 Brooks Mews, W1 (Bond St.), 020-7495 4774; fax 7491 3545;
www.atozrestaurants.com
◪ "Excellent" Modern Italian cooking and "warm", service
lure loyalists to this "sleek, subtle, elegant and cool" A-Z
Group–owned venue in a quiet Mayfair mews that's a "hip,
reinvigorating place for lunch" and "not buzzy in the
evenings"; still, dissenters get tetchy about "overpriced"
fare and "deteriorating service."

Tentazioni ⊠   25   19   22   £41
Lloyd's Wharf, 2 Mill St., SE1 (London Bridge/Tower Hill),
020-7237 1100; fax 7237 1100; www.tentazioni.co.uk
■ "Some of the best rustic Modern Italian cooking in
London" with a "fab wine list" of "unusual" "beauties" to
boot draws fans to this "intimate" venue in a "hard-to-
find", converted warehouse behind Butler's Wharf where
service is "conscientious" "without being overpowering";

"it's not cheap, but it's worth the splurge" agree acolytes who also confide that at £36 for five courses, the "amazing set tasting menu is well worth trying."

Tenth Restaurant & Bar, The ⊠   – – – VE

Royal Garden Hotel, 10th fl., 2-24 Kensington High St., W8 (High St. Kensington), 020-7361 1910; fax 7361 1921; www.royalgardenhotel.co.uk

There's a "spectacular view of Kensington Gardens" and the Serpentine from this 10th-floor dining room of the Royal Gardens Hotel on a corner of Hyde Park, and when you add in a "creative" Modern European–Eclectic menu and service that's "super-attentive, without suffocating" it amounts to a "delightful" place to spend a "summer evening"; P.S. the 'Manhattan' jazz nights on the last Saturday of each month are "not to be missed."

Terminus   16 14 15 £28

Great Eastern Hotel, Liverpool St., EC2 (Liverpool St.), 020-7618 7400; fax 7618 7401

☑ "Dependable – no more, no less" – sums up the Modern British–Eclectic brasserie menu on offer at this "buzzing", "loud" train-themed Conran Group venue in the Great Eastern Hotel by Liverpool Street Station; it's "good for an informal lunch" – plus "you can have a breakfast meeting without being overheard"; still, others stop short at "restaurant prices for a cafe location."

Terrace, The   ▽ 21 16 17 £37

33C Holland St., W8 (High St. Kensington), 020-7937 3224; fax 7937 3323

■ This "tiny place tucked down a quiet Kensington street" is "loved locally" for its "elegant, but casual" setting, "attentive service" and "consistently good" Modern British cooking – even if "the menu choice is limited"; "given its few tables" are "somewhat close together", you may "feel like joining your neighbour's conversation."

Terrace   22 20 21 £36

Le Meridien Piccadilly, 2nd fl., 21 Piccadilly, W1 (Green Park/ Piccadilly Circus), 020-7851 3085; fax 7851 3090

☑ With its "wonderful glasshouse atmosphere", this "relaxed", "lovely" conservatory dining room in the Le Meridien Piccadilly "doesn't make you feel as though you're in a hotel" and what's more, it offers "surprisingly good" French fare and "wonderful afternoon tea"; but it doesn't sit well with a few who find it a "bit reserved" with "so-so food."

Texas Embassy Cantina   12 14 15 £21

1 Cockspur St., SW1 (Charing Cross/Piccadilly Circus), 020-7925 0077; fax 7925 0444; www.texasembassy.com

☑ It "scratches an itch for homesick American expats", but whether this two-level "Tex-Mex right smack" next to

Trafalgar Square is "worthy of that designation" is up for grabs; "yee-haw", it's "cheesy, but fun" shout enthusiasts, and a "close approximation" of a "taste of home", so "round up the kids and chow down!"; but others run for the border, advising "avoid like the Alamo."

T.G.I. Friday's ◑   10 11 13 £20

96-98 Bishop's Bridge Rd., W2 (Bayswater/Queensway), 020-7229 8600; fax 7727 4150
25-29 Coventry St., W1 (Piccadilly Circus), 020-7839 6262; fax 7839 6296
6 Bedford St., WC2 (Charing Cross/Covent Garden), 020-7379 0585; fax 7240 3239
www.tgifridays.com

☑ "Hard to beat for a filling meal" "without spending your whole salary" attest those thankful for this "casual" chain with "basic" American fare and "friendly" staff that makes a "fun after-work hangout", a "standby with the kids" and offers "a bit of home" to "expats"; still, it's "all way toooo rushed", "faux-cheery" and "predictable" for some tastes.

Thai on the River   18 19 19 £33

Unit 4, Chelsea Wharf, 15 Lots Rd., SW10 (Fulham Broadway/ Sloane Sq.), 020-7351 1151; fax 7823 3390; www.thaiontheriver.co.uk

☑ Thanks to "fetching views" of the Thames with some tables placed near the "swanky Chelsea" Harbour, this "cosy" 10-year-old Thai is a "local favourite"; the "food is excellent" ("never changes, but always good") with a "good-value Sunday buffet" for £13.50, plus "service is good and it's not overpriced – it's an all-around deal"; but others float off in another direction, declaring the "service lacklustre."

Thai Pavilion   20 16 19 £23

42 Rupert St., W1 (Leicester Sq./Piccadilly Circus), 020-7287 6333; fax 7587 0484; www.thaipavilion.com ◑
82 Kennington Rd., SE11 (Lambeth North), 020-7587 0455; fax 7587 0484; www.pavilioneast.com

☑ A "must-stop" for "pretty darn good" food with "fantastic flavours" – "have the waitress design your menu, you will be in good hands!" – this tri-level "Thai right off Shaftesbury Avenue" and younger, "excellent branch in Lambeth" hit the mark for many who either "get a table on the top floor [of Rupert Street] and sit cross-legged on cushions" or opt for regular seating; still, the disenchanted deem it "nothing to get excited about."

Thai Square   17 17 14 £24

21-24 Cockspur St., SW1 (Charing Cross/Piccadilly Circus), 020-7839 4000; fax 7839 0839
347-349 Upper St., N1 (Angel), 020-7704 2000; fax 7704 2277

(continued)

(continued)
Thai Square
136-138 Minories, EC3 (Tower Hill), 020-7680 1111;
fax 7680 1112 🖂
www.thaipot.co.uk
▰ "Big" and "noisy", the Trafalgar Square "SW1 flagship
location" of this Thai trio has a "majestic", "theatrical"
look, and for many remains a "tasty" option for "splendid",
"good-value" dishes "served up" with "fierce flavours"
and "charm"; but others opine that the younger siblings
in Islington and Tower Hill (with a DJ on Thursdays and
Fridays) "are reliable, but a bit anonymous."

Thierry's 🖂 – | – | – | E
342 King's Rd., SW3 (Sloane Sq./South Kensington),
020-7352 3365; fax 7352 3365
"Surprisingly charming", this low-key King's Road French
bistro "deserves more credit than it gets" thanks to "very
good", "authentic bourgeois cuisine" and a setting that
evokes a "corner of France"; whilst a few feel the "price
is a bit high for what it is", others think it's "worth it now and
again for a nice romantic dinner *à deux*"; P.S. it can be
"empty early evening, but it gets busy later."

THYME 🖂 27 | 18 | 23 | £45
14 Clapham Park Rd., SW4 (Clapham Common), 020-7627 2468;
fax 7627 2424; www.thymeandspace.com
▰ "They manage to surprise and delight every time" fawn
followers who find it's "worth the trip" to Clapham for this
"interesting dining experience" with "attentive service" and
a meal comprised of a "lot of small", "sophisticated" New
French dishes; the "exquisite flavours" are an "absolute
must for food and wine lovers" – most notably the "marathon
tasting menu" – so expect to "run up the bill quickly";
P.S. never mind the "Ikea-like decor" – at press time, plans
were underway to move to the new Hospital multimedia
centre in Covent Garden this autumn.

Tiger Lil's 14 | 12 | 12 | £19
75 Bishop's Bridge Rd., W2 (Bayswater/Queensway),
020-7221 2622; fax 7221 2399
16A Southside Clapham Common, SW4 (Clapham Common),
020-7720 5433; fax 7622 5995
270 Upper St., N1 (Highbury & Islington), 020-7226 1118;
fax 7288 1108
www.tigerlils.com
▰ "The food is wok you make of it" at this "novelty" Asian-
Eclectic trio where diners "choose their own raw materials"
from a "good variety of fish, meat, veg and noodles" and
then watch the "friendly chefs" create a "stir-fry frenzy";
whilst it's "not so good" for "romantic dates", the "all-you-
can-eat" concept is "excellent if you're hungry", on "a
budget" or "you have young children" to amuse.

Timo　　22　15　15　£39
343 Kensington High St., W8 (High St. Kensington),
020-7603 3888; fax 7603 8111; www.atozrestaurants.com
■ Part of the A-Z stable, this "pleasant" "great find in an unlikely part of Kensington High Street" offers an "excellently executed" menu of Italian fare as well as "creative options"; it "helps ring the changes" in the neighbourhood agree aesthetes who give the "classy, contemporary with a twist" setting a thumb's up, but others snipe the "small" space "lacks atmosphere."

Tokyo Diner ●　　17　12　16　£14
2 Newport Pl., WC2 (Leicester Sq.), 020-7287 8777;
fax 7434 1415
◪ Fans of this little sushi "jewel" in Chinatown ("run by a charming Englishman", Richard Hill) "wish there were more of them", praising "delicious, home-cooked Japanese" fare that's "great to stoke up" on "without breaking the bank"; however, a minority think there "are better alternatives", pointing to a "limited menu" and "indifferent service."

Tom Aikens ☒　　25　23　24　£73
43 Elystan St., SW3 (South Kensington), 020-7584 2003
◪ It's "nice to have Mr. Aikens back in London" after his departure from Pied à Terre a few years back enthuse those enamoured with the "amazing culinary experience" provided by the eponymous chef at this "welcome addition" to Chelsea, an "exciting place" for people "serious about food" where "artistic" New French fare is served in an "elegant, Zen-ish setting"; "close, but no cigar" claim sceptics who fret about "frosty service (hardly a smiling face)" and "too many swishy patterns on the plate."

Tom's Delicatessen　　19　14　13　£20
226 Westbourne Grove, W11 (Notting Hill Gate), 020-7221 8818;
fax 7221 7717
■ Be it "Kate Moss or Robbie Williams", "you never know who" you'll "bump into" at this "celebrity-laden" all-day BYO deli/diner from Tom Conran, set in "informal", "crowded but charming" Notting Hill premises where "interesting [Eclectic] offerings" are "worth the wait" for a table; it's "fantastic for brunch" at the weekends and "in summer, be charmed by the little garden at the back"

Tootsies　　14　11　13　£18
120 Holland Park Ave., W11 (Holland Park), 020-7229 8567
35 Haven Green, W5 (Ealing Broadway), 020-8566 8200;
fax 8991 1491
148 Chiswick High Rd., W4 (Turnham Green), 020-8747 1869;
fax 8987 0686
35 James St., W1 (Bond St.), 020-7486 1611; fax 7935 4957
48 High St., SW19 (Wimbledon), 020-8946 4135

(continued)

(continued)
Tootsies

147 Church Rd., SW13 (Hammersmith), 020-8748 3630;
fax 8748 7098
107 Old Brompton Rd., SW7 (South Kensington), 020-7581 8942;
fax 7590 0979
177 New King's Rd., SW6 (Parsons Green), 020-7736 4023
36-38 Abbeville Rd, SW4 (Clapham South), 020-8772 6646;
fax 8772 0672
196-198 Haverstock Hill, NW3 (Belsize Park), 020-7431 3812;
fax 7794 8478
Additional locations throughout London
☑ For a "no-frills burger" in a "diner-style atmosphere",
this "laid-back" "Americanised" chain "does what it does
well", and whilst the "decor varies widely by location" (from
"decent" to "bland"), "child-friendly" staff are applauded
for coping when it's "heaving" with "kiddies"; in sum, it's
"reliable when you're in the mood for this sort of thing."

Toto's
25 | 22 | 22 | £50

Walton Hse., Walton St. at Lennox Garden Mews, SW3
(Knightsbridge), 020-7589 2062; fax 7581 9668
■ "Mouth-watering" fare, an "impressive wine list",
"polished staff" that "cater to your every whim" and a
"bustling", "superb ambience" "all combine to underline
the dependable joys" of this "classy" 21-year-old Italian in a
Chelsea mews; whether you choose "the high-ceilinged
room downstairs or the intimate, spartan area upstairs",
"it's lovely for a romantic evening" and a "great place to
eat and drink comfortably" – plus there's a "nice little patio
at the back" for lunch only.

Troubadour, The
15 | 20 | 15 | £17

265 Old Brompton Rd., SW5 (Earl's Court), 020-7370 1434;
fax 7341 6329; www.troubadour.co.uk
☑ "Feel bohemian even if you're not" at this "chilled-out",
"cramped" 50-year-old Earl's Court all-day coffeehouse
with a "funky" decor where "beatniks and writers" enjoy
"hearty" Modern British–Eclectic fare from a "solid, country
pub–style" menu, with "amazing breakfasts"; a "quaint
garden" and a recently expanded "gorgeous deli next door"
complete the picture.

Truc Vert
20 | 14 | 14 | £24

42 N. Audley St., W1 (Bond St.), 020-7491 9988; fax 7491 7717
■ "Watch the world go by" at this "little bit of France in
W1", a "small", "relaxed" Gallic restaurant-cum-shop in
"modest" Mayfair premises with rustic, "chic countryside
decor" where a daily changing bistro menu of "healthy,
filling comfort food" ensures it "gets very busy" at "peak
hours" (hence service speed is "dependent on the time you
arrive"); P.S. "locals go" for the "delicious deli" offerings,
like "freshly baked bread on the premises."

TSUNAMI 🛂   27 21 18 £38

5-7 Voltaire Rd., SW4 (Clapham North), 020-7978 1610;
fax 7978 1591

◪ "Killer cocktails, a cool vibe and delicious food" sums
up the mix at this "stylish" spot in an "unstylish part of
Clapham" where Ken Sam, "an ex-Nobu chef", prepares
"magnificently fresh", "creative sushi combos" that are
"elegantly constructed and skilfully executed", along with
"brilliant" cooked Japanese fare; nonetheless, a few get
stirred up by "tables too close together" or those near the
door – "social Siberia" – and "deafening noise levels."

Turnmills Top Floor 🛂   – – – E

63 Clerkenwell Rd., EC1 (Farringdon), 020-7608 3220;
fax 7250 1057; www.turnmills.co.uk

Revamped with a spot-on bohemian feel, this Eclectic venue
on the top floor of a Clerkenwell building has replaced
longtime occupant Gaudí; velvet drapes, chandeliers and
mirrors set the stage for a sensibly priced, globe-trotting
menu with some unconventional combinations, plus the
short wine list starts at £12.50; N.B. the basement is a
popular clubbing haunt.

Tuttons Brasserie ●   15 13 16 £25

11-12 Russell St., WC2 (Covent Garden), 020-7836 4141;
fax 7379 9979

■ "A mixed crowd of tourists and Brits on a night out"
sit "shoulder to shoulder" at this "old faithful", all-day
brasserie in Covent Garden that "serves its purpose" as
a "cheap and cheerful" pit stop for "middle-of-the-road"
Modern British fare, whether you're "with children" or "have
a show in the area."

Two Brothers Fish 🛂   ▽ 24 11 18 £19

297-303 Regent's Park Rd., N3 (Finchley Central), 020-8346 0469;
fax 8343 1978

■ Even though they take "no bookings" at dinner and fin
fans must "be prepared to queue", this unassuming Finchley
seafooder is "worth the schlep" for "terrific" fish 'n' chips
that "exceed expectations for value" – all "served with
a smile"; P.S. "if it's good enough for Madonna, it's good
enough for me!"

202   19 18 14 £22

202 Westbourne Grove, W11 (Notting Hill Gate), 020-7727 2722;
fax 7792 9217

◪ Conduct a "tête-à-tête" over a "yummy brunch" or "rub
shoulders with" the "model-pose crowd" – either way,
much like sibling Nicole's, designer Nicole Fahri's shop 'n'
dine venture, this "convivial" Modern European spot with
American touches in Notting Hill is the "place to be seen,
especially on weekends"; the "basic dishes" add up to a
"good neighbourhood place" – "if you can wait out the

queue" and sometimes "attitudinal staff", plus there's a patio, too.

UBON ⊠   26   22   20   £55
34 Westferry Circus, E14 (Canary Wharf), 020-7719 7800; fax 7719 7801; www.noburestaurants.com
■ "Easier to book" and "less pretentious than its anagram in Mayfair", Nobu's "phenomenal little sister" in Canary Wharf is "every bit as good" when it comes to the "fabulous" Japanese–South American fusion fare (including the "signature miso black cod") – and may even be "a touch better" thanks to the "fantastic view over the Thames"; this is "expense-account eating and worth the price – if somebody else pays"; but a minority claim it's "hardly a life-changing experience" and feel it "lacks the buzz" of its famous sibling.

Uli ⊠   ▽ 24   13   21   £26
16 All Saints Rd., W11 (Ladbroke Grove), 020-7727 7511
■ In unassuming premises near Portobello Road, this "homely" spot, whose name means 'strength' in Chinese, is distinguished by a "tasty", "no-nonsense" Pan-Asian menu with a cache of "creative" dishes, along with "attentive, knowledgeable service", "mainly by the proprietor"; P.S. it's also "a takeaway favourite."

Union Cafe ⊠   20   15   19   £29
96 Marylebone Ln., W1 (Bond St.), 020-7486 4860; fax 7486 4860; www.brinkleys.com
■ "An unexpected neighbourhood treat" in Marylebone, this "lively", "favourite everyday place" where "you don't feel hassled or rushed by waiters" also boasts a Modern British–Eclectic menu of "imaginative", "good value" fare; "it's the right" choice "if you fancy something quick" paired with "attractively priced wines", "set at retail, not restaurant prices."

Vale, The   –   –   –   E
99 Chippenham Rd., W9 (Maida Vale), 020-7266 0990; fax 7286 7224
"Good that it remains something of a local secret" insist insiders smitten by this Maida Vale "gem" in a conservatory with "creative" tucker and "attentive", "friendly staff"; the "regularly changing" Modern British menu with "excellent value set meals ought to pack it out every day", but, as yet, to no a-vale.

VAMA ◐   26   20   19   £36
438 King's Rd., SW10 (Sloane Sq.), 020-7565 8500; fax 7565 8501; www.vama.co.uk
■ "It was a bud, now blooming" encore enthusiasts "absolutely blown away" by chef Andy Varma's "delicate, innovative" Northwest Punjabi cooking (definitely "not your mother's curry takeaway") at this "contemporary",

"chichi" World's Ender; the "stylish", "soothing setting" and "cordial, leisurely service" heighten the "memorable meal", making this "superb" venue a "shining star in the constellation"; still, a few feel "service can be spotty"; P.S. it's "a hike from Sloane Square tube."

Vasco & Piero's Pavilion ⌧   ▽ 21 | 12 | 20 | £33
15 Poland St., W1 (Oxford Circus), 020-7437 8774; fax 7437 0467; www.vascosfood.com
■ It's been around for decades, nonetheless, "not everyone knows about" this low-key, "homey" Soho Italian with "pleasant service" owned by Vasco Matteucci; it's "reliable" for "genuine" Tuscan cooking, including homemade pasta from a menu that changes twice daily, and while it's all "fairly priced", the £14.50 set "lunch is an impressive" offer.

Veeraswamy ◗   21 | 19 | 19 | £37
Victory House, 99-101 Regent St., W1 (Piccadilly Circus), 020-7734 1401; fax 7439 8434; www.realindianfood.com
☑ "Bold colours make the decor warm and exotic" at this "enthralling" 79-year-old Indian in a "convenient Piccadilly location" where an "upscale" Northwest Frontier menu works "for those both experienced and unfamiliar with the cuisine", served by "cordial" "waiters in regional dress"; but a handful find it "too dear for what it is", and snipe that service "can be slow" and "disinterested."

Verbanella ◗   17 | 16 | 20 | £36
30 Beauchamp Pl., SW3 (Knightsbridge), 020-7584 1107; fax 7589 9662; www.verbanella.com
☑ "Hearty" Traditional Italian dishes are on offer at this "charming and homey little townhouse" in Knightsbridge with "warm, genial service"; loyalists reveal that the "menu is modest, but well done", plus it makes a "great lunch spot after shopping at Harrod's"; still, the unconvinced deem it "a throwback to an era best left behind."

Viet Hoa ◗   21 | 7 | 14 | £18
70-72 Kingsland Rd., E2 (Old St.), 020-7729 8293; fax 7729 8293
☑ Never mind the "appalling decor that's worse than a school canteen" and staff that are "brutally efficient rather than friendly" – it "kind of adds to the experience" at this "popular Vietnamese haunt", "one of the bright spots on Kingsland Road"; thanks to a "wide variety" of "relatively cheap, super-tasty", "unusual and traditional dishes", the "food is good enough to justify the hike"; P.S. it's "best to go in a big group."

Villandry   19 | 16 | 14 | £36
170 Great Portland St., W1 (Great Portland St.), 020-7631 3131; fax 7631 3030; www.villandry.com
☑ "The mix works well" at this "bustling", "cramped" restaurant "at the back of a gourmet deli" on Great Portland Street: there's a "trendy" crowd, "good celebrity spotting"

and an "enjoyable" Modern British–Eclectic menu that "constantly changes and surprises", plus you can pop in "after doing a shop in the food store"; still, a handful vent that it's "let down" by "excruciatingly slow", "erratic service"; N.B. there's also a relaxed cafe/bar next door.

Vine, The   ∇ 18 | 16 | 15 | £22
86 Highgate Rd., NW5 (Kentish Town B.R.), 020-7209 0038; fax 7209 9001
☑ "Snuck away not far from" Parliament Hill, this "decent gastro-pub" with a "cool worn" look, complete with leather sofas and a fireplace, and a "warm attitude", also boasts a "lovely garden" that makes it a "great summer venue"; whilst you won't find a more friendly, fun, funky" spot "for a Sunday afternoon session", most maintain that the Modern British–European fare "can be hit-or-miss."

Vineyard at Stockcross   ∇ 22 | 22 | 24 | £68
Vineyard at Stockcross, Stockcross, Newbury, Berkshire, 01635 528770; fax 01635 528398; www.the-vineyard.co.uk
■ "Sheer magic" is at work at this "grown-up" dining room in Sir Peter Michael's Berkshire hotel, which summons up that "rare mix of English country house [setting] and American efficiency"; the "great" Modern British–Classic French menu mesmerises mavens with "top-class flavours" whilst the wine list, laden with selections from the owner's Sonoma County vineyard, is "to die for."

Vingt-Quatre ◐   13 | 11 | 13 | £23
325 Fulham Rd., SW10 (South Kensington), 020-7376 7224; fax 7352 2643
☑ "Open 24/7", this "cracking little restaurant" in Fulham Road delivers "good", Eclectic "just-what-you-feel-like food" that's "unrivalled for that early morning fry-up" and a "must for Sunday brunch" and "post-pub/club munchies"; "pumping tunes" set the mood "late at night" when you can "rub elbows" with "interesting people"; still, detractors declare "if it was named after how long you'd want to spend over a meal, it would be called *demi-heure!*"

Vrisaki ⊠   – | – | – | M
73 Myddelton Rd., N22 (Bounds Green/Wood Green), 020-8889 8760
"Authentic, traditional" Greek cooking is the magnet at this humble-looking "good spot" in Wood Green that's "excellent for mezze"; grazers groan there's one caveat: "dishes are large!" so order accordingly or you'll leave lamenting "never had so much food in my life."

WAGAMAMA   19 | 14 | 16 | £16
26A Kensington High St., W8 (High St. Kensington), 020-7376 1717
101A Wigmore St., W1 (Bond St./Oxford Circus), 020-7409 0111
10A Lexington St., W1 (Oxford Circus/Piccadilly Circus), 020-7292 0990

(continued)

WAGAMAMA

1 Tavistock St., WC2 (Covent Garden), 020-7836 3330;
fax 7240 8846
4A Streatham St., WC1 (Holborn/Tottenham Court Rd.),
020-7323 9223; fax 7436 7834
Harvey Nichols, 109-125 Knightsbridge, SW1
(Knightsbridge), 020-7201 8000; fax 7201 8080
40 Parkfield St., N1 (Angel), 020-7226 2664
11 Jamestown Rd., NW1 (Camden Town), 020-7428 0800;
fax 7482 4887
109 Fleet St., EC4 (Blackfriars/St. Paul's), 020-7583 7889 🅂
1A Ropemaker St., EC2 (Moorgate), 020-7588 2688 🅂
www.wagamama.com
Additional locations throughout London

■ "Love my 'Mama'" exclaim enthusiasts of this "slick" "express Japanese with style", a "lifesaver" for "nosh" "on the go" with "cafeteria-style seating", "fast food that doesn't leave you dissatisfied" (including "slurpily delicious" noodles) and "ridiculously" speedy service ("the geek in me likes the wireless ordering"); it's "nothing flash", but it's a "winning combination" – and "guaranteed to make you happy without making a dent in the pocket."

Waldo's Dining Room 🅂   ∇ 24 26 25 £64

Cliveden Hotel, Taplow, Berkshire, 01628 668561;
fax 01628 661837; www.clivedenhouse.co.uk

■ Perhaps "the first thing that strikes you is the feeling of intimacy as you step downstairs into the dining room" within the "grand setting" of Berkshire's historic Cliveden Hotel – "you really feel like you are lord of the manor here"; and "what luxury" awaits, from the "exceptional" New French fare at "breathtaking prices" to the "comprehensive wine selection" to "exemplary service."

Wapping Food   19 25 17 £36

Wapping Hydraulic Power Station, Wapping Wall, E1
(Wapping), 020-7680 2080

■ "The ultimate in industrial chic", this "unusual" Wapping venue, set in a "roomy", "disused power station, complete with machinery" and "bizarre art" exhibits, "always has something new to look at" – especially if you "go for a long, lazy lunch" "on a sunny day, when the light floods through the windows"; also "worth investigating": the Modern Euro–Eclectic cooking with "imaginative flavour combinations" and the "very Antipodean wine selection."

Waterloo Fire Station   13 13 10 £25

150 Waterloo Rd., SE1 (Waterloo), 020-7620 2226; fax 7633 9161

◪ "Fun, loud" and "lively", this "quirky" "old fire station" near Waterloo with big tables and church pew seating is a "social spot" "to meet friends" for "tasty", "cheap, pub"-like Modern European fare" like "bangers and mash"; but it's a flaming disappointment to others who fume about "bar food for restaurant prices."

WATERSIDE INN ☒ 27 25 27 £86

Waterside Inn, Ferry Rd., Berkshire, Bray-on-Thames, Berkshire, 01628 620691; fax 01628 784710; www.waterside-inn.co.uk

■ "You expect excellence and you get it" at Michel Roux's "romantic" "fantasy" setting "on the banks of the Thames" in Berkshire that's "marvellous in every respect"; "top marks all round" are awarded for "faultless" French cooking – the "magic in the kitchen always dazzles" – "served with "subtlety and distinction"; it's "just what you would expect of an English country inn": "perfect for an indulgent lunch on a sunny weekend" and "superb" if you "stay the night in one of the beautiful rooms" with "outlandish prices."

Waterway ▽ 16 19 13 £34

54 Formosa St., W9 (Warwick Ave.), 020-7266 3557; fax 7266 3579; www.thewaterway.co.uk

☒ Set in "an excellent location (especially in summer)" overlooking the Grand Union Canal in Maida Vale, this boisterous gastro-pub is "a good place to go with a group"; the dining area offers a "creative", yet "not exceptional" French menu, but it's the "amateur staff" who "seem to change on a weekly basis" that "cast a shadow" over the experience.

Wells, The 20 17 14 £37

30 Well Walk, NW3 (Hampstead), 020-7794 3785

☒ "Hampstead's salvation" proclaim supporters smitten by the "adventurous", "high-quality" Modern European "brasserie-style food" – and "some very good wines too" – at this "popular" yearling on the first floor of a "cosy", "wonderful" 200-year-old inn; that said, sceptics feel "let down by haphazard service", concluding "it's still a pub" "trying to be fancy."

Westbourne, The 17 16 11 £23

101 Westbourne Park Villas, W2 (Royal Oak/Westbourne Park), 020-7221 1332; fax 7243 8081

☒ Still a "see-and-be-seen place" for "very tasty" Modern European–Eclectic fare, this "lively", "bohemian [Notting] Hillbillie hangout" with "chilled surroundings" and "the feel of a provincial French cafe" is "always crowded" with "good-looking babes"; still, the less-enchanted snipe that the fare is "just a sideline" and knock the "ostentatiously indifferent" staff who "think they are all celebrities"; P.S. it's "best for lazy weekend lunches."

Wheeler's, St. James's ☒ 21 16 19 £44

12A Duke of York St., SW1 (Piccadilly Circus), 020-7930 2460; fax 8839 2394

■ At 53 years and counting, "the last of this once-famous chain" in St James's, now part of the Marco Pierre White empire, remains a "charming" "glimpse of lost England", with "superbly executed" Modern British–Classic French seafood – like "quintessential Dover sole" – served up in "what must be the world's narrowest dining room"; still, gripers grouse that it's a "boring" "time warp"; N.B. at press time, it was sold to Matthew Brown, formerly of Belvedere.

White Swan Pub & Dining Room ⊠   − | − | − | E

108 Fetter Ln., EC4 (Chancery Ln./Farringdon), 020-7242 9696; www.thewhiteswanlondon.com

Tom and Ed Martin, who also own The Wells, recently took over this popular journalists' hangout, previously called Mucky Duck, gave it a refurb and returned it to its original name; they also recruited chef Jason Scrimshaw (ex Bibendum) who offers punchy Modern British cooking with European influences in the bright, mirror-ceilinged first-floor dining room, along with a shorter, simpler menu in the ground-floor bar; N.B. closed weekends.

Wilton's ⊠   24 | 23 | 24 | £60

55 Jermyn St., SW1 (Green Park/Piccadilly Circus), 020-7629 9955; fax 7495 6233; www.wiltons.co.uk

■ "The sun never sets on this corner of the British empire", a "traditional" "remnant – a fine one – of old-world dining" at "new-world prices" in St. James's – whose post "face-lift" "charm has endless longevity", especially "if you fancy rubbing elbows with a lord or lady"; from Jerome Ponchelle's "top-class" Modern British fare – dominated by "seafood so fresh you'd think there's a lake on the roof" "served in the genteel English manner" to the "wonderful" "men's club"–type atmosphere, it rarely "fails to satisfy."

Windows on the World   18 | 23 | 18 | £53

Hilton Park Lane, 22 Park Ln., W1 (Hyde Park Corner), 020-7208 4021; fax 7208 4144

◪ This 28th-floor restaurant/bar atop the Park Lane Hilton is "worth it" for the "amazing views over the Queen's back garden" alone, then "add in attentive" staff and "enjoyable" French offerings and you have an "excellent romantic evening"; still, it's not tops for all – "very average" fume a few – "but on the other hand", the "sky-high location" has to be seen to believed."

Wòdka ◑   19 | 16 | 18 | £36

12 St. Albans Grove, W8 (High St. Kensington), 020-7937 6513; fax 7937 8621; www.wodka.co.uk

■ "Nobody leaves sober or unsatisfied" after "enjoying the delights" of "delicious Polish cuisine with a modern twist" and "fabulous" vodka selection ("never knew there were so many types!") at this "noisy" "gem" in a "quiet Kensington neighbourhood" staffed with "great-looking" "Eastern European model"-types; it's a "fun place to bring a group" so join the "hip", "young crowd" "having a blast" – you're in for a "serious good time"; P.S. lunch is "quiet."

Wolseley, The ◐   19 25 20 £41
160 Piccadilly, W1 (Green Park), 020-7499 6996;
www.thewolseley.com

☑ "A chic atmosphere prevails" at this "welcome addition to Piccadilly" previously occupied by China House (once the "showroom for a defunct luxury British car named Wolseley") and now run by two maestros formerly from The Ivy, Chris Corbin and Jeremy King; admirers adore the "A-list" crowd and Modern European "comfort food" and note while it's "tricky to get a table", it's "fab day and night"; but detractors declare the "fare is not as good as the buzz" and find "service slow – unless you're a celeb."

Wong Kei ◐⇗   13 6 6 £12
41-43 Wardour St., W1 (Leicester Sq./Piccadilly Circus),
020-7437 8408

☑ "Low scores should not distract from the usefulness" of this "fast, furious fun" "Chinatown experience" where "the rudest waiters on earth" are "seen as entertainment", the Cantonese "food has never been less than good and cheap" and you "sit at tables with strangers" – "which could be a good or bad thing"; even with the "recent refurb", there's "nothing like it": it's "as popular as ever."

Yatra ◐▨   – – – VE
34 Dover St., W1 (Green Park), 020-7493 0200; fax 7493 4228;
www.yatra.co.uk

Though recently spruced up, the waterfall in the entrance remains, which adds to the "charm" of this comfortably rustic Indian eatery in Mayfair named after the ancient Sanskrit word for 'spiritual journey'; the fare is "fabulous", albeit "expensive", and diners have the option of "sitting cross-legged at floor-level" or European-style seating; Bar Bollywood, the lounge downstairs, offers live entertainment.

Yauatcha   – – – M
15 Broadwick St., W1 (Oxford Circus), 020-7494 8888; fax 7494 8889

Culinary legend Alan Yau maintains his reputation as an innovator with this sleek, bi-level operation in the new Ford Motor Company headquarters in Soho, boasting a teahouse on the ground floor offering over 100 varieties of leaves and French-inspired pastries, and a dim sum spot in the basement with Chinese victuals for lunch and dinner from chef Cheong Wah Soon from Yau's hot spot Hakkasan; N.B. check out the retail store selling tea and paraphernalia.

Yellow River Cafe   ▽ 13 11 14 £22
206 Upper St., N1 (Highbury & Islington), 020-7354 8833;
fax 7704 1890

■ The only branch left standing in Islington of this once three-strong chain, this Pan-Asian cafe has retained respected chef Ken Hom, offering a selection of "cheap", "standard" fare; but foes suggest the kitchen "has slipped recently" and surmise that this "every type of cuisine" concept "simply doesn't work"; N.B. it serves all day from Friday to Sunday.

Ye Olde Cheshire Cheese   14 | 24 | 16 | £22

145 Fleet St., EC4 (Blackfriars), 020-7353 6170; fax 7353 0845;
www.yeoldecheshirecheese.com

◩ "Steeped in a great, historic atmosphere", this "lovely quaint pub" in Fleet Street "throws you back over 300 years", and even if the Traditional British fare "has little to offer in the way of sophistication", it's a London "landmark" with the "wonderful smell of coal fires in the winter" and "must be seen to be believed"; still, a few feel it should be dubbed "ye olde touriste trappe."

Yoshino ⍓   23 | 16 | 19 | £24

3 Piccadilly Pl., W1 (Piccadilly Circus), 020-7287 6622;
fax 7287 1733

◪ It's "hard to find, but worth it", say fans of this "true purist's Japanese restaurant" in an alley near Piccadilly Circus with an "affordable" menu "a cut above others in the same price range"; if a handful claim it's "overrated" with "average" victuals, the fact it's "usually filled with Japanese faces" reassures most.

Yo! Sushi ⍓   15 | 14 | 13 | £22

Whiteleys, Unit 218, 151 Queensway, W2 (Bayswater),
020-7727 9392; fax 7727 9390
Unit R07, Paddington Station, W2 (Paddington), 020-7706 9550
Selfridges, 400 Oxford St., W1 (Bond St.), 020-7318 3944;
fax 7318 3885
52 Poland St., W1 (Oxford Circus), 020-7287 0443; fax 7439 3660
11-13 Bayley St., WC1 (Tottenham Court Rd.), 020-7636 0076;
fax 7439 3663
Fulham Broadway Ctr., 1st fl., Fulham Rd., SW6
(Fulham Broadway), 020-7385 6077; fax 7385 9584
Harvey Nichols, 5th fl., Knightsbridge, SW1 (Knightsbridge),
020-7235 5000; fax 7318 3885
County Hall, Unit 3B, Belvedere Rd., SE1 (Westminster),
020-7928 8871; fax 7928 5619
Unit 2, N1 Ctr., 39 Parkfield St., N1 (Angel), 020-7359 3502
95 Farringdon Rd., EC1 (Farringdon), 020-7841 0785; fax 7841 0798
www.yosushi.com
Additional locations throughout London

◪ "What a kick – tons of people are intently absorbed in pulling the right" "little boat of sushi" "off the rack" as it "whizzes around the conveyor belts" at this "kitschy", "funky" outfit, with the added amusement of a "hilarious, talking robot" as a "drinks dispenser"; whilst some snipe it's "not bad for a chain, but it's not a tip-top" raw fish bar either, even they concede "can't beat it for convenience."

ZAFFERANO   25   19   22   £53

*15 Lowndes St., SW1 (Knightsbridge), 020-7235 5800;
fax 7235 1971*

◪ "Each time is special" laud loyalists who "fight for
a reservation" at this "gourmet's delight" with a "lofty
reputation" in Belgravia where chef Andrew Needham
delivers "heavenly *Italiano*" "food to ooh and aah about",
boosted by an "impressive wine list" and "attentive service";
the "intimate" setting is "well-suited for a dinner where
you'd like to chat and it can even be a bit romantic"; but
quibblers believe it's "coasting" and say the "tight quarters"
make you "feel like a sardine when it's busy"; N.B. at press
time, plans were underway to add an adjoining deli and bar.

Zaika   24   23   20   £47

*1 Kensington High St., W8 (High St. Kensington), 020-7795 6533;
fax 7937 8854; www.zaika-restaurant.co.uk*

◪ "Not your typical Indian", Claudio Pulze and Raj Sharma's
"plush", yet "comfortable" Kensington venue in a "massive
former bank" offers "attentive service" along with a small
menu of "perfectly matched, complex tastes" – a "melt-in-
your-mouth mixture of subtlety and fire"; but a handful
harrumph it's "much ado about nothing", insisting it's "lost
its pizzazz"; N.B. the post-*Survey* departure of chef Vineet
Bhatia may impact the above Food rating.

Zamoyski   –   –   –   E

85 Fleet Rd., NW3 (Belsize Park), 020-7794 4792

Spot on "for a cold winter's night", this "family-style" Belsize
Park venue enters its third decade earning appreciation
for "big portions" of "excellent" Polish fare that's "lighter
than might be expected", plus a wide "selection of vodka";
P.S. there's live folk singing on weekend nights.

Zen Central ◐   23   16   20   £43

*20 Queen St., W1 (Green Park), 020-7629 8089; fax 7493 6181;
www.zencentralrestaurant.com*

◪ With "innovative", "upper-class [multiregional] fare"
and "pleasant service", this well-established Mayfair
Mandarin is a "wonderful find", and even if some feel the
"decor needs an upgrade" and the menu is "pricey for
what it is", followers feel this "first-tier" Zen outpost is
"part of the A-team for London Chinese" venues.

ZeNW3 ◐   19   15   18   £35

*83-84 Hampstead High St., NW3 (Hampstead), 020-7794 7863;
fax 7794 6956; www.zenw3.com*

◪ To acolytes, this Hampstead Zen outpost is an "oasis in
a culinary desert", proffering an "extensive, innovative
menu" of "light Chinese food" (plus some Japanese dishes
"if the whim takes you") and "friendly staff who are nice to
children"; but bashers beg to differ, suggesting it's "well
past its sell-by date" and "badly needs a lick of paint."

Zetter Restaurant & Rooms   – | – | – | E |

The Zetter, 86-88 Clerkenwell Rd., EC1 (Farringdon),
020-7324 4455; fax 7324 4445; www.thezetter.com

Formerly a warehouse, this five-story Clerkenwell hotel boasts 59 bedrooms, plus a spacious Italian restaurant with an attractive curved marble bar and two private rooms; gutsy Italian cooking from Megan Jones (most recently at Moro) is supported by a varied wine list (including an eclectic selection by the glass) and bottled spring water drawn from an old borehole beneath the building; N.B. the name originates from the Zetter football pools family.

Ziani ●   23 | 17 | 22 | £37 |

45 Radnor Walk, SW3 (Sloane Sq.), 020-7351 5297; fax 7244 8387

☑ Expect "elbow-to-elbow seating" at this "tiny, boisterous and busy" Italian trattoria in Chelsea (affiliated with Carpaccio and Como Lario) where "friendly" staff "treat you like family" ("so eat, eat!") and the "traditional", "reliable" fare is "amazingly cheap for the quality"; but the "cramped shoebox" setting is too "hectic" for a few who also feel "rushed out the door."

Zilli Fish ●▣   20 | 15 | 17 | £33 |

36-40 Brewer St., W1 (Piccadilly Circus), 020-7734 8649
8-18 Wild St., WC2 (Covent Garden/Holborn),
020-7240 0011
www.zillialdo.com

☑ Yes, "it can get packed" with "media trendies" at celeb chef Aldo Zilli's "cosy, bustling" Soho Italian and Covent Garden sib (which also boasts a wood-burning pizza oven) where "the fish is delish" and "staff greet you with a smile" ("they love people who enjoy their food here"); but a vocal minority maintain the "menu could be a bit more interesting."

Zimzun   ▽ 16 | 20 | 19 | £20 |

Retail Ctr., Fulham Rd., SW6 (Fulham Broadway), 020-7385 4555;
fax 7386 8555; www.zimzun.co.uk

■ "It's easy to roll home" from this "fun, stylish" Thai venue housed in the first floor of a new shopping centre above Fulham Broadway underground station; the "large square" communal "tables give the restaurant a very Asian feel" and it's decorated "with little touches you don't expect", plus the "fast meals" are "interesting" and "affordable" (there's even a set lunch for under £6).

Zinc Bar & Grill   15 | 16 | 14 | £28 |

11 Jerdan Pl., SW6 (Fulham Broadway), 020-7386 2250;
fax 7386 2260
21 Heddon St., W1 (Oxford Circus/Piccadilly Circus),
020-7255 8899; fax 7255 8888 ▣
www.conran.com

☑ There are "no pretensions" at this "relaxed" Conran Group eatery off Regent Street where a "simple" menu of

Modern British–Euro bistro fare makes it "a reasonable option" for "a quick bite after shopping" or "meeting up with old friends"; still, the less-convinced snipe "service can be spotty" and "food can vary"; P.S. the "smart", younger Fulham branch is especially "good if you want to sit outside in summer" and sip "sparkling drinks."

Zizzi   15 15 14 £20

231 Chiswick High Rd., W4 (Chiswick), 020-874 7940 ◗
110-116 Wigmore St., W1 (Bond St.), 020-7935 2336 ◗
35-38 Paddington St., W1 (Baker St.), 020-7224 1450 ◗
33-41 Charlotte St., W1 (Goodge St.), 020-7436 9440 ◗
73-75 The Strand, WC2 (Charing Cross), 020-7240 1717;
fax 7379 9753 ◗
20 Bow St., WC2 (Holborn), 020-7836 6101
35-37 Battersea, SW11 (Clapham South),
020-7924 7311 ◖
194-196 Earl's Court Rd., SW5 (Earl's Court),
020-7370 1999 ◗
87 Allitsen Rd., NW8 (St. John's Wood), 020-7722 7296
1-3 Hampstead Ln., N6 (Highgate), 020-8347 0090 ◗
Additional locations throughout London

◪ A "steady-Eddy", this "family-orientated", "yummier than average chain" "never fails to deliver good" Modern Italian "fare at reasonable prices"; the "cosy atmosphere is accented by wood-burning ovens", resulting in "crispy pizzas with delicious toppings" that "satisfy even the hungriest" – you can't help but "leave with a warm feeling"; still, a handful feel it's "starting to lack flavour and flair" and lament "nonexistent service."

Zucca   19 17 17 £29

188 Westbourne Grove, W11 (Notting Hill Gate), 020-7727 0060;
fax 7727 0069

◪ For "a quiet hideaway" with "simple", "solid" Modern Italian cooking and "some interesting dishes", fans zero in on this "fashionably dark", "cosy" Notting Hill trattoria with "friendly service" that makes "you feel like you've found some place unique"; nevertheless, a handful scoff that "it's nothing to call mama about" and conclude that "service needs to be kicked up a notch"; N.B. takeaway is for pizzas only.

Zuccato   ▽ 12 13 14 £23

O₂ Ctr., 255 Finchley Rd., NW3 (Finchley Rd.), 020-7431 1799;
fax 7431 7198 ◗
41 Bow Ln., EC4 (Mansion House), 020-7329 6364;
fax 7329 6336 ⊠
www.etruscagroup.co.uk

■ Whether it be "a quick snack before a film" or a stop for "some pasta and a glass of wine around the corner from the office", this "inexpensive" Modern Italian duo in the City and the O₂ Centre on Finchley Road make a "cute", "comfortable", "very reasonable place to eat"; "could do much better" opine an unimpressed minority.

ZUMA
| 24 | 23 | 19 | £55 |

5 Raphael St., SW7 (Knightsbridge), 020-7584 1010;
fax 7584 5005; www.zumarestaurant.com

■ "You can never get a booking for good reason" at this "swanky" Knightsbridge Japanese no-smoking "hot spot" heaving with a "*très* bling-bling crowd" and specialising in "gorgeous food" served by "professional staff"; "sorry Nobu, I found a new lover" sigh admirers, smitten by the "delectable sushi", "ambrosial dishes" from the robata grill and the "eye-candy feast" in the "hip" sake bar; it's "not for the faint-walleted", still, "you feel you've been somewhere special"; N.B. at press time, plans were afoot to open a sib named Roka in Fitzrovia with Japanese BBQ.

subscribe to zagat.com

Indexes

CUISINES
LOCATIONS
SPECIAL FEATURES

CUISINES

African
Mandola (W11)

Argentinean
El Gaucho (multi. loc.)
Gaucho Grill (multi. loc.)

Asian
Asia de Cuba (WC2)
Cicada (EC1)
dim t (N6)
e&o (W11)
east@west (WC2)
Eight Over Eight (SW3)
Great Eastern (EC2)
Jim Thompson's (multi. loc.)
L'Etranger (SW7)
Singapura (multi. loc.)
Taman gang (W1)
Tampopo (SW10)
Tiger Lil's (multi. loc.)
Uli (W11)
Yellow River (N1)

Australian
Osia (SW1)

Belgian
Abbaye (EC1)
Belgo Centraal (multi. loc.)
Bierodrome (multi. loc.)

Brazilian
Rodizio Rico (W2)

British (Modern)
Adam St. (WC2)
Admiralty (WC2)
Alastair Little (W1)
Anchor & Hope (SE1)
Anglesea Arms (W6)
Annie's (multi. loc.)
Approach Tavern (E2)
Atlantic B&G (W1)
Axis (WC2)
Balans (multi. loc.)
Balham Kitchen (SW12)
Bank Aldwych (WC2)
Bankside (SE1)
Bank West./Zander (SW1)
Barnsbury (N1)

Belvedere (W8)
Brackenbury (W6)
Bradley's (NW3)
Brinkley's (SW10)
Browns (multi. loc.)
Builders Arms (SW3)
Bush Bar & Grill (W12)
Cafe at Sotheby's (W1)
Chez Bruce (SW17)
Clarke's (W8)
Collection (SW3)
Cow Din. Rm. (W2)
Dan's (SW3)
Dibbens (EC1)
Duke of Cambridge (N1)
Duke of Clarence (SW5)
1802 (E14)
Engineer (NW1)
ffiona's (W8)
Fifth Floor (SW1)
First Floor (W11)
Fishmarket (EC2)
Fish Shop/St. John (EC1)
Frederick's (N1)
Frontline (W2)
Glaister's Bar (SW10)
Glasshouse (Kew)
Globe (NW3)
Gravetye Manor (W. Sus)
Groucho Club (W1)
Hartwell House (Bucks)
Havelock Tavern (W14)
Home House (W1)
Hush (W1)
Ifield (SW10)
Ivy, The (WC2)
Joe's (SW3)
Joe's Rest. (SW1)
Julie's (W11)
Just Gladwins (EC3)
Kensington Place (W8)
Lansdowne (NW1)
Launceston Pl. (W8)
Le Caprice (SW1)
Le Deuxieme (WC2)
Palmerston (SE22)
People's Palace (SE1)
Polygon B&G (SW4)
Portrait (WC2)
Prince Bonaparte (W2)

Prism (EC3)
Pug (W4)
Ransome's Dock (SW11)
Redmonds (SW14)
Restaurant 7 (SE1)
Rhodes 24 (EC2)
Richard Corrigan (W1)
Rowley's (SW1)
R.S.J. (SE1)
Savoy Grill (WC2)
Sir Charles Napier (Oxon)
Smiths/Top Floor (EC1)
Snows on Green (W6)
Soho House (W1)
Sonny's (SW13)
St. John (EC1)
St. John Bread/Wine (E1)
Tate Gallery (SW1)
Terminus (EC2)
Terrace, The (W8)
Tom's Deli (W11)
Troubadour (SW5)
Tuttons Brass. (WC2)
Union Cafe (W1)
Vale (W9)
Villandry (W1)
Vine (NW5)
Vineyard/Stock. (Berks)
Wheeler's (SW1)
Wilton's (SW1)
Zinc B&G (W1)

British (Traditional)
Abbeville (SW4)
Annabel's (W1)
Bentley's (W1)
Boisdale (multi. loc.)
Brian Turner (W1)
Browns (multi. loc.)
Butlers Wharf (SE1)
Chelsea Bun (multi. loc.)
Cow Din. Rm. (W2)
Fish! (SE1)
Fish Shop/St. John (EC1)
Fortnum's Fountain (W1)
French Horn (Berks)
Goring Din. Rm. (SW1)
Green's (SW1)
Grenadier (SW1)
Grill Room (W1)
Grumbles (SW1)
Guinea Grill (W1)
Inn The Park (SW1)

Kew Grill (Kew)
Langan's Bistro (W1)
Langan's Brass. (W1)
Maggie Jones's (W8)
Mark's Club (W1)
Notting Grill (W11)
Odin's (W1)
Porters (WC2)
Quality Chop (EC1)
Rib Room/Oyster (SW1)
Richoux (multi. loc.)
Ritz (W1)
Rivington Grill (EC2)
Rowley's (SW1)
Rules (WC2)
Scotts (W1)
Shepherd's (SW1)
Simpson's (WC2)
Smiths/Dining Rm. (EC1)
White Swan (EC4)
Wilton's (SW1)
Ye Olde Cheshire (EC4)

Burmese
Mandalay (W2)

Chinese
(* dim sum specialist)
Chuen Cheng Ku (W1)*
ECapital (W1)
Four Seasons Chin. (W2)
Fung Shing (WC2)
Golden Dragon (W1)*
Good Earth (multi. loc.)
Gung-Ho (NW6)
Hakkasan (W1)*
Harbour City (W1)*
Hunan (SW1)
Imperial China (WC2)
Imperial City (EC3)
Jade Garden (W1)*
Joy King Lau (WC2)*
Kai Mayfair (W1)
Lee Ho Fook (W1)*
Mandarin Kitchen (W2)
Mao Tai (multi. loc.)
Memories of China (multi. loc.)
Mr. Chow (SW1)
Mr. Kong (WC2)
New Culture Rev. (multi. loc.)
New World (W1)*
Opera (NW3)*
Oriental (W1)*
Poons (multi. loc.)

Princess Garden (W1)
Royal China (multi. loc.)*
Singapore Garden (NW6)
Song Que Café (E2)
Wong Kei (W1)
Yauatcha (W1)*
Zen Central (W1)
ZeNW3 (NW3)

Chophouse
Black & Blue (multi. loc.)
Butlers Wharf (SE1)
Christopher's (WC2)
El Gaucho (multi. loc.)
Gaucho Grill (multi. loc.)
Kew Grill (Kew)
Notting Grill (W11)
Pope's Eye (multi. loc.)
Quality Chop (EC1)
Rib Room/Oyster (SW1)
Rules (WC2)
Smiths/Top Floor (EC1)
Smiths/Dining Rm. (EC1)
Smollensky's (multi. loc.)
Sophie's Steak (SW10)

Cuban
Asia de Cuba (WC2)

Danish
Lundum's (SW7)

Eclectic
Archipelago (W1)
Aura Kitchen (SW1)
Aurora (EC2)
Axis (WC2)
Bibendum Oyster (SW3)
Bistrot 190 (SW7)
Blakes (SW7)
Blue Print (SE1)
Books for Cooks (W11)
Boxwood Café (SW1)
Brinkley's (SW10)
Cafe Med (multi. loc.)
Cantina Vinopolis (SE1)
Canyon (Richmond)
Collection (SW3)
Ebury Wine Bar (SW1)
Electric Brasserie (W11)
Engineer (NW1)
Enterprise (SW3)
Fifth Floor Cafe (SW1)
First Floor (W11)

Food for Thought (WC2)
Giraffe (multi. loc.)
Hoxton Apprentice (N1)
Ifield (SW10)
Kanteen/K-West (W14)
Kettners (W1)
Lanes (W1)
Lanesborough (SW1)
Lansdowne (NW1)
Light House (SW19)
Lonsdale, The (W11)
Mosimann's (SW1)
Motcombs (SW1)
MVH (SW13)
Naked Turtle (SW14)
Oxo Tower (SE1)
Pomegranates (SW1)
Providores/Tapa (W1)
Randall & Aubin (W1)
Ransome's Dock (SW11)
Raoul's (W9)
Spoon+ (W1)
Sugar Club (W1)
Tenth Rest. (W8)
Terminus (EC2)
Tiger Lil's (multi. loc.)
Troubadour (SW5)
Turnmills (EC1)
Union Cafe (W1)
Villandry (W1)
Vingt-Quatre (SW10)
Wapping Food (E1)
Westbourne (W2)

Fish 'n' Chips
Fish! (SE1)
Fish Shop/St. John (EC1)
Geales Fish (W8)
Livebait (multi. loc.)
Nautilus Fish (NW6)
North Sea (WC1)
Rudland Stubbs (EC1)
Scotts (W1)
Seashell (NW1)
Sweetings (EC4)
Two Brothers Fish (N3)

French (Bistro)
Bibendum Oyster (SW3)
Bistrot 190 (SW7)
Café Boheme (W1)
Café des Amis (WC2)
Cafe Rouge (multi. loc.)

Chez Gérard (multi. loc.)
French House (W1)
Glaister's Bar (SW10)
Grumbles (SW1)
Incognico (WC2)
La Bouchée (SW7)
Langan's Bistro (W1)
La Poule au Pot (SW1)
Le Boudin Blanc (W1)
Le Petit Max (SW11)
L'Escargot (W1)
Monsieur Max (Hampton Hill)
Pat. Valerie (multi. loc.)
Racine (SW3)
Simply Nico (SW1)
Thierry's (SW3)
Truc Vert (W1)

French (Brasserie)
Brasserie Roux (SW1)
Brass. St. Quentin (SW3)
Cheyne Walk (SW3)
Chez Gérard (multi. loc.)
La Brasserie (SW3)
Langan's Brass. (W1)
La Trouvaille (N1)
Le Palais du Jardin (WC2)
Malmaison Hotel Bar (EC1)
Quaglino's (SW1)

French (Classic)
Almeida (N1)
Annabel's (W1)
Aubergine (SW10)
Belair House (SE21)
Brasserie Roux (SW1)
Brass. St. Quentin (SW3)
Chez Bruce (SW17)
Chez Gérard (multi. loc.)
Foliage (SW1)
La Bouchée (SW7)
La Brasserie (SW3)
Langan's Brass. (W1)
La Poule au Pot (SW1)
La Trouvaille (multi. loc.)
L'Aventure (NW8)
Le Boudin Blanc (W1)
Le Café du Marché (EC1)
Le Colombier (SW3)
Le Gavroche (W1)
Le Palais du Jardin (WC2)
Le Petit Max (SW11)
Le Pont de la Tour (SE1)

L'Estaminet (WC2)
Les Trois Garcons (E1)
Le Suquet (SW3)
Lobster Pot (SE11)
Lou Pescadou (SW5)
Mirabelle (W1)
Mon Plaisir (WC2)
Monsieur Max (Hampton Hill)
Odin's (W1)
Oslo Court (NW8)
Poissonnerie/l'Ave. (SW3)
Racine (SW3)
Ritz (W1)
Stratford's (W8)
Terrace (W1)
Thierry's (SW3)
Vineyard/Stock. (Berks)
Waterside Inn (Berks)
Wheeler's (W1)
Windows on World (W1)

French (New)
Aubergine (SW10)
Belvedere (W8)
Berkeley Sq. Café (W1)
Bibendum (SW3)
Bleeding Heart (EC1)
Café des Amis (WC2)
Capital Rest. (SW3)
Cellar Gascon (EC1)
Club Gascon (EC1)
Coq d'Argent (EC2)
Criterion Grill (W1)
Crivelli's Garden (WC2)
Deca (W1)
1880 (SW7)
Fat Duck (Berks)
Foliage (SW1)
Gordon Ramsay/Claridge (W1)
Gordon Ramsay/68 Royal (SW3)
Greenhouse (W1)
Incognico (WC2)
La Trompette (W4)
La Trouvaille (W1)
Le Cercle (SW1)
Le Manoir/Q.S. (Oxon)
Le Mercury (N1)
L'Escargot (W1)
Le Soufflé (W1)
L'Etranger (SW7)
LMNT (E8)
L'Oranger (SW1)
Mon Plaisir (WC2)

Morgan M (N7)
Morton's (W1)
Nathalie (SW3)
Novelli/City (EC4)
Odette's (NW1)
1 Lombard St. (EC3)
One-O-One (SW1)
Orrery (W1)
Patterson's (W1)
Pearl (WC1)
Pétrus (SW1)
Pied à Terre (W1)
Plateau (E14)
Putney Bridge (SW15)
Roussillon (SW1)
Sketch (W1)
Square (W1)
Terrace (W1)
Thyme (SW4)
Tom Aikens (SW3)
Waldo's (Berks)
Waterside Inn (Berks)
Waterway (W9)

Greek
Costas Grill (W8)
Daphne (NW1)
Greek Valley (NW8)
Halepi (multi. loc.)
Lemonia (NW1)
Real Greek (multi. loc.)
Vrisaki (N22)

Hamburgers
Arkansas Cafe (E1)
Big Easy (SW3)
Black & Blue (multi. loc.)
Ed's Easy Diner (multi. loc.)
Gourmet Burger (multi. loc.)
Hard Rock Cafe (W1)
Joe Allen (WC2)
Kettners (W1)
Lucky 7 (W2)
PJ's B&G (multi. loc.)
Planet Hollywood (W1)
Smollensky's (multi. loc.)
Sophie's Steak (SW10)
Sticky Fingers (W8)
T.G.I. Friday's (multi. loc.)
Tootsies (multi. loc.)
Vingt-Quatre (SW10)

Hungarian
Gay Hussar (W1)

Indian
Benares (W1)
Bengal Clipper (SE1)
Bombay Bicycle (SW12)
Bombay Brasserie (SW7)
Cafe Lazeez (multi. loc.)
Cafe Spice (E1)
Chor Bizarre (W1)
Chowki Bar (W1)
Chutney Mary (SW10)
Chutney's (NW1)
Cinnamon Club (SW1)
Deya (W1)
Ginger (W2)
Gopal's of Soho (W1)
Kastoori (SW17)
Khan's (W2)
Khan's/Kensington (SW7)
Lahore Kebab (multi. loc.)
La Porte des Indes (W1)
Ma Goa (multi. loc.)
Malabar (W8)
Malabar Junction (WC1)
Masala Zone (multi. loc.)
Mela (WC2)
Memories of India (multi. loc.)
Mint Leaf (SW1)
Noor Jahan (multi. loc.)
Painted Heron (multi. loc.)
Parsee (N19)
Quilon (SW1)
Rani (N3)
Rasa (multi. loc.)
Rasoi Vineet Bhatia (SW3)
Ravi Shankar (multi. loc.)
Red Fort (W1)
River Spice (E1)
Salloos (SW1)
Sarkhel's (SW18)
Soho Spice (W1)
Star of India (SW5)
Tamarind (W1)
Vama (SW10)
Veeraswamy (W1)
Yatra (W1)
Zaika (W8)

Irish
Richard Corrigan (W1)

Italian
Abbey Rd. Pub (NW8)
A Cena (Twickenham)
Alba (EC1)

Cuisine Index

Al Duca (SW1)
Alloro (W1)
Al San Vincenzo (W2)
Aperitivo (multi. loc.)
Arancia (SE16)
Ark (W8)
Artigiano (NW3)
Ask Pizza (multi. loc.)
Assaggi (W2)
Bertorelli (multi. loc.)
Brunello (SW7)
Buona Sera (multi. loc.)
Cantina del Ponte (SE1)
Caraffini (SW1)
Caravaggio (EC3)
Carluccio's (multi. loc.)
Carpaccio (SW3)
Casale Franco (N1)
Cecconi's (W1)
Cipriani (W1)
Como Lario (SW1)
Daphne's (SW3)
De Cecco (SW6)
Del Buongustaio (SW15)
Diverso (W1)
Eco (SW4)
Edera (W11)
Elistano (SW3)
Emporio Armani (SW3)
Enoteca Turi (SW15)
Essenza (W11)
Floriana (SW3)
Friends (SW10)
Getti (multi. loc.)
Gia (SW3)
Green Olive (W9)
Grissini (SW1)
Harry's Bar (W1)
Il Bordello (E1)
Il Convivio (SW1)
Il Falconiere (SW7)
Isola (SW1)
Kettners (W1)
L'Accento Ital. (W2)
La Famiglia (SW10)
La Fontana (SW1)
Latium (W1)
L'Incontro (SW1)
Little Italy (W1)
Locanda Locatelli (W1)
Locanda Otto. (W8)
Lucio (SW3)
Luigi's (WC2)
Made in Italy (SW3)

Manicomio (SW3)
Mediterraneo (W11)
Metrogusto (N1)
Mimmo d'Ischia (SW1)
Monte's (SW1)
Montpeliano (SW7)
Monza (SW3)
Neal Street (WC2)
Oak (W2)
Oliveto (SW1)
Olivo (SW1)
Orso (WC2)
Osteria Antica (SW11)
Osteria Basilico (W11)
Paolo (W1)
Passione (W1)
Pellicano (SW3)
Pizza Express (multi. loc.)
Pizza Metro (SW11)
Pizza Pomodoro (multi. loc.)
Quadrato (E14)
Quirinale (SW1)
Quod (SW1)
Quo Vadis (W1)
Red Pepper (W9)
Refettorio (EC4)
Riccardo's (SW3)
Riva (SW13)
River Cafe (W6)
Rosmarino (NW8)
Sale e Pepe (SW1)
Salusbury Pub (NW6)
Sambuca (SW1)
San Lorenzo (SW3)
San Lorenzo Fuor. (SW19)
Santa Lucia (SW10)
Santini (SW1)
Sartoria (W1)
Scalini (SW3)
Shumi (SW1)
Signor Sassi (SW1)
Signor Zilli (W1)
Spago (SW7)
Spiga (W1)
Spighetta (W1)
Strada (multi. loc.)
TECA (W1)
Tentazioni (SE1)
Timo (W8)
Toto's (SW3)
Vasco & Piero's (W1)
Verbanella (SW3)
Zafferano (SW1)
Zetter (EC1)

Ziani (SW3)
Zilli Fish (multi. loc.)
Zizzi (multi. loc.)
Zucca (W11)
Zuccato (multi. loc.)

Japanese
Abeno Museum (WC1)
Benihana (multi. loc.)
Cafe Japan (NW11)
City Miyama (EC4)
Defune (W1)
Hi Sushi (multi. loc.)
Ikeda (W1)
Ikkyu (W1)
itsu (multi. loc.)
Jin Kichi (NW3)
Kiku (W1)
Koi (W8)
Kulu Kulu Sushi (multi. loc.)
Matsuri (multi. loc.)
Mitsukoshi (SW1)
Miyama (W1)
Moshi Moshi (multi. loc.)
Nobu (W1)
Noto (EC2)
Sakura (W1)
Satsuma (W1)
Sumosan (W1)
Tatsuso (EC1)
Tokyo Diner (WC2)
Tsunami (SW4)
Ubon (E14)
Wagamama (multi. loc.)
Yo! Sushi (multi. loc.)
Zuma (SW7)

Kosher
Bloom's (NW11)
Reubens (W1)
Six-13 (W1)
Solly's (NW11)

Malaysian
Champor (SE1)
Melati (W1)
Nyonya (W11)
Silks & Spice (multi. loc.)
Singapore Garden (NW6)
Sri Nam (E14)

Mediterranean
Angela Hartnett's (W1)
Atlantic B&G (W1)
Cafe Med (multi. loc.)

Camden Brasserie (NW1)
Cantaloupe (EC2)
Cantina del Ponte (SE1)
Cantina Vinopolis (SE1)
Citrus (W1)
Crivelli's Garden (WC2)
Cru (N1)
Eagle (EC1)
Fifteen (N1)
Fifth Floor Cafe (SW1)
Levant (W1)
Little Bay (multi. loc.)
L'Oranger (SW1)
Maggiores (WC2)
Manor (W11)
Monte's (SW1)
Moro (EC1)
Nicole's (W1)
Oxo Tower Brass. (SE1)
Pescatori (W1)
Rocket (multi. loc.)

Mexican
Cactus Blue (SW3)
Cafe Pacifico (WC2)
Canyon (Richmond)
La Perla (multi. loc.)
Santa Fe (N1)
Texas Embassy (SW1)

Middle Eastern
Al Bustan (SW7)
Al Hamra (W1)
Alounak (multi. loc.)
Al Sultan (W1)
Al Waha (W2)
Aziz (SW6)
Beiteddine (SW1)
Chintamani (SW1)
Dish Dash (SW12)
Efes Kebab House (W1)
Fairuz (multi. loc.)
Fakhreldine (multi. loc.)
Frontline (W2)
Gallipoli (N1)
Ishbilia (SW1)
Iznik (N5)
Kandoo (W2)
Levant (W1)
Levantine (W2)
Maroush (multi. loc.)
Noura (SW1)
Ozer (W1)

Pasha (N1)
Sofra (multi. loc.)
Solly's (NW11)
Tas (SE1)

Modern European
Abingdon, The (W8)
Admiral Codrington (SW3)
Allium (SW1)
Andrew Edmunds (W1)
Angela Hartnett's (W1)
Aurora (EC2)
Avenue (SW1)
Babylon (W8)
Banquette (WC2)
Bistrot 190 (SW7)
Blandford St. (W1)
Bluebird (SW3)
Blue Print (SE1)
Circus (W1)
Clerkenwell (EC1)
Criterion Grill (W1)
Don (EC4)
Draper's Arms (N1)
Drones (multi. loc.)
Ebury Din. Rm. (SW1)
1880 (SW7)
Embassy (W1)
Enterprise (SW3)
Exmouth Grill (EC1)
Foliage (SW1)
Gate (W6)
George (W1)
Indigo (WC2)
Ivy, The (WC2)
J. Sheekey (WC2)
Just St. James's (SW1)
Le Cafe du Jardin (WC2)
Le Caprice (SW1)
Le Palais du Jardin (WC2)
Lola's (N1)
Mash (W1)
Nicole's (W1)
noble rot. (W1)
Notting Hill Brass. (W11)
Novelli/City (EC4)
number 10 (W10)
Odette's (NW1)
1 Lombard Brass. (EC3)
Oriel (SW1)
People's Palace (SE1)
Red Rm./Waterstones (W1)
Royal Exchange (EC3)

Salisbury Tavern (SW6)
Seraphin/Wine (N1)
Six-13 (W1)
Sugar Reef (W1)
Tenth Rest. (W8)
202 (W11)
Vine (NW5)
Wapping Food (E1)
Waterloo Fire (SE1)
Wells (NW3)
Westbourne (W2)
Wolseley (W1)
Zinc B&G (multi. loc.)

Moroccan
Gallipoli (N1)
Momo (W1)
Original Tagine (W1)
Pasha (SW7)

North African
Aziz (SW6)
Levant (W1)
Levantine (W2)
Momo (W1)
Moro (EC1)
Souk (WC2)

North American
Arkansas Cafe (E1)
Ashbells (W11)
Banquette (WC2)
Big Easy (SW3)
Bodeans (multi. loc.)
Chelsea Bun (multi. loc.)
Christopher's (WC2)
Hard Rock Cafe (W1)
Harlem (W2)
Joe Allen (WC2)
Lucky 7 (W2)
PJ's B&G (multi. loc.)
Planet Hollywood (W1)
Rainforest Cafe (W1)
Reubens (W1)
Smollensky's (multi. loc.)
Sophie's Steak (SW10)
Sticky Fingers (W8)
T.G.I. Friday's (multi. loc.)
Tootsies (multi. loc.)

Pacific Rim
Blakes (SW7)
Cactus Blue (SW3)

I-Thai (W2)
Mju (SW1)
Oxo Tower Brass. (SE1)
Pacific Oriental (EC2)
Polygon B&G (SW4)
Sugar Club (W1)
Yellow River (N1)

Peruvian
Fina Estampa (SE1)

Pizza
Ask Pizza (multi. loc.)
Buona Sera (SW11)
Cantina del Ponte (SE1)
Casale Franco (N1)
Eco (multi. loc.)
Friends (SW10)
Kettners (W1)
La Porchetta Pizza (multi. loc.)
Made in Italy (SW3)
Oak (W2)
Oliveto (SW1)
Orso (WC2)
Pizza Express (multi. loc.)
Pizza Metro (SW11)
Pizza on Park (SW1)
Pizza Pomodoro (multi. loc.)
Red Pepper (W9)
Rocket (multi. loc.)
Spago (SW7)
Spiga (W1)
Spighetta (W1)
Strada (multi. loc.)
Zizzi (multi. loc.)
Zucca (W11)

Polish
Baltic (SE1)
Daquise (SW7)
Wòdka (W8)
Zamoyski (NW3)

Russian
Potemkin (EC1)

Scottish
Boisdale (multi. loc.)

Seafood
Belgo Centraal (multi. loc.)
Bentley's (W1)
Bibendum Oyster (SW3)
Bluebird (SW3)

Cafe Fish (W1)
Chamberlain's (EC3)
Fish! (SE1)
Fish Hoek (W4)
Fishmarket (EC2)
Fish Shop/St. John (EC1)
FishWorks (W4)
Geales Fish (W8)
Green's (SW1)
J. Sheekey (WC2)
Le Pont de la Tour (SE1)
Le Suquet (SW3)
Livebait (multi. loc.)
Lobster Pot (SE11)
Lou Pescadou (SW5)
Manzi's (WC2)
One-O-One (SW1)
Pescatori (W1)
Poissonnerie/l'Ave. (SW3)
Randall & Aubin (multi. loc.)
Rasa (W1)
Rudland Stubbs (EC1)
Scotts (W1)
Seashell (NW1)
Stratford's (W8)
Sweetings (EC4)
Two Brothers Fish (N3)
Wheeler's (SW1)
Wilton's (SW1)
Zilli Fish (multi. loc.)

Small Plates
Aperitivo (multi. loc.)
Cellar Gascon (EC1)
Chintamani (SW1)
Club Gascon (EC1)
east@west (WC2)
El Blason (SW3)
Fina Estampa (SE1)
Fino (W1)
Hunan (SW1)
La Rueda (multi. loc.)
Le Cercle (SW1)
Lonsdale, The (W11)
Meson Don Felipe (SE1)
Moro (EC1)
Providores/Tapa (W1)
Shumi (SW1)
Thyme (SW4)

South African
Fish Hoek (W4)

South American
Armadillo (E8)
Cactus Blue (SW3)
1492 (SW6)
La Piragua (N1)

Spanish
Cambio de Tercio (SW5)
Cigala (WC1)
El Blason (SW3)
El Pirata (W1)
Eyre Brothers (EC2)
Fino (W1)
Galicia (W10)
La Rueda (multi. loc.)
Lomo (SW10)
Meson Don Felipe (SE1)
Moro (EC1)
Rebato's (SW8)

Swedish
Garbo's (W1)
Lundum's (SW7)

Thai
Bangkok (SW7)
Ben's Thai (W9)
Blue Elephant (SW6)
Busaba Eathai (multi. loc.)
Busabong (SW10)
Chiang Mai (W1)
Churchill Arms (W8)
Crazy Bear (W1)
Esarn Kheaw (W12)
I-Thai (W2)
Mango Tree (SW1)

Nahm (SW1)
Patara (multi. loc.)
Pepper Tree (multi. loc.)
Silks & Spice (multi. loc.)
Sri Nam (E14)
Sri Siam City (EC2)
Sri Thai Soho (W1)
Sugar Hut (SW6)
Thai on the River (SW10)
Thai Pavilion (multi. loc.)
Thai Square (multi. loc.)
Zimzun (SW6)

Vegetarian
Blah! Blah! Blah! (W12)
Chutney's (NW1)
Eat & Two Veg (W1)
Food for Thought (WC2)
Gate (W6)
itsu (W1)
Kastoori (SW17)
Lanesborough (SW1)
Mildreds (W1)
Pied à Terre (W1)
Rani (N3)
Rasa (multi. loc.)
Ravi Shankar (multi. loc.)
Roussillon (SW1)
Sri Nam (E14)

Vietnamese
Bam-Bou (W1)
Nam Long-Le Shaker (SW5)
Saigon (W1)
Song Que Café (E2)
Viet Hoa (E2)

LOCATIONS

CENTRAL LONDON

Belgravia
Beiteddine
Boxwood Café
Drones
Ebury Wine Bar
Grenadier
Grissini
Il Convivio
Ishbilia
Lanesborough
Memories of China
Mimmo d'Ischia
Motcombs
Nahm
Oliveto
One-O-One
Pat. Valerie
Pétrus
Pizza on Park
Rib Room/Oyster
Salloos
Santini
Zafferano

Bloomsbury/Fitzrovia
Abeno Museum
Archipelago
Ask Pizza
Bam-Bou
Bertorelli
Busaba Eathai
Carluccio's
Chez Gérard
Cigala
Crazy Bear
Efes Kebab House
Fino
Hakkasan
Ikkyu
Lahore Kebab
La Perla
Latium
Malabar Junction
Mash
North Sea
Paolo
Passione
Pescatori

Pied à Terre
Poons
Rasa
Spoon+
Villandry
Wagamama
Yo! Sushi
Zizzi

Chinatown
Chuen Cheng Ku
ECapital
Fung Shing
Golden Dragon
Harbour City
Imperial China
Jade Garden
Joy King Lau
Lee Ho Fook
Manzi's
Mr. Kong
New World
Poons
Tokyo Diner
Wong Kei

Covent Garden/Holborn
Adam St.
Admiralty
Asia de Cuba
Axis
Bank Aldwych
Banquette
Belgo Centraal
Bertorelli
Bierodrome
Bleeding Heart
Browns
Café des Amis
Cafe Pacifico
Cafe Rouge
Chez Gérard
Christopher's
east@west
Food for Thought
Gaucho Grill
Indigo
Ivy, The
Joe Allen

J. Sheekey
Kulu Kulu Sushi
La Perla
La Porchetta Pizza
Le Cafe du Jardin
Le Deuxieme
Le Palais du Jardin
L'Estaminet
Livebait
Luigi's
Maggiores
Matsuri
Mon Plaisir
Neal Street
New Culture Rev.
Orso
Pat. Valerie
Pearl
Pizza Express
PJ's B&G
Poons
Porters
Rules
Savoy Grill
Simpson's
Smollensky's
Sofra
Strada
T.G.I. Friday's
Tuttons Brass.
Wagamama
Zilli Fish
Zizzi

Knightsbridge
Brass. St. Quentin
Cafe Rouge
Capital Rest.
Emporio Armani
Fifth Floor
Fifth Floor Cafe
Floriana
Foliage
Good Earth
Isola
Joe's Rest.
Maroush
Mju
Monte's
Montpeliano
Monza
Mosimann's
Mr. Chow

Patara
Pat. Valerie
Pizza Express
Pizza Pomodoro
Racine
Richoux
Sale e Pepe
San Lorenzo
Signor Sassi
Verbanella
Wagamama
Yo! Sushi
Zuma

Marylebone
Black & Blue
Blandford St.
Carluccio's
Chutney's
Defune
Deya
Eat & Two Veg
Fairuz
Garbo's
Getti
Giraffe
Home House
Jim Thompson's
Kandoo
Langan's Bistro
La Porte des Indes
La Rueda
Levant
Locanda Locatelli
Mandalay
Maroush
Momo
Odin's
Original Tagine
Orrery
Ozer
Pat. Valerie
Providores/Tapa
Ravi Shankar
Reubens
Royal China
Seashell
Six-13
Sofra
Spighetta
Strada
Tootsies
Union Cafe

Location Index

Tower Bridge/Wapping
Arancia
Bengal Clipper
Blue Print
Browns
Butlers Wharf
Cantina del Ponte
Champor
Il Bordello
Le Pont de la Tour
River Spice
Smollensky's
Tentazioni

Waterloo/Southwark/Kennington
Anchor & Hope
Chez Gérard
Livebait
Lobster Pot
Meson Don Felipe
Painted Heron
People's Palace
Rebato's
R.S.J.
Tas
Thai Pavilion
Waterloo Fire

NORTH/NORTH WEST LONDON

Camden Town/Kentish Town/Primrose Hill
Aperitivo
Belgo Centraal
Camden Brasserie
Daphne
Engineer
Lansdowne
Lemonia
New Culture Rev.
Odette's
Vine
Wagamama

Gung-Ho
Halepi
Hi Sushi
Jin Kichi
Little Bay
Nautilus Fish
Opera
Salusbury Pub
Singapore Garden
Tootsies
Wells
Zamoyski
ZeNW3

Golders Green/Finchley
Bloom's
Cafe Japan
Ed's Easy Diner
Jim Thompson's
Lahore Kebab
Rani
Solly's
Two Brothers Fish
Zuccato

Highgate/Muswell Hill/Tufnell Park
dim t
Giraffe
Parsee
Vrisaki
Zizzi

Islington
Almeida
Barnsbury
Bierodrome
Browns
Cafe Med
Carluccio's
Casale Franco
Draper's Arms
Duke of Cambridge
Frederick's
Gallipoli
Giraffe
Iznik
La Piragua

Hampstead/Kilburn/Swiss Cottage
Artigiano
Ask Pizza
Black & Blue
Bradley's
Gaucho Grill
Giraffe
Globe
Good Earth
Gourmet Burger

South Kensington
Al Bustan
Ask Pizza
Babylon
Bangkok
Bibendum
Bibendum Oyster
Bistrot 190
Black & Blue
Blakes
Bombay Brasserie
Cactus Blue
Cafe Lazeez
Collection
Daquise
Duke of Clarence
1880
El Gaucho
Gia
Il Falconiere
Joe's
Khan's/Kensington
Kulu Kulu Sushi
La Bouchée
La Brasserie

L'Etranger
Lucio
Lundum's
Memories of India
Noor Jahan
Pasha
Patara
Spago
Star of India
Tootsies

Wandsworth/Balham/ Wimbledon
Balham Kitchen
Chez Bruce
Dish Dash
Jim Thompson's
Kastoori
Light House
Pepper Tree
San Lorenzo Fuor.
Sarkhel's
Strada
Tootsies

WEST LONDON

Bayswater
Alounak
Al San Vincenzo
Al Waha
Fairuz
Fakhreldine
Four Seasons Chin.
Ginger
Gourmet Burger
Halepi
I-Thai
Khan's
L'Accento Ital.
Mandarin Kitchen
Mandola
Poons
Rodizio Rico
Royal China
T.G.I. Friday's
Tiger Lil's
Yo! Sushi

Chiswick
Annie's
Ask Pizza

Cafe Med
Cafe Rouge
Fish Hoek
FishWorks
Giraffe
Gourmet Burger
La Trompette
Monsieur Max
Pug
Silks & Spice
Tootsies

Hammersmith
Carluccio's
Gate
River Cafe
Smollensky's
Tootsies

Kensington
Abingdon, The
Ark
Ask Pizza
Balans
Black & Blue
Brunello

Location Index

Churchill Arms
Clarke's
Edera
ffiona's
Giraffe
Kensington Place
Koi
Launceston Pl.
Locanda Otto.
Maggie Jones's
Memories of China
Pat. Valerie
Pizza Express
Sticky Fingers
Stratford's
Tenth Rest.
Terrace, The
Timo
Wagamama
Wòdka
Zaika

Lonsdale, The
Lucky 7
Malabar
Manor
Mediterraneo
New Culture Rev.
Noor Jahan
Notting Grill
Notting Hill Brass.
number 10
Nyonya
Oak
Osteria Basilico
Pizza Express
Prince Bonaparte
Tom's Deli
Tootsies
202
Uli
Westbourne
Zucca

Notting Hill/Holland Park

Ashbells
Ask Pizza
Assaggi
Belvedere
Books for Cooks
Cafe Med
Cafe Rouge
Costas Grill
Cow Din. Rm.
e&o
Electric Brasserie
Essenza
First Floor
Galicia
Geales Fish
Harlem
Julie's
Ladbroke Arms

Olympia

Alounak
Havelock Tavern
Pope's Eye

Paddington

Frontline
Levantine

Shepherd's Bush

Anglesea Arms
Blah! Blah! Blah!
Brackenbury
Bush Bar & Grill
Cafe Rouge
Esarn Kheaw
Kanteen/K-West
Snows on Green
Zizzi

IN THE COUNTRY

Fat Duck
French Horn
Gravetye Manor
Hartwell House
Le Manoir/Q.S.

Sir Charles Napier
Vineyard/Stock.
Waldo's
Waterside Inn

SPECIAL FEATURES

(Indexes list the best in each category. Multi-location restaurants' features may vary by location.)

All-Day Dining

Al Bustan (SW7)
Aperitivo (multi. loc.)
Ask Pizza (multi. loc.)
Banquette (WC2)
Belgo Centraal (WC2)
Bibendum Oyster (SW3)
Big Easy (SW3)
Black & Blue (multi. loc.)
Browns (multi. loc.)
Busaba Eathai (multi. loc.)
Cafe Lazeez (multi. loc.)
Cafe Rouge (multi. loc.)
Carluccio's (multi. loc.)
Chelsea Bun (SW10)
Chowki Bar (W1)
Chuen Cheng Ku (W1)
Cipriani (W1)
Ed's Easy Diner (multi. loc.)
Efes Kebab House (W1)
El Pirata (W1)
Fifth Floor Cafe (SW1)
Food for Thought (WC2)
Hi Sushi (NW3)
Hoxton Apprentice (N1)
Imperial City (EC3)
Indigo (WC2)
Inn The Park (SW1)
Ishbilia (SW1)
itsu (multi. loc.)
Joe Allen (WC2)
Joe's (SW3)
La Brasserie (SW3)
La Rueda (W1)
Le Cercle (SW1)
Lee Ho Fook (W1)
Le Manoir/Q.S. (Oxon)
Levant (W1)
Lucky 7 (W2)
Mildreds (W1)
New Culture Rev. (multi. loc.)
Noura (SW1)
Oriel (SW1)
Orso (WC2)
Ozer (W1)
Pat. Valerie (multi. loc.)
Pizza Express (multi. loc.)

Pizza on Park (SW1)
PJ's B&G (SW3)
Planet Hollywood (W1)
Porters (WC2)
Portrait (WC2)
Rainforest Cafe (W1)
Randall & Aubin (multi. loc.)
Richoux (multi. loc.)
Royal China (multi. loc.)
Royal Exchange (EC3)
Rules (WC2)
Satsuma (W1)
Seashell (NW1)
Smollensky's (multi. loc.)
Solly's (NW11)
Sophie's Steak (SW10)
Souk (WC2)
Sticky Fingers (W8)
St. John Bread/Wine (E1)
Tas (SE1)
Terrace (W1)
Texas Embassy (SW1)
T.G.I. Friday's (W1)
Tom's Deli (W11)
Tootsies (multi. loc.)
Truc Vert (W1)
Tuttons Brass. (WC2)
Villandry (W1)
Vingt-Quatre (SW10)
Wagamama (multi. loc.)
Wolseley (W1)
Wong Kei (W1)
Yellow River (N1)
Ye Olde Cheshire (EC4)
Yo! Sushi (multi. loc.)
Zinc B&G (multi. loc.)
Zuccato (NW3)

Breakfast

(See also Hotel Dining)
Asia de Cuba (WC2)
Balans (multi. loc.)
Balham Kitchen (SW12)
Bank Aldwych (WC2)
Bank West./Zander (SW1)
Bistrot 190 (SW7)
Bluebird (SW3)

Books for Cooks (W11)
Cafe at Sotheby's (W1)
Café Boheme (W1)
Cafe Rouge (multi. loc.)
Carluccio's (multi. loc.)
Chelsea Bun (multi. loc.)
Cinnamon Club (SW1)
Coq d'Argent (EC2)
Cru (N1)
Eat & Two Veg (W1)
Eco (SW9)
Ed's Easy Diner (multi. loc.)
Electric Brasserie (W11)
Emporio Armani (SW3)
Engineer (NW1)
Fifth Floor Cafe (SW1)
Food for Thought (WC2)
Fortnum's Fountain (W1)
Giraffe (multi. loc.)
Grissini (SW1)
Harlem (W2)
Hartwell House (Bucks)
Inn The Park (SW1)
Joe's (SW3)
Joe's Rest. (SW1)
La Brasserie (SW3)
Little Bay (multi. loc.)
Lucky 7 (W2)
Mash (W1)
1 Lombard Brass. (EC3)
Oriel (SW1)
Pat. Valerie (multi. loc.)
Pizza on Park (SW1)
Portrait (WC2)
Raoul's (W9)
Richoux (multi. loc.)
Royal Exchange (EC3)
Simply Nico (SW1)
Simpson's (WC2)
Sketch (W1)
St. John Bread/Wine (E1)
Tom's Deli (W11)
Tootsies (multi. loc.)
Troubadour (SW5)
Truc Vert (W1)
Tuttons Brass. (WC2)
202 (W11)
Villandry (W1)
Vingt-Quatre (SW10)
Wolseley (W1)

Brunch
Abbeville (SW4)
Abingdon, The (W8)

Admiral Codrington (SW3)
Admiralty (WC2)
Angela Hartnett's (W1)
Annie's (multi. loc.)
Ashbells (W11)
Avenue (SW1)
Aziz (SW6)
Balans (multi. loc.)
Balham Kitchen (SW12)
Bank Aldwych (WC2)
Barnsbury (N1)
Belvedere (W8)
Bistrot 190 (SW7)
Bluebird (SW3)
Blue Elephant (SW6)
Brasserie Roux (SW1)
Browns (multi. loc.)
Bush Bar & Grill (W12)
Butlers Wharf (SE1)
Cactus Blue (SW3)
Canyon (Richmond)
Cecconi's (W1)
Chelsea Bun (multi. loc.)
Christopher's (WC2)
Chutney Mary (SW10)
Clarke's (W8)
Clerkenwell (EC1)
Coq d'Argent (EC2)
Cru (N1)
1802 (E14)
Enterprise (SW3)
Exmouth Grill (EC1)
Fifth Floor Cafe (SW1)
First Floor (W11)
1492 (SW6)
Garbo's (W1)
Giraffe (multi. loc.)
Harlem (W2)
Joe Allen (WC2)
Joe's (SW3)
Joe's Rest. (SW1)
La Brasserie (SW3)
Lanesborough (SW1)
Le Caprice (SW1)
L'Etranger (SW7)
Lucky 7 (W2)
Lundum's (SW7)
Manor (W11)
Mash (W1)
Motcombs (SW1)
Nathalie (SW3)
Nicole's (W1)
Osteria Antica (SW11)

Business Dining

Cheeseboards

Monsieur Max (Hampton Hill)
noble rot. (W1)
Orrery (W1)
Pétrus (SW1)
Pied à Terre (W1)
Plateau (E14)
Putney Bridge (SW15)
Refettorio (EC4)
Richard Corrigan (W1)
Ritz (W1)
Riva (SW13)
River Cafe (W6)
Roussillon (SW1)
Royal Exchange (EC3)
Santini (SW1)
Sartoria (W1)
Savoy Grill (WC2)
Sir Charles Napier (Oxon)
Sketch (W1)
Smiths/Dining Rm. (EC1)
Sonny's (SW13)
Square (W1)
St. John Bread/Wine (E1)
Tom Aikens (SW3)
Vale (W9)
Vineyard/Stock. (Berks)
Waldo's (Berks)
Waterside Inn (Berks)
Waterway (W9)
Windows on World (W1)
Zafferano (SW1)

Child-Friendly

(Besides the normal fast-food
places; * children's menu
available)
Abbeville (SW4)
Abbey Rd. Pub (NW8)
Abingdon, The (W8)
A Cena (Twickenham)*
Al Bustan (SW7)
Al Duca (SW1)
Almeida (N1)
Arkansas Cafe (E1)
Asia de Cuba (WC2)*
Ask Pizza (multi. loc.)
Axis (WC2)*
Babylon (W8)*
Balham Kitchen (SW12)*
Bank Aldwych (WC2)*
Bank West./Zander (SW1)*
Banquette (WC2)
Belair House (SE21)*

Belgo Centraal (multi. loc.)*
Benihana (multi. loc.)*
Bibendum (SW3)*
Big Easy (SW3)*
Bloom's (NW11)*
Bluebird (SW3)*
Blue Elephant (SW6)
Bodeans (W1)*
Boxwood Café (SW1)*
Brasserie Roux (SW1)
Browns (multi. loc.)*
Buona Sera (multi. loc.)*
Cafe Fish (W1)*
Cafe Med (multi. loc.)*
Cafe Pacifico (WC2)*
Cafe Rouge (multi. loc.)*
Cantina del Ponte (SE1)*
Canyon (Richmond)*
Caraffini (SW1)
Carluccio's (multi. loc.)*
Carpaccio (SW3)
Casale Franco (N1)
Champor (SE1)
Chelsea Bun (multi. loc.)*
Chez Bruce (SW17)
Chez Gérard (EC1)
Christopher's (WC2)*
Chuen Cheng Ku (W1)
Churchill Arms (W8)
Cigala (WC1)
Cinnamon Club (SW1)
Circus (W1)
Clerkenwell (EC1)
Crivelli's Garden (WC2)
Daphne's (SW3)
Deca (W1)
Del Buongustaio (SW15)
Dish Dash (SW12)
Draper's Arms (N1)*
Drones (SW1)
Duke of Cambridge (N1)
Duke of Clarence (SW5)
Eagle (EC1)
e&o (W11)
Ebury Din. Rm. (SW1)
ECapital (W1)
Edera (W11)
Ed's Easy Diner (multi. loc.)*
Electric Brasserie (W11)
Elistano (SW3)
Enoteca Turi (SW15)
Exmouth Grill (EC1)
Fifteen (N1)

Special Feature Index

Fifth Floor Cafe (SW1)
Fino (W1)
Fish! (SE1)*
Fish Shop/St. John (EC1)
Fortnum's Fountain (W1)*
Frederick's (N1)*
Giraffe (multi. loc.)*
Gourmet Burger (multi. loc.)*
Grenadier (SW1)
Grill Room (W1)*
Hakkasan (W1)
Hard Rock Cafe (W1)*
Hoxton Apprentice (N1)
Indigo (WC2)*
Inn The Park (SW1)
itsu (multi. loc.)
Jim Thompson's (multi. loc.)*
Joe Allen (WC2)
Joe's Rest. (SW1)
Julie's (W11)*
Just St. James's (SW1)*
Kanteen/K-West (W14)
Kensington Place (W8)*
Kettners (W1)
Kew Grill (Kew)*
La Brasserie (SW3)
La Famiglia (SW10)*
Lanes (W1)*
Lanesborough (SW1)*
La Porchetta Pizza (N1)
La Trompette (W4)*
Le Caprice (SW1)
Le Manoir/Q.S. (Oxon)*
Le Petit Max (SW11)
L'Etranger (SW7)
Livebait (multi. loc.)*
Locanda Locatelli (W1)
Lola's (N1)
Lucky 7 (W2)*
Made in Italy (SW3)
Manicomio (SW3)
Maroush (multi. loc.)
Masala Zone (multi. loc.)*
Mediterraneo (W11)
Mela (WC2)
Mitsukoshi (SW1)
Nathalie (SW3)
New Culture Rev. (multi. loc.)
Nobu (W1)
Noura (SW1)
Oliveto (SW1)
Orso (WC2)
Osia (SW1)

Oxo Tower Brass. (SE1)
Pellicano (SW3)
People's Palace (SE1)*
Pepper Tree (multi. loc.)
Pizza Express (multi. loc.)
Pizza Metro (SW11)
Pizza on Park (SW1)
PJ's B&G (multi. loc.)*
Planet Hollywood (W1)*
Porters (WC2)*
Quadrato (E14)*
Quaglino's (SW1)*
Quality Chop (EC1)
Quilon (SW1)
Quirinale (SW1)
Rainforest Cafe (W1)*
Randall & Aubin (SW10)
Ransome's Dock (SW11)
Raoul's (W9)
Rasa (multi. loc.)
Rasoi Vineet Bhatia (SW3)
Real Greek (EC1)
Redmonds (SW14)*
Red Pepper (W9)
Restaurant 7 (SE1)*
Reubens (W1)*
Riccardo's (SW3)
Richoux (multi. loc.)*
Ritz (W1)*
Riva (SW13)
River Cafe (W6)
Rocket (multi. loc.)*
Rodizio Rico (W2)
Rosmarino (NW8)
Royal China (multi. loc.)
Rules (WC2)
Sale e Pepe (SW1)
Salisbury Tavern (SW6)
San Lorenzo (SW3)
San Lorenzo Fuor. (SW19)
Santa Fe (N1)*
Sarkhel's (SW18)*
Seashell (NW1)*
Sir Charles Napier (Oxon)*
Six-13 (W1)
Smiths/Top Floor (EC1)
Smollensky's (multi. loc.)*
Solly's (NW11)*
Sonny's (SW13)*
Sophie's Steak (SW10)*
Spago (SW7)*
Spiga (W1)
Spighetta (W1)

Sticky Fingers (W8)*
Strada (multi. loc.)*
Tampopo (SW10)*
Tentazioni (SE1)*
Texas Embassy (SW1)*
T.G.I. Friday's (multi. loc.)*
Thierry's (SW3)
Tiger Lil's (multi. loc.)*
Tom's Deli (W11)
Tootsies (multi. loc.)*
Truc Vert (W1)
Tsunami (SW4)
Tuttons Brass. (WC2)*
Two Brothers Fish (N3)*
202 (W11)
Ubon (E14)
Uli (W11)
Villandry (W1)
Vineyard/Stock. (Berks)*
Vingt-Quatre (SW10)
Wagamama (multi. loc.)*
Waterside Inn (Berks)*
Wòdka (W8)
Wolseley (W1)
Yauatcha (W1)
Yellow River (N1)*
Yo! Sushi (multi. loc.)*
Zafferano (SW1)
Zizzi (N6)*
Zucca (W11)
Zuccato (NW3)*
Zuma (SW7)

Critic-Proof
(Get lots of business despite so-so food)
Ask Pizza (multi. loc.)
Browns (multi. loc.)
Cafe Rouge (multi. loc.)
Hard Rock Cafe (W1)
Richoux (multi. loc.)
T.G.I. Friday's (multi. loc.)
Yo! Sushi (multi. loc.)
Zizzi (multi. loc.)

Delivery/Takeaway
(D=delivery, T=takeaway)
Al Bustan (SW7) (D, T)
Al Hamra (W1) (D, T)
Alounak (multi. loc.) (D, T)
Al Waha (W2) (T)
Arkansas Cafe (E1) (T)
Ask Pizza (multi. loc.) (T)

Bangkok (SW7) (T)
Beiteddine (SW1) (D, T)
Benihana (W1) (T)
Ben's Thai (W9) (T)
Big Easy (SW3) (T)
Bloom's (NW11) (D, T)
Blue Elephant (SW6) (D, T)
Busabong (SW10) (T)
Cafe Fish (W1) (T)
Cafe Japan (NW11) (T)
Cafe Lazeez (multi. loc.) (T)
Cafe Spice (E1) (D, T)
Cantina del Ponte (SE1) (T)
Carluccio's (multi. loc.) (D, T)
Chelsea Bun (multi. loc.) (T)
Chintamani (SW1) (T)
Chor Bizarre (W1) (D, T)
Chuen Cheng Ku (W1) (T)
Churchill Arms (W8) (T)
Chutney Mary (SW10) (T)
Cigala (WC1) (D, T)
Defune (W1) (T)
Eat & Two Veg (W1) (T)
ECapital (W1) (T)
Ed's Diner (multi. loc.) (D, T)
Efes Kebab House (W1) (D, T)
Esarn Kheaw (W12) (T)
Fairuz (multi. loc.) (D, T)
Fakhreldine (multi. loc.) (D, T)
Friends (SW10) (T)
Garbo's (W1) (T)
Gaucho Grill (multi. loc.) (T)
Geales Fish (W8) (T)
Giraffe (multi. loc.) (T)
Golden Dragon (W1) (T)
Gourmet Burger (multi. loc.) (T)
Halepi (multi. loc.) (T)
Harbour City (W1) (T)
Hard Rock Cafe (W1) (T)
Hunan (SW1) (T)
Ikeda (W1) (T)
Il Falconiere (SW7) (T)
Imperial City (EC3) (T)
Inn The Park (SW1) (T)
Ishbilia (SW1) (D, T)
itsu (multi. loc.) (D, T)
Jin Kichi (NW3) (T)
Khan's (W2) (T)
Khan's/Kensington (SW7) (D, T)
Kiku (W1) (T)
Koi (W8) (T)
Kulu Kulu Sushi (multi. loc.) (T)
Lahore Kebab (multi. loc.) (D, T)

Hakkasan (W1)
Inn The Park (SW1)
Joe's Rest. (SW1)
Le Cercle (SW1)
Le Colombier (SW3)
Manicomio (SW3)
Matsuri (multi. loc.)
Mildreds (W1)
Mitsukoshi (SW1)
Mon Plaisir (WC2)
New Culture Rev. (multi. loc.)
Nicole's (W1)
Oriel (SW1)
Pat. Valerie (multi. loc.)
Porters (WC2)
Portrait (WC2)
Providores/Tapa (W1)
Randall & Aubin (multi. loc.)
Red Rm./Waterstones (W1)
Restaurant 7 (SE1)
Richoux (multi. loc.)
St. John Bread/Wine (E1)
Tampopo (SW10)
Terminus (EC2)
Tom's Deli (W11)
Truc Vert (W1)
Villandry (W1)
Wagamama (multi. loc.)
Wolseley (W1)
Yauatcha (W1)
Yellow River (N1)
Yo! Sushi (multi. loc.)

Entertainment

(Call for days and times of performances)

Abbaye (EC1) (jazz)
Adam St. (WC2) (varies)
Ashbells (W11) (jazz)
Atlantic B&G (W1) (DJ)
Aura Kitchen (SW1) (DJ)
Axis (WC2) (jazz)
Baltic (SE1) (jazz)
Bank Aldwych (WC2) (jazz)
Bank West./Zander (SW1) (DJ)
Belair House (SE21) (jazz)
Big Easy (SW3) (guitar)
Bluebird (SW3) (DJ/piano)
Bombay Brass. (SW7) (piano)
Cactus Blue (SW3) (DJ)
Café Boheme (W1) (jazz)
Cafe Fish (W1) (piano)

Cantaloupe (EC2) (DJ)
Canyon (Richmond) (piano)
Chintamani (SW1) (DJ)
Chutney Mary (SW10) (jazz)
Circus (W1) (DJ)
Coq d'Argent (EC2) (jazz)
Cru (N1) (jazz)
Duke of Clar. (SW5) (quiz nights)
Efes Kebab (W1) (belly dancing)
1802 (E14) (DJ)
Embassy (W1) (dancing)
Fish! (SE1) (jazz)
Globe (NW3) (cabaret)
Goring Din. Rm. (SW1) (piano)
Greek Valley (NW8) (bouzouki)
Hakkasan (W1) (DJ)
Halepi (NW3) (Greek)
Hard Rock Cafe (W1) (bands)
Harlem (W2) (DJ)
Hartwell House (Bucks) (piano)
Ishbilia (SW1) (belly dancing)
Joe Allen (WC2) (jazz/piano)
Kettners (W1) (piano)
Lanes (W1) (piano)
Lanesborough (SW1) (jazz)
Langan's Brass. (W1) (jazz)
La Porte des Indes (W1) (jazz)
La Rueda (multi. loc.) (varies)
Le Cafe du Jardin (WC2) (piano)
Le Café du Marché (EC1) (jazz)
Le Caprice (SW1) (piano)
Le Pont de la Tour (SE1) (piano)
Le Soufflé (W1) (piano)
Levant (W1) (belly dancing)
Levantine (W2) (belly dancing)
Little Italy (W1) (DJ)
Ma Goa (SW15) (Goan music)
Maroush (multi. loc.) (Lebanese)
Mash (W1) (DJ)
Meson Don Felipe (SE1) (guitar)
Mirabelle (W1) (piano)
Naked Turtle (SW14) (jazz)
noble rot. (W1) (DJ)
Notting Hill Brass. (W11) (jazz)
Oxo Tower Brass. (SE1) (jazz)
Pizza/Park (SW1) (cabaret/jazz)
Pizza Pomodoro (multi.) (bands)
PJ's B&G (WC2) (jazz)
Planet Hollywood (W1) (DJ)
Prince Bonaparte (W2) (DJ)
Quaglino's (SW1) (jazz)
Rib/Oyster (SW1) (piano/singer)

Ritz (W1) (band)
Sartoria (W1) (jazz singer/piano)
Silks & Spice (EC4) (varies)
Simpson's (WC2) (piano)
Sketch (W1) (DJ)
Smiths/Top Floor (EC1) (DJ)
Smollensky's (multi.) (DJ/piano)
Soho Spice (W1) (DJ)
Souk (WC2) (belly dancing)
Sugar Reef (W1) (nightclub)
Sumosan (W1) (DJ)
Tas (SE1) (guitar)
Terrace (W1) (piano)
Thai Sq. (multi. loc.) (DJ/disco)
Vine./Stock. (Berks) (jazz/piano)
Windows on World (W1) (band)
Zamoyski (NW3) (guitar/singer)
Zinc B&G (multi. loc.) (DJ/jazz)

Fireplaces

Abbeville (SW4)
Abbey Rd. Pub (NW8)
Admiral Codrington (SW3)
Angela Hartnett's (W1)
Anglesea Arms (W6)
Approach Tavern (E2)
Balham Kitchen (SW12)
Bam-Bou (W1)
Barnsbury (N1)
Belair House (SE21)
Bistrot 190 (SW7)
Bleeding Heart (EC1)
Builders Arms (SW3)
Cambio de Tercio (SW5)
Cheyne Walk (SW3)
Christopher's (WC2)
Cicada (EC1)
Clerkenwell (EC1)
Crazy Bear (W1)
Daphne's (SW3)
Draper's Arms (N1)
Edera (W11)
Fat Duck (Berks)
French Horn (Berks)
Gravetye Manor (W. Sus)
Grenadier (SW1)
Havelock Tavern (W14)
I-Thai (W2)
Julie's (W11)
La Poule au Pot (SW1)
Le Cercle (SW1)
Le Manoir/Q.S. (Oxon)
Lemonia (NW1)

L'Escargot (W1)
LMNT (E8)
Malmaison Hotel Bar (EC1)
Manicomio (SW3)
Maroush (SW3)
Mediterraneo (W11)
Naked Turtle (SW14)
Prince Bonaparte (W2)
Richard Corrigan (W1)
Rules (WC2)
Salusbury Pub (NW6)
Sir Charles Napier (Oxon)
Sonny's (SW13)
Vine (NW5)
Waldo's (Berks)
Waterside Inn (Berks)
Waterway (W9)
Wells (NW3)
Westbourne (W2)

Game in Season

Abbeville (SW4)
Admiralty (WC2)
Alastair Little (W1)
Almeida (N1)
Andrew Edmunds (W1)
Angela Hartnett's (W1)
Archipelago (W1)
Aurora (EC2)
Avenue (SW1)
Axis (WC2)
Barnsbury (N1)
Belvedere (W8)
Berkeley Sq. Café (W1)
Bibendum (SW3)
Blandford St. (W1)
Bluebird (SW3)
Boxwood Café (SW1)
Brackenbury (W6)
Brasserie Roux (SW1)
Brass. St. Quentin (SW3)
Brian Turner (W1)
Butlers Wharf (SE1)
Caraffini (SW1)
Caravaggio (EC3)
Carpaccio (SW3)
Cecconi's (W1)
Cellar Gascon (EC1)
Chutney Mary (SW10)
Cinnamon Club (SW1)
Circus (W1)
Club Gascon (EC1)
Criterion Grill (W1)

Embassy (W1)
Enoteca Turi (SW15)
Enterprise (SW3)
Exmouth Grill (EC1)
Fat Duck (Berks)
ffiona's (W8)
Fifteen (N1)
Fino (W1)
Foliage (SW1)
French Horn (Berks)
Frontline (W2)
Glasshouse (Kew)
Gordon Ramsay/Claridge (W1)
Gordon Ramsay/68 Royal (SW3)
Goring Din. Rm. (SW1)
Gravetye Manor (W. Sus)
Green Olive (W9)
Green's (SW1)
Grenadier (SW1)
Grill Room (W1)
Hartwell House (Bucks)
Havelock Tavern (W14)
Inn The Park (SW1)
Julie's (W11)
Kensington Place (W8)
Kew Grill (Kew)
La Famiglia (SW10)
La Fontana (SW1)
Lanesborough (SW1)
Langan's Bistro (W1)
Langan's Brass. (W1)
La Poule au Pot (SW1)
La Trompette (W4)
Le Cercle (SW1)
Le Gavroche (W1)
Le Manoir/Q.S. (Oxon)
Le Pont de la Tour (SE1)
L'Escargot (W1)
Le Soufflé (W1)
L'Etranger (SW7)
L'Incontro (SW1)
Locanda Locatelli (W1)
L'Oranger (SW1)
Lundum's (SW7)
Mirabelle (W1)
Monsieur Max (Hampton Hill)
Monza (SW3)
Morgan M (N7)
Moro (EC1)
Motcombs (SW1)
MVH (SW13)
Nathalie (SW3)

Neal Street (WC2)
noble rot. (W1)
Notting Grill (W11)
Odette's (NW1)
Olivo (SW1)
1 Lombard St. (EC3)
Orrery (W1)
Oslo Court (NW8)
Osteria Antica (SW11)
Oxo Tower (SE1)
Passione (W1)
People's Palace (SE1)
Pétrus (SW1)
Pied à Terre (W1)
Polygon B&G (SW4)
Pomegranates (SW1)
Prism (EC3)
Providores/Tapa (W1)
Putney Bridge (SW15)
Quirinale (SW1)
Racine (SW1)
Randall & Aubin (W1)
Ransome's Dock (SW11)
Rhodes 24 (EC2)
Richard Corrigan (W1)
Ritz (W1)
Riva (SW13)
River Cafe (W6)
Roussillon (SW1)
Rules (WC2)
Santini (SW1)
Sartoria (W1)
Savoy Grill (WC2)
Scalini (SW3)
Scotts (W1)
Shepherd's (SW1)
Simpson's (WC2)
Sir Charles Napier (Oxon)
Sketch (W1)
Smiths/Dining Rm. (EC1)
Snows on Green (W6)
Sonny's (SW13)
Square (W1)
St. John (EC1)
Tate Gallery (SW1)
Tom Aikens (SW3)
Toto's (SW3)
Villandry (W1)
Waldo's (Berks)
Waterside Inn (Berks)
Wilton's (SW1)
Zafferano (SW1)

Special Feature Index

Historic Places
(Year opened; * building)
1571 Royal Exchange (EC3)*
1598 Gravetye Manor (W. Sus)*
1662 Bleeding Heart (EC1)*
1667 Ye Olde Cheshire (EC4)*
1700 Admiralty (WC2)*
1700 Cru (N1)*
1740 Richard Corrigan (W1)*
1742 Grenadier (SW1)*
1742 Wilton's (SW1)
1798 Rules (WC2)*
1802 1802 (E14)*
1828 Simpson's (WC2)
1850 El Blason (SW3)*
1851 Scotts (W1)
1867 Kettners (W1)
1881 Duke of Cambridge (N1)*
1889 Foliage (SW1)*
1889 Savoy Grill (WC2)
1889 Sweetings (EC4)
1897 Angela Hartnett's (W1)*
1900 Frontline (W2)*
1906 Ritz (W1)
1910 Waterloo Fire (SE1)*
1913 Bertorelli (multi. loc.)
1916 Bentley's (W1)
1923 Bluebird (SW3)*
1926 Pat. Valerie (multi. loc.)
1926 Veeraswamy (W1)
1928 Manzi's (WC2)
1931 Grill Room (W1)
1935 Lee Ho Fook (W1)
1939 Geales Fish (W8)
1940 Daphne (NW1)*
1940 Paolo (W1)*
1942 Mon Plaisir (WC2)
1947 Daquise (SW7)
1950 Fortnum's Fountain (W1)
1950 People's Palace (SE1)*
1951 Costas Grill (W8)

Hotel Dining
Baglioni
    Brunello (SW7)
Berkeley Hotel
    Boxwood Café (SW1)
    Pétrus (SW1)
Blakes Hotel
    Blakes (SW7)
Capital Hotel, The
    Capital Rest. (SW3)
Carlton Tower
    Grissini (SW1)
    Rib Room/Oyster (SW1)
Churchill InterContinental
    Locanda Locatelli (W1)
Claridge's Hotel
    Gordon Ramsay/Claridge
    (W1)
Cliveden Hotel
    Waldo's (Berks)
Connaught Hotel, The
    Angela Hartnett's (W1)
Crowne Plaza
    Refettorio (EC4)
Crowne Plaza St. James
    Quilon (SW1)
Dolphin Square Hotel
    Allium (SW1)
Dorchester, The
    Grill Room (W1)
    Oriental (W1)
Four Seasons Hotel
    Lanes (W1)
Four Seasons Canary Wharf
    Quadrato (E14)
French Horn Hotel
    French Horn (Berks)
Gore Hotel
    Bistrot 190 (SW7)
Goring Hotel, The
    Goring Din. Rm. (SW1)
Gravetye Manor Hotel
    Gravetye Manor (W. Sus)
Great Eastern Hotel
    Aurora (EC2)
    Fishmarket (EC2)
    Terminus (EC2)
Halkin Hotel
    Nahm (SW1)
Hartwell House
    Hartwell House (Bucks)
Hempel Hotel
    I-Thai (W2)
Hilton Park Lane
    Windows on World (W1)
Holiday Inn
    Lahore Kebab (WC1)
Hotel Inter-Continental
    Le Soufflé (W1)
K-West Hotel
    Kanteen/K-West (W14)

subscribe to zagat.com

Special Feature Index

Late Dining

Soho Spice (W1) (midnight)
Tokyo Diner (WC2) (midnight)
Vingt-Quatre (SW10) (24 hrs.)
Wolseley (W1) (midnight)
Zilli Fish (W1) (midnight)
Zuccato (NW3) (midnight)

No-Smoking Sections

Admiralty (WC2)
Almeida (N1)
Archipelago (W1)
Arkansas Cafe (E1)
Ask Pizza (multi. loc.)
Balans (multi. loc.)
Bankside (SE1)
Belgo Centraal (WC2)
Benihana (SW3)
Berkeley Sq. Café (W1)
Bierodrome (WC2)
Big Easy (SW3)
Black & Blue (multi. loc.)
Blandford St. (W1)
Bombay Brasserie (SW7)
Brass. St. Quentin (SW3)
Brian Turner (W1)
Brinkley's (SW10)
Browns (multi. loc.)
Cactus Blue (SW3)
Cafe Fish (W1)
Cafe Lazeez (multi. loc.)
Cafe Rouge (multi. loc.)
Cafe Spice (E1)
Camden Brasserie (NW1)
Cantaloupe (EC2)
Cantina Vinopolis (SE1)
Canyon (Richmond)
Capital Rest. (SW3)
Caraffini (SW1)
Caravaggio (EC3)
Carpaccio (SW3)
Casale Franco (N1)
Chamberlain's (EC3)
Champor (SE1)
Chelsea Bun (SW11)
Chez Gérard (multi. loc.)
Chowki Bar (W1)
Chuen Cheng Ku (W1)
Chutney Mary (SW10)
Citrus (W1)
Clerkenwell (EC1)
Como Lario (SW1)
Cru (N1)
Dan's (SW3)
Daphne's (SW3)

Daquise (SW7)
De Cecco (SW6)
Defune (W1)
Dish Dash (SW12)
Draper's Arms (N1)
Duke of Cambridge (N1)
Eat & Two Veg (W1)
ECapital (W1)
Ed's Easy Diner (NW3)
Enoteca Turi (SW15)
Eyre Brothers (EC2)
Fakhreldine (W1)
Fifth Floor Cafe (SW1)
First Floor (W11)
Fish! (SE1)
Fish Hoek (W4)
Fish Shop/St. John (EC1)
Floriana (SW3)
Fortnum's Fountain (W1)
Frederick's (N1)
Fung Shing (WC2)
Getti (multi. loc.)
Harbour City (W1)
Hard Rock Cafe (W1)
Hi Sushi (W1)
Hunan (SW1)
Incognico (WC2)
Indigo (WC2)
Joe Allen (WC2)
Kai Mayfair (W1)
Khan's (W2)
Khan's/Kensington (SW7)
Koi (W8)
Lahore Kebab (multi. loc.)
Lanes (W1)
La Porchetta Pizza (N1)
L'Aventure (NW8)
Le Cercle (SW1)
Lee Ho Fook (W1)
Le Soufflé (W1)
L'Etranger (SW7)
Light House (SW19)
Little Italy (W1)
Livebait (multi. loc.)
Lucky 7 (W2)
Malabar Junction (WC1)
Mango Tree (SW1)
Manor (W11)
Mao Tai (multi. loc.)
Maroush (SW3)
Mela (WC2)
Melati (W1)
Memories of India (multi. loc.)

Metrogusto (N1)
Mimmo d'Ischia (SW1)
Mju (SW1)
Monsieur Max (Hampton Hill)
Motcombs (SW1)
Naked Turtle (SW14)
Nathalie (SW3)
Nautilus Fish (NW6)
New Culture Rev. (multi. loc.)
Nicole's (W1)
Nobu (W1)
Notting Grill (W11)
Noura (SW1)
Odin's (W1)
Oriel (SW1)
Original Tagine (W1)
Orso (WC2)
Pacific Oriental (EC2)
Painted Heron (SW10)
Parsee (N19)
Patara (multi. loc.)
Pat. Valerie (multi. loc.)
Patterson's (W1)
Pepper Tree (SW18)
Pescatori (W1)
Pizza Express (multi. loc.)
Pizza on Park (SW1)
Pizza Pomodoro (EC2)
Planet Hollywood (W1)
Poons (WC2)
Pope's Eye (multi. loc.)
Porters (WC2)
Quadrato (E14)
Quality Chop (EC1)
Quilon (SW1)
Racine (SW3)
Ransome's Dock (SW11)
Raoul's (W9)
Ravi Shankar (NW1)
Reubens (W1)
Riccardo's (SW3)
Richoux (multi. loc.)
River Spice (E1)
Rocket (W1)
Rudland Stubbs (EC1)
Santa Fe (N1)
Sarkhel's (SW18)
Seashell (NW1)
Shepherd's (SW1)
Smollensky's (multi. loc.)
Sofra (W1)
Soho Spice (W1)
Solly's (NW11)

Sri Nam (E14)
Sri Siam City (EC2)
Sticky Fingers (W8)
Strada (multi. loc.)
Sumosan (W1)
Tas (SE1)
Tenth Rest. (W8)
Terminus (EC2)
Terrace (W1)
T.G.I. Friday's (multi. loc.)
Thierry's (SW3)
Two Brothers Fish (N3)
Union Cafe (W1)
Vale (W9)
Verbanella (SW3)
Vineyard/Stock. (Berks)
Windows on World (W1)
Yatra (W1)
Yellow River (N1)
Yoshino (W1)
Zamoyski (NW3)
Zizzi (multi. loc.)
Zuccato (NW3)

Noteworthy Newcomers

Allium (SW1)
Anchor & Hope (SE1)
Ashbells (W11)
Balham Kitchen (SW12)
Banquette (WC2)
Brunello (SW7)
Cheyne Walk (SW3)
Cipriani (W1)
Crazy Bear (W1)
Deya (W1)
east@west (WC2)
Ebury Din. Rm. (SW1)
1880 (SW7)
Essenza (W11)
Exmouth Grill (EC1)
1492 (SW6)
Harlem (W2)
Hoxton Apprentice (N1)
INC Bar (SE10)
Inn The Park (SW1)
Kanteen/K-West (W14)
Kew Grill (Kew)
Latium (W1)
Le Cercle (SW1)
Le Petit Max (SW11)
Levantine (W2)
Lucio (SW3)
Malmaison Hotel Bar (EC1)
Manicomio (SW3)

Morgan M (N7)
Nathalie (SW3)
Novelli/City (EC4)
number 10 (W10)
Palmerston (SE22)
Patterson's (W1)
Pearl (WC1)
Plateau (E14)
Raoul's (W9)
Rasoi Vineet Bhatia (SW3)
Refettorio (EC4)
Rhodes 24 (EC2)
River Spice (E1)
Santa Lucia (SW10)
Shumi (SW1)
Taman gang (W1)
Tampopo (SW10)
Turnmills (EC1)
Wolseley (W1)
Yauatcha (W1)
Zetter (EC1)
Zimzun (SW6)

Offbeat

Alounak (multi. loc.)
Annie's (multi. loc.)
Aperitivo (multi. loc.)
Approach Tavern (E2)
Archipelago (W1)
Arkansas Cafe (E1)
Asia de Cuba (WC2)
Belgo Centraal (multi. loc.)
Benihana (multi. loc.)
Bierodrome (multi. loc.)
Blah! Blah! Blah! (W12)
Bloom's (NW11)
Blue Elephant (SW6)
Boisdale (multi. loc.)
Books for Cooks (W11)
Cambio de Tercio (SW5)
Cellar Gascon (EC1)
Chor Bizarre (W1)
Chowki Bar (W1)
Club Gascon (EC1)
Costas Grill (W8)
Crazy Bear (W1)
Cru (N1)
Daquise (SW7)
Dish Dash (SW12)
ffiona's (W8)
Fifteen (N1)
FishWorks (W4)
Food for Thought (WC2)
Hoxton Apprentice (N1)

itsu (multi. loc.)
Jim Thompson's (multi. loc.)
Kulu Kulu Sushi (multi. loc.)
La Porte des Indes (W1)
Le Cercle (SW1)
Les Trois Garcons (E1)
Levant (W1)
Levantine (W2)
LMNT (E8)
Lola's (N1)
Lucky 7 (W2)
Maggie Jones's (W8)
Mju (SW1)
Momo (W1)
Moro (EC1)
Moshi Moshi (EC2)
MVH (SW13)
Nahm (SW1)
Nautilus Fish (NW6)
Ozer (W1)
Pizza Metro (SW11)
Polygon B&G (SW4)
Providores/Tapa (W1)
Quality Chop (EC1)
Rainforest Cafe (W1)
Randall & Aubin (W1)
Ransome's Dock (SW11)
Real Greek (EC1)
Richard Corrigan (W1)
Rivington Grill (EC2)
Sale e Pepe (SW1)
Sketch (W1)
Solly's (NW11)
Souk (WC2)
Spoon+ (W1)
St. John (EC1)
St. John Bread/Wine (E1)
Sugar Club (W1)
Tate Gallery (SW1)
Tom's Deli (W11)
Troubadour (SW5)
Truc Vert (W1)
Tsunami (SW4)
Wagamama (multi. loc.)
Wapping Food (E1)
Yo! Sushi (multi. loc.)

Outdoor Dining

(G=garden; P=patio;
PV=pavement; T=terrace;
W=waterside)
Abbaye (EC1) (P)
Abbeville (SW4) (P)

Abbey Rd. Pub (NW8) (P)
Admiral Codrington (SW3) (P)
Al Hamra (W1) (P)
Anglesea Arms (W6) (P)
Approach Tavern (E2) (G)
Archipelago (W1) (P)
Ark (W8) (T)
Arkansas Cafe (E1) (PV)
Artigiano (NW3) (PV)
Babylon (W8) (T)
Balham Kitchen (SW12) (PV)
Bam-Bou (W1) (T)
Bank West./Zander (SW1) (T)
Belair House (SE21) (T)
Belvedere (W8) (T)
Berkeley Sq. Café (W1) (P)
Blandford St. (W1) (PV)
Blue Print (SE1) (T, W)
Brackenbury (W6) (P)
Brian Turner (W1) (P)
Builders Arms (SW3) (PV)
Butlers Wharf (SE1) (T)
Cantina del Ponte (SE1) (T, W)
Canyon (Richmond) (P, T)
Caraffini (SW1) (PV)
Casale Franco (N1) (P)
Chamberlain's (EC3) (PV)
Churchill Arms (W8) (P)
Coq d'Argent (EC2) (G, T)
Costas Grill (W8) (G)
Dan's (SW3) (G)
Daphne's (SW3) (G)
Eagle (EC1) (PV)
Edera (W11) (P)
1802 (E14) (T, W)
Eight Over Eight (SW3) (PV)
El Gaucho (SW3) (T)
Elistano (SW3) (PV)
El Pirata (W1) (PV)
Engineer (NW1) (G)
Exmouth Grill (EC1) (PV)
Fifth Floor Cafe (SW1) (T)
FishWorks (W4) (G, T)
Getti (multi. loc.) (PV)
Gravetye Manor (W. Sus) (G)
Hard Rock Cafe (W1) (T)
Havelock Tavern (W14) (G, PV)
Hoxton Apprentice (N1) (T)
Hush (W1) (P)
Inn The Park (SW1) (P, T)
Ishbilia (SW1) (PV)
Joe's (SW3) (PV)
Julie's (W11) (P, PV)

Kandoo (W2) (G)
La Famiglia (SW10) (G)
Lansdowne (NW1) (PV)
La Poule au Pot (SW1) (PV)
La Trompette (W4) (P)
La Trouvaille (W1) (PV)
Le Boudin Blanc (W1) (T)
Le Colombier (SW3) (T)
Le Manoir/Q.S. (Oxon) (G, P, T)
Le Pont de la Tour (SE1) (T, W)
L'Oranger (SW1) (P)
Lundum's (SW7) (T)
Made in Italy (SW3) (T)
Manicomio (SW3) (PV)
Mao Tai (SW3) (PV)
Mediterraneo (W11) (PV)
Mildreds (W1) (PV)
Mirabelle (W1) (P)
Monza (SW3) (PV)
Moro (EC1) (PV)
Motcombs (SW1) (PV)
Notting Grill (W11) (T)
Odette's (NW1) (G, PV)
Orrery (W1) (T)
Osteria Antica (SW11) (PV)
Osteria Basilico (W11) (P)
Oxo Tower (SE1) (T, W)
Oxo Tower Brass. (SE1) (T, W)
Ozer (W1) (PV)
Painted Heron (multi. loc.) (T)
Passione (W1) (PV)
Pellicano (SW3) (PV)
Pizza on Park (SW1) (PV)
PJ's B&G (multi. loc.) (PV)
Plateau (E14) (T)
Porters (WC2) (PV)
Quadrato (E14) (T)
Ransome's Dock (SW11) (T, W)
Real Greek (EC1) (PV)
Riccardo's (SW3) (P)
Ritz (W1) (T)
River Cafe (W6) (P)
Royal China (E14) (W)
Sambuca (SW1) (PV)
San Lorenzo Fuor. (SW19) (P)
Santini (SW1) (T)
Scotts (W1) (PV)
Sir Charles Napier (Oxon) (G, T)
Smiths/Top Floor (EC1) (T)
Spoon+ (W1) (G, T)
Sweetings (EC4) (PV)
Texas Embassy (SW1) (PV)
Thai on the River (SW10) (P, W)

Tom's Deli (W11) (G)
Toto's (SW3) (G)
202 (W11) (G, PV)
Uli (W11) (P)
Vama (SW10) (P)
Villandry (W1) (PV)
Vine (NW5) (G)
Vineyard/Stock. (Berks) (T, W)
Wapping Food (E1) (G, P)
Waterway (W9) (P, T)
Westbourne (W2) (T)
Zucca (W11) (PV)

People-Watching
Admiral Codrington (SW3)
Angela Hartnett's (W1)
Asia de Cuba (WC2)
Avenue (SW1)
Bam-Bou (W1)
Bangkok (SW7)
Belvedere (W8)
Bibendum (SW3)
Bibendum Oyster (SW3)
Blakes (SW7)
Bluebird (SW3)
Boxwood Café (SW1)
Cafe at Sotheby's (W1)
Caraffini (SW1)
Cecconi's (W1)
Cellar Gascon (EC1)
Christopher's (WC2)
Cinnamon Club (SW1)
Cipriani (W1)
Circus (W1)
Club Gascon (EC1)
Daphne's (SW3)
Drones (SW1)
e&o (W11)
Eight Over Eight (SW3)
Electric Brasserie (W11)
Emporio Armani (SW3)
Fifteen (N1)
Fifth Floor Cafe (SW1)
Fino (W1)
Gordon Ramsay/Claridge (W1)
Gordon Ramsay/68 Royal (SW3)
Hakkasan (W1)
Hush (W1)
Ivy, The (WC2)
Joe's (SW3)
J. Sheekey (WC2)
Kensington Place (W8)

La Famiglia (SW10)
Langan's Bistro (W1)
Langan's Brass. (W1)
La Trompette (W4)
Le Caprice (SW1)
Le Cercle (SW1)
Le Gavroche (W1)
L'Incontro (SW1)
Locanda Locatelli (W1)
Mirabelle (W1)
Momo (W1)
Nicole's (W1)
Nobu (W1)
Orso (WC2)
Osia (SW1)
Pasha (SW7)
Pétrus (SW1)
PJ's B&G (SW3)
Providores/Tapa (W1)
Quaglino's (SW1)
Racine (SW3)
Riccardo's (SW3)
River Cafe (W6)
San Lorenzo (SW3)
Santini (SW1)
Savoy Grill (WC2)
Shumi (SW1)
Sketch (W1)
Smiths/Top Floor (EC1)
Sophie's Steak (SW10)
Spoon+ (W1)
Sumosan (W1)
Timo (W8)
Tom Aikens (SW3)
Tom's Deli (W11)
Tsunami (SW4)
202 (W11)
Vingt-Quatre (SW10)
Waterside Inn (Berks)
Wilton's (SW1)
Wolseley (W1)
Yauatcha (W1)
Zafferano (SW1)
Zetter (EC1)
Zilli Fish (W1)
Zinc B&G (W1)
Zuma (SW7)

Power Scenes
Angela Hartnett's (W1)
Aurora (EC2)
Avenue (SW1)
Bank Aldwych (WC2)

Special Feature Index

Belvedere (W8)
Blue Print (SE1)
Boxwood Café (SW1)
Caravaggio (EC3)
Cecconi's (W1)
Cinnamon Club (SW1)
Cipriani (W1)
Circus (W1)
Club Gascon (EC1)
Daphne's (SW3)
Drones (SW1)
east@west (WC2)
Gordon Ramsay/Claridge (W1)
Gordon Ramsay/68 Royal (SW3)
Goring Din. Rm. (SW1)
Greenhouse (W1)
Green's (SW1)
Grill Room (W1)
Ivy, The (WC2)
J. Sheekey (WC2)
Lanes (W1)
Langan's Brass. (W1)
Launceston Pl. (W8)
Le Caprice (SW1)
Le Gavroche (W1)
Le Manoir/Q.S. (Oxon)
Le Pont de la Tour (SE1)
Le Soufflé (W1)
L'Incontro (SW1)
Mirabelle (W1)
Nahm (SW1)
Neal Street (WC2)
Nobu (W1)
Odin's (W1)
1 Lombard St. (EC3)
Pétrus (SW1)
Prism (EC3)
Rhodes 24 (EC2)
Ritz (W1)
San Lorenzo (SW3)
Savoy Grill (WC2)
Shepherd's (SW1)
Sketch (W1)
Spoon+ (W1)
Square (W1)
Tom Aikens (SW3)
Waterside Inn (Berks)
Wheeler's (SW1)
Wilton's (SW1)
Wolseley (W1)
Zafferano (SW1)
Zuma (SW7)

Pre-Theatre Menus

(Call for prices and times)
Al Duca (SW1)
Almeida (N1)
Angela Hartnett's (W1)
Asia de Cuba (WC2)
Atlantic B&G (W1)
Axis (WC2)
Baltic (SE1)
Bank Aldwych (WC2)
Bank West./Zander (SW1)
Belgo Centraal (NW1)
Benihana (SW3)
Bluebird (SW3)
Brasserie Roux (SW1)
Brass. St. Quentin (SW3)
Browns (multi. loc.)
Bush Bar & Grill (W12)
Café Boheme (W1)
Café des Amis (WC2)
Cafe Fish (W1)
Cafe Med (multi. loc.)
Cantina del Ponte (SE1)
Chez Gérard (multi. loc.)
Chintamani (SW1)
Chor Bizarre (W1)
Christopher's (WC2)
Cinnamon Club (SW1)
Circus (W1)
Clerkenwell (EC1)
Criterion Grill (W1)
Dibbens (EC1)
Embassy (W1)
Fish Hoek (W4)
Fish Shop/St. John (EC1)
Food for Thought (WC2)
Frederick's (N1)
Gordon Ramsay/Claridge (W1)
Goring Din. Rm. (SW1)
Grill Room (W1)
Incognico (WC2)
Indigo (WC2)
Isola (SW1)
Joe Allen (WC2)
La Bouchée (SW7)
Lanesborough (SW1)
La Trouvaille (multi. loc.)
Le Boudin Blanc (W1)
Le Deuxieme (WC2)
L'Escargot (W1)
L'Estaminet (WC2)
L'Etranger (SW7)
Lola's (N1)

L'Oranger (SW1)
Ma Goa (SW15)
Manzi's (WC2)
Mash (W1)
Matsuri (SW1)
Mela (WC2)
Orso (WC2)
Oxo Tower Brass. (SE1)
Pasha (N1)
Patterson's (W1)
Pearl (WC1)
People's Palace (SE1)
Porters (WC2)
Quaglino's (SW1)
Quod (SW1)
Quo Vadis (W1)
Racine (SW3)
Rani (N3)
Red Fort (W1)
Richard Corrigan (W1)
Richoux (multi. loc.)
Ritz (W1)
R.S.J. (SE1)
Salisbury Tavern (SW6)
Savoy Grill (WC2)
Signor Zilli (W1)
Smollensky's (multi. loc.)
Sofra (multi. loc.)
Spoon+ (W1)
Sri Thai Soho (W1)
Stratford's (W8)
Sugar Club (W1)
Sugar Reef (W1)
Tamarind (W1)
Tampopo (SW10)
Thai Pavilion (W1)
Thierry's (SW3)
Tiger Lil's (SW4)
Tokyo Diner (WC2)
Tuttons Brass. (WC2)
Vasco & Piero's (W1)
Veeraswamy (W1)
Villandry (W1)
Waterloo Fire (SE1)
Yatra (W1)
Zaika (W8)
Zilli Fish (WC2)

Private Rooms
(Call for capacity)
Abbaye (EC1)
Abbeville (SW4)
Abbey Rd. Pub (NW8)

Admiralty (WC2)
Alastair Little (W1)
Allium (SW1)
Alloro (W1)
Almeida (N1)
Angela Hartnett's (W1)
Aperitivo (W1)
Archipelago (W1)
Atlantic B&G (W1)
Balham Kitchen (SW12)
Baltic (SE1)
Bam-Bou (W1)
Belgo Centraal (WC2)
Belvedere (W8)
Benares (W1)
Benihana (multi. loc.)
Berkeley Sq. Café (W1)
Blakes (SW7)
Bluebird (SW3)
Blue Elephant (SW6)
Bodeans (W1)
Bombay Bicycle (SW12)
Boxwood Café (SW1)
Brasserie Roux (SW1)
Brian Turner (W1)
Cactus Blue (SW3)
Cafe Spice (E1)
Cambio de Tercio (SW5)
Cantina Vinopolis (SE1)
Capital Rest. (SW3)
Chez Bruce (SW17)
Chintamani (SW1)
Chor Bizarre (W1)
Christopher's (WC2)
Chuen Cheng Ku (W1)
Chutney Mary (SW10)
Cinnamon Club (SW1)
Cipriani (W1)
Circus (W1)
Clerkenwell (EC1)
Cru (N1)
Dan's (SW3)
Daphne's (SW3)
Deca (W1)
Dish Dash (SW12)
Drones (SW1)
e&o (W11)
east@west (WC2)
Ebury Din. Rm. (SW1)
Edera (W11)
1880 (SW7)
1802 (E14)
Eight Over Eight (SW3)

Embassy (W1)
Fairuz (W1)
Garbo's (W1)
Gordon Ramsay/Claridge (W1)
Goring Din. Rm. (SW1)
Gravetye Manor (W. Sus)
Greenhouse (W1)
Green Olive (W9)
Green's (SW1)
Guinea Grill (W1)
Hakkasan (W1)
Hard Rock Cafe (W1)
Hartwell House (Bucks)
Hush (W1)
Il Convivio (SW1)
I-Thai (W2)
itsu (SW3)
Ivy, The (WC2)
Julie's (W11)
Just St. James's (SW1)
Kai Mayfair (W1)
Kensington Place (W8)
La Famiglia (SW10)
Lanesborough (SW1)
La Porte des Indes (W1)
La Poule au Pot (SW1)
La Trouvaille (multi. loc.)
Launceston Pl. (W8)
Le Colombier (SW3)
Le Gavroche (W1)
Le Manoir/Q.S. (Oxon)
Lemonia (NW1)
Le Pont de la Tour (SE1)
L'Escargot (W1)
L'Estaminet (WC2)
Les Trois Garcons (E1)
Le Suquet (SW3)
L'Etranger (SW7)
L'Incontro (SW1)
Lola's (N1)
L'Oranger (SW1)
Lundum's (SW7)
Made in Italy (SW3)
Malmaison Hotel Bar (EC1)
Manor (W11)
Mao Tai (SW6)
Masala Zone (N1)
Matsuri (multi. loc.)
Memories of China (SW1)
Memories of India
Mimmo d'Ischia (SW1)
Mint Leaf (SW1)
Mirabelle (W1)

Mitsukoshi (SW1)
Momo (W1)
Mon Plaisir (WC2)
Montpeliano (SW7)
Morgan M (N7)
Motcombs (SW1)
Mr. Chow (SW1)
MVH (SW13)
Nahm (SW1)
Nathalie (SW3)
Neal Street (WC2)
noble rot. (W1)
Nobu (W1)
Notting Grill (W11)
number 10 (W10)
1 Lombard St. (EC3)
1 Lombard Brass. (EC3)
One-O-One (SW1)
Oriental (W1)
Palmerston (SE22)
Pasha (SW7)
Passione (W1)
Patterson's (W1)
Pearl (WC1)
Pellicano (SW3)
Pétrus (SW1)
Pied à Terre (W1)
Plateau (E14)
Poissonnerie/l'Ave. (SW3)
Prism (EC3)
Quadrato (E14)
Quaglino's (SW1)
Quo Vadis (W1)
Rainforest Cafe (W1)
Rasoi Vineet Bhatia (SW3)
Real Greek (EC1)
Rib Room/Oyster (SW1)
Richard Corrigan (W1)
Ritz (W1)
Rivington Grill (EC2)
Rocket (multi. loc.)
Roussillon (SW1)
Royal China (multi. loc.)
Rules (WC2)
San Lorenzo Fuor. (SW19)
Santa Fe (N1)
Santini (SW1)
Sartoria (W1)
Savoy Grill (WC2)
Scotts (W1)
Shumi (SW1)
Sir Charles Napier (Oxon)
Six-13 (W1)

Sketch (W1)
Smiths/Top Floor (EC1)
Smiths/Dining Rm. (EC1)
Solly's (NW11)
Souk (WC2)
Square (W1)
Star of India (SW5)
St. John (EC1)
Sugar Club (W1)
Tatsuso (EC1)
Tentazioni (SE1)
Texas Embassy (SW1)
Thai Square (SW1)
Thierry's (SW3)
Timo (W8)
Vale (W9)
Vasco & Piero's (W1)
Veeraswamy (W1)
Vineyard/Stock. (Berks)
Waterloo Fire (SE1)
Waterside Inn (Berks)
Wells (NW3)
Wheeler's (SW1)
Wilton's (SW1)
Wòdka (W8)
Yatra (W1)
Ye Olde Cheshire (EC4)
Yoshino (W1)
Zafferano (SW1)
Zilli Fish (WC2)
Zuma (SW7)

Pubs/Microbreweries
Abbeville (SW4)
Abbey Rd. Pub (NW8)
Admiral Codrington (SW3)
Anchor & Hope (SE1)
Anglesea Arms (W6)
Approach Tavern (E2)
Barnsbury (N1)
Builders Arms (SW3)
Churchill Arms (W8)
Cow Din. Rm. (W2)
Draper's Arms (N1)
Duke of Cambridge (N1)
Duke of Clarence (SW5)
Eagle (EC1)
Engineer (NW1)
Enterprise (SW3)
Gate (W6)
Grenadier (SW1)
Havelock Tavern (W14)
Lansdowne (NW1)

Mash (W1)
Oak (W2)
Palmerston (SE22)
Prince Bonaparte (W2)
Salisbury Tavern (SW6)
Salusbury Pub (NW6)
Vine (NW5)
Waterway (W9)
Wells (NW3)
Westbourne (W2)
White Swan (EC4)
Ye Olde Cheshire (EC4)

Pudding Specialists
Alastair Little (W1)
Almeida (N1)
Angela Hartnett's (W1)
Asia de Cuba (WC2)
Aubergine (SW10)
Aurora (EC2)
Belvedere (W8)
Bibendum Oyster (SW3)
Blakes (SW7)
Boxwood Café (SW1)
Capital Rest. (SW3)
Chez Bruce (SW17)
Cipriani (W1)
Clarke's (W8)
Club Gascon (EC1)
east@west (WC2)
Embassy (W1)
Fat Duck (Berks)
Fifth Floor (SW1)
Foliage (SW1)
Fortnum's Fountain (W1)
Glasshouse (Kew)
Gordon Ramsay/Claridge (W1)
Gordon Ramsay/68 Royal (SW3)
Lanes (W1)
Lanesborough (SW1)
La Trompette (W4)
Le Cercle (SW1)
Le Gavroche (W1)
Le Manoir/Q.S. (Oxon)
Le Soufflé (W1)
Locanda Locatelli (W1)
L'Oranger (SW1)
Mirabelle (W1)
Nobu (W1)
Orrery (W1)
Osia (SW1)
Pat. Valerie (multi. loc.)
Pétrus (SW1)

Plateau (E14)
Providores/Tapa (W1)
Richard Corrigan (W1)
Richoux (multi. loc.)
Ritz (W1)
River Cafe (W6)
Savoy Grill (WC2)
Sketch (W1)
Spoon+ (W1)
Square (W1)
Thyme (SW4)
Tom Aikens (SW3)
Waterside Inn (Berks)
Wolseley (W1)
Zafferano (SW1)
Zuma (SW7)

Quiet Conversation

Al Sultan (W1)
Aubergine (SW10)
Aurora (EC2)
Axis (WC2)
Banquette (WC2)
Belair House (SE21)
Benares (W1)
Bengal Clipper (SE1)
Bentley's (W1)
Berkeley Sq. Café (W1)
Blakes (SW7)
Brian Turner (W1)
Capital Rest. (SW3)
Dan's (SW3)
east@west (WC2)
1880 (SW7)
Embassy (W1)
Foliage (SW1)
Goring Din. Rm. (SW1)
Green's (SW1)
Hartwell House (Bucks)
Il Convivio (SW1)
Indigo (WC2)
Lanes (W1)
Lanesborough (SW1)
Launceston Pl. (W8)
Le Gavroche (W1)
Le Manoir/Q.S. (Oxon)
L'Oranger (SW1)
Lundum's (SW7)
Mitsukoshi (SW1)
Mju (SW1)
Nahm (SW1)
Nathalie (SW3)
Odin's (W1)

One-O-One (SW1)
Oriental (W1)
Orrery (W1)
Quadrato (E14)
Quirinale (SW1)
Ritz (W1)
Roussillon (SW1)
Salloos (SW1)
Scotts (W1)
Sketch (W1)
Stratford's (W8)
Waterside Inn (Berks)
Wilton's (W1)
Windows on World (W1)

Romantic Places

Andrew Edmunds (W1)
Angela Hartnett's (W1)
Aurora (EC2)
Belvedere (W8)
Blakes (SW7)
Blue Elephant (SW6)
Brunello (SW7)
Capital Rest. (SW3)
Cellar Gascon (EC1)
Chintamani (SW1)
Chutney Mary (SW10)
Cipriani (W1)
Clarke's (W8)
Club Gascon (EC1)
Crazy Bear (W1)
Criterion Grill (W1)
Daphne's (SW3)
Drones (SW1)
Frederick's (N1)
French Horn (Berks)
Glasshouse (Kew)
Gordon Ramsay/Claridge (W1)
Gordon Ramsay/68 Royal (SW3)
Gravetye Manor (W. Sus)
Hakkasan (W1)
Hartwell House (Bucks)
Julie's (W11)
Lanesborough (SW1)
La Poule au Pot (SW1)
Launceston Pl. (W8)
L'Aventure (NW8)
Le Café du Marché (EC1)
Le Caprice (SW1)
Le Cercle (SW1)
Le Gavroche (W1)
Le Manoir/Q.S. (Oxon)
Le Pont de la Tour (SE1)

Les Trois Garcons (E1)
Locanda Locatelli (W1)
L'Oranger (SW1)
Lundum's (SW7)
Maggie Jones's (W8)
Mirabelle (W1)
Momo (W1)
Nobu (W1)
Odette's (NW1)
Odin's (W1)
Orrery (W1)
Pétrus (SW1)
Pied à Terre (W1)
Pomegranates (SW1)
Prism (EC3)
Richard Corrigan (W1)
Ritz (W1)
River Cafe (W6)
Roussillon (SW1)
San Lorenzo (SW3)
Shumi (SW1)
Sketch (W1)
Snows on Green (W6)
Square (W1)
Tom Aikens (SW3)
Toto's (SW3)
Waterside Inn (Berks)
Windows on World (W1)
Zafferano (SW1)
Zuma (SW7)

Senior Appeal

Al Duca (SW1)
Angela Hartnett's (W1)
Aubergine (SW10)
Belair House (SE21)
Belvedere (W8)
Bentley's (W1)
Berkeley Sq. Café (W1)
Bibendum (SW3)
Bloom's (NW11)
Boxwood Café (SW1)
Brasserie Roux (SW1)
Brass. St. Quentin (SW3)
Brian Turner (W1)
Cafe at Sotheby's (W1)
Capital Rest. (SW3)
Cecconi's (W1)
Citrus (W1)
Dan's (SW3)
Deca (W1)
Drones (SW1)
Floriana (SW3)

Foliage (SW1)
Fortnum's Fountain (W1)
Glasshouse (Kew)
Gordon Ramsay/Claridge (W1)
Gordon Ramsay/68 Royal (SW3)
Goring Din. Rm. (SW1)
Gravetye Manor (W. Sus)
Green's (SW1)
Grill Room (W1)
Hartwell House (Bucks)
Ivy, The (WC2)
J. Sheekey (WC2)
Kai Mayfair (W1)
Lanes (W1)
Lanesborough (SW1)
Langan's Bistro (W1)
La Poule au Pot (SW1)
Launceston Pl. (W8)
Le Caprice (SW1)
Le Gavroche (W1)
Le Manoir/Q.S. (Oxon)
Le Soufflé (W1)
L'Etranger (SW7)
L'Incontro (SW1)
L'Oranger (SW1)
Lundum's (SW7)
Manzi's (WC2)
Mimmo d'Ischia (SW1)
Mirabelle (W1)
Montpeliano (SW7)
Motcombs (SW1)
Neal Street (WC2)
Noura (SW1)
Odin's (W1)
One-O-One (SW1)
Oriental (W1)
Orrery (W1)
Pat. Valerie (multi. loc.)
Pétrus (SW1)
Poissonnerie/l'Ave. (SW3)
Quadrato (E14)
Quirinale (SW1)
Racine (SW3)
Red Fort (W1)
Red Rm./Waterstones (W1)
Reubens (W1)
Rib Room/Oyster (SW1)
Richoux (multi. loc.)
Ritz (W1)
Riva (SW13)
Rosmarino (NW8)
Rowley's (SW1)

Rules (WC2)
Santini (SW1)
Sartoria (W1)
Savoy Grill (WC2)
Scalini (SW3)
Scotts (W1)
Shepherd's (SW1)
Simpson's (WC2)
Square (W1)
Stratford's (W8)
Tate Gallery (SW1)
Tom Aikens (SW3)
Toto's (SW3)
Waldo's (Berks)
Waterside Inn (Berks)
Wilton's (SW1)
Wolseley (W1)
Zafferano (SW1)
Zen Central (W1)

Set-Price Menus
(Call for prices and times)
Abbey Rd. Pub (NW8)
A Cena (Twickenham)
Admiral Codrington (SW3)
Alastair Little (W1)
Al Duca (SW1)
Allium (SW1)
Alloro (W1)
Almeida (N1)
Angela Hartnett's (W1)
Anglesea Arms (W6)
Archipelago (W1)
Aubergine (SW10)
Aurora (EC2)
Avenue (SW1)
Axis (WC2)
Belvedere (W8)
Benares (W1)
Benihana (NW3)
Berkeley Sq. Café (W1)
Bibendum (SW3)
Blue Elephant (SW6)
Brass. St. Quentin (SW3)
Brian Turner (W1)
Butlers Wharf (SE1)
Cafe Japan (NW11)
Cafe Lazeez (EC1)
Cafe Spice (E1)
Cantina del Ponte (SE1)
Caravaggio (EC3)
Chez Bruce (SW17)
Chez Gérard (multi. loc.)

Chintamani (SW1)
Chor Bizarre (W1)
Christopher's (WC2)
Chutney Mary (SW10)
Cigala (WC1)
Cinnamon Club (SW1)
Cipriani (W1)
Circus (W1)
Citrus (W1)
City Miyama (EC4)
Clarke's (W8)
Clerkenwell (EC1)
Club Gascon (EC1)
Coq d'Argent (EC2)
Crazy Bear (W1)
Criterion Grill (W1)
Dan's (SW3)
Deca (W1)
Deya (W1)
Drones (SW1)
Ebury Din. Rm. (SW1)
ECapital (W1)
Edera (W11)
1880 (SW7)
1802 (E14)
Eight Over Eight (SW3)
El Pirata (W1)
Embassy (W1)
Enoteca Turi (SW15)
Essenza (W11)
Exmouth Grill (EC1)
Fat Duck (Berks)
Fifteen (N1)
Fino (W1)
Fish Shop/St. John (EC1)
Floriana (SW3)
Foliage (SW1)
French Horn (Berks)
Frontline (W2)
Gaucho Grill (W1)
Gia (SW3)
Glasshouse (Kew)
Gordon Ramsay/Claridge (W1)
Gordon Ramsay/68 Royal (SW3)
Goring Din. Rm. (SW1)
Gravetye Manor (W. Sus)
Great Eastern (EC2)
Grill Room (W1)
Halepi (NW3)
Hartwell House (Bucks)
Hush (W1)
Il Convivio (SW1)

Tom Aikens (SW3)
Toto's (SW3)
Vama (SW10)
Vasco & Piero's (W1)
Veeraswamy (W1)
Vineyard/Stock. (Berks)
Waldo's (Berks)
Waterside Inn (Berks)
Windows on World (W1)
Yoshino (W1)
Zafferano (SW1)
Zaika (W8)
Zilli Fish (multi. loc.)

Singles Scenes

Admiral Codrington (SW3)
Asia de Cuba (WC2)
Atlantic B&G (W1)
Aura Kitchen (SW1)
Avenue (SW1)
Balans (multi. loc.)
Bank Aldwych (WC2)
Bank West./Zander (SW1)
Belgo Centraal (multi. loc.)
Bierodrome (multi. loc.)
Big Easy (SW3)
Bistrot 190 (SW7)
Bluebird (SW3)
Brinkley's (SW10)
Browns (multi. loc.)
Buona Sera (SW3)
Cactus Blue (SW3)
Cafe Pacifico (WC2)
Cantaloupe (EC2)
Cecconi's (W1)
Cellar Gascon (EC1)
Christopher's (WC2)
Circus (W1)
Collection (SW3)
Dish Dash (SW12)
Draper's Arms (N1)
e&o (W11)
Ebury Wine Bar (SW1)
Eight Over Eight (SW3)
Engineer (NW1)
Enterprise (SW3)
Fifteen (N1)
Fifth Floor Cafe (SW1)
Fino (W1)
First Floor (W11)
Gia (SW3)
Hakkasan (W1)
Hush (W1)

Just St. James's (SW1)
Kettners (W1)
La Perla (multi. loc.)
La Rueda (multi. loc.)
Le Cercle (SW1)
Manor (W11)
Maroush (multi. loc.)
Momo (W1)
Moro (EC1)
Motcombs (SW1)
Nam Long-Le Shaker (SW5)
noble rot. (W1)
Nobu (W1)
Oriel (SW1)
Osia (SW1)
Oxo Tower (SE1)
Oxo Tower Brass. (SE1)
Pizza on Park (SW1)
PJ's B&G (SW3)
Putney Bridge (SW15)
Quaglino's (SW1)
Sketch (W1)
Smiths/Top Floor (EC1)
Sophie's Steak (SW10)
Spiga (W1)
Spighetta (W1)
Spoon+ (W1)
Sticky Fingers (W8)
Sugar Reef (W1)
Sumosan (W1)
Terminus (EC2)
Texas Embassy (SW1)
Waterloo Fire (SE1)
Waterway (W9)
Zinc B&G (multi. loc.)
Zuma (SW7)

Sleepers

(Good to excellent food, but
little known)
A Cena (Twickenham)
Al San Vincenzo (W2)
Al Waha (W2)
Archipelago (W1)
Busabong (SW10)
Chutney's (NW1)
City Miyama (EC4)
Cru (N1)
ECapital (W1)
Esarn Kheaw (W12)
Fina Estampa (SE1)
FishWorks (W4)
Gopal's of Soho (W1)

Green Olive (W9)
Havelock Tavern (W14)
Ikeda (W1)
I-Thai (W2)
La Fontana (SW1)
L'Incontro (SW1)
Locanda Otto. (W8)
Ma Goa (multi. loc.)
Mandola (W11)
Nautilus Fish (NW6)
Osteria Antica (SW11)
Parsee (N19)
Pope's Eye (multi. loc.)
Potemkin (EC1)
Prism (EC3)
Ravi Shankar (multi. loc.)
Rivington Grill (EC2)
Salisbury Tavern (SW6)
San Lorenzo Fuor. (SW19)
Six-13 (W1)
Sonny's (SW13)
Stratford's (W8)
Terrace, The (W8)
Two Brothers Fish (N3)
Uli (W11)
Vasco & Piero's (W1)
Vineyard/Stock. (Berks)
Waldo's (Berks)

Smoking Prohibited

(May be permissible at bar)
Angela Hartnett's (W1)
Banquette (WC2)
Books for Cooks (W11)
Boxwood Café (SW1)
Busaba Eathai (multi. loc.)
Cafe at Sotheby's (W1)
Chez Bruce (SW17)
Clarke's (W8)
Crivelli's Garden (WC2)
Fat Duck (Berks)
Fifteen (N1)
Food for Thought (WC2)
Giraffe (multi. loc.)
Glasshouse (Kew)
Gordon Ramsay/Claridge (W1)
Gordon Ramsay/68 Royal (SW3)
Gravetye Manor (W. Sus)
Hartwell House (Bucks)
Inn The Park (SW1)
itsu (multi. loc.)
Jim Thompson's (multi. loc.)

La Trompette (W4)
Le Manoir/Q.S. (Oxon)
Mandalay (W2)
Masala Zone (multi. loc.)
Mildreds (W1)
Morgan M (N7)
Moshi Moshi (multi. loc.)
Nyonya (W11)
Pétrus (SW1)
Portrait (WC2)
Providores/Tapa (W1)
Rainforest Cafe (W1)
Rasa (multi. loc.)
Rasoi Vineet Bhatia (SW3)
Restaurant 7 (SE1)
Rules (WC2)
Satsuma (W1)
Savoy Grill (WC2)
Sir Charles Napier (Oxon)
Spighetta (W1)
Tampopo (SW10)
Tom Aikens (SW3)
Tom's Deli (W11)
Truc Vert (W1)
202 (W11)
Villandry (W1)
Wagamama (multi. loc.)
Yauatcha (W1)
Yo! Sushi (multi. loc.)
Zuma (SW7)

Special Occasions

Almeida (N1)
Angela Hartnett's (W1)
Asia de Cuba (WC2)
Aubergine (SW10)
Avenue (SW1)
Belvedere (W8)
Berkeley Sq. Café (W1)
Bibendum (SW3)
Blakes (SW7)
Blue Elephant (SW6)
Brunello (SW7)
Capital Rest. (SW3)
Cecconi's (W1)
Chez Bruce (SW17)
Chutney Mary (SW10)
Cinnamon Club (SW1)
Cipriani (W1)
Clarke's (W8)
Club Gascon (EC1)
Crazy Bear (W1)
Criterion Grill (W1)

Special Feature Index

Daphne's (SW3)
Drones (SW1)
east@west (WC2)
Fifteen (N1)
Fino (W1)
Foliage (SW1)
French Horn (Berks)
Glasshouse (Kew)
Gordon Ramsay/Claridge (W1)
Gordon Ramsay/68 Royal (SW3)
Goring Din. Rm. (SW1)
Gravetye Manor (W. Sus)
Grill Room (W1)
Hartwell House (Bucks)
Ivy, The (WC2)
J. Sheekey (WC2)
Lanesborough (SW1)
La Trompette (W4)
Launceston Pl. (W8)
Le Caprice (SW1)
Le Cercle (SW1)
Le Gavroche (W1)
Le Manoir/Q.S. (Oxon)
Le Pont de la Tour (SE1)
Le Soufflé (W1)
Locanda Locatelli (W1)
L'Oranger (SW1)
Lundum's (SW7)
Mirabelle (W1)
Momo (W1)
Nahm (SW1)
Neal Street (WC2)
Nobu (W1)
Oriental (W1)
Orrery (W1)
Osia (SW1)
Pétrus (SW1)
Pied à Terre (W1)
Plateau (E14)
Providores/Tapa (W1)
Quaglino's (SW1)
Rasoi Vineet Bhatia (SW3)
Richard Corrigan (W1)
Ritz (W1)
River Cafe (W6)
San Lorenzo (SW3)
Santini (SW1)
Sartoria (W1)
Savoy Grill (WC2)
Sketch (W1)
Smiths/Top Floor (EC1)
Smiths/Dining Rm. (EC1)
Spoon+ (W1)

Square (W1)
Thyme (SW4)
Tom Aikens (SW3)
Ubon (E14)
Vineyard/Stock. (Berks)
Waterside Inn (Berks)
Wilton's (SW1)
Windows on World (W1)
Zafferano (SW1)
Zaika (W8)
Zuma (SW7)

Tea Service

(See also Hotel Dining)
Bibendum Oyster (SW3)
Books for Cooks (W11)
Brasserie Roux (SW1)
Cafe at Sotheby's (W1)
Capital Rest. (SW3)
Carluccio's (W1)
Chor Bizarre (W1)
Cipriani (W1)
Criterion Grill (W1)
Crivelli's Garden (WC2)
1802 (E14)
Emporio Armani (SW3)
Fifth Floor Cafe (SW1)
Food for Thought (WC2)
Goring Din. Rm. (SW1)
Hartwell House (Bucks)
Joe's Rest. (SW1)
La Brasserie (SW3)
Lanesborough (SW1)
Le Cercle (SW1)
Momo (W1)
Nicole's (W1)
Pat. Valerie (multi. loc.)
Porters (WC2)
Portrait (WC2)
Randall & Aubin (SW10)
Red Rm./Waterstones (W1)
Restaurant 7 (SE1)
Richoux (multi. loc.)
Ritz (W1)
Royal Exchange (EC3)
Sketch (W1)
Terrace (W1)
Tom's Deli (W11)
202 (W11)
Vineyard/Stock. (Berks)
Wolseley (W1)
Yauatcha (W1)

Special Feature Index

Trendy

Admiral Codrington (SW3)
Alloro (W1)
Anchor & Hope (SE1)
Angela Hartnett's (W1)
Aperitivo (W1)
Ashbells (W11)
Asia de Cuba (WC2)
Assaggi (W2)
Aura Kitchen (SW1)
Avenue (SW1)
Axis (WC2)
Baltic (SE1)
Bam-Bou (W1)
Belgo Centraal (multi. loc.)
Belvedere (W8)
Benares (W1)
Bibendum (SW3)
Bibendum Oyster (SW3)
Bierodrome (multi. loc.)
Blakes (SW7)
Boxwood Café (SW1)
Busaba Eathai (multi. loc.)
Bush Bar & Grill (W12)
Cafe at Sotheby's (W1)
Cafe Lazeez (multi. loc.)
Canyon (Richmond)
Caraffini (SW1)
Carluccio's (multi. loc.)
Cecconi's (W1)
Cellar Gascon (EC1)
Cheyne Walk (SW3)
Chez Bruce (SW17)
Chintamani (SW1)
Christopher's (WC2)
Cicada (EC1)
Cinnamon Club (SW1)
Cipriani (W1)
Circus (W1)
Clarke's (W8)
Club Gascon (EC1)
Crazy Bear (W1)
Criterion Grill (W1)
Daphne's (SW3)
Drones (SW1)
e&o (W11)
ECapital (W1)
Edera (W11)
Eight Over Eight (SW3)
Electric Brasserie (W11)
Elistano (SW3)
Emporio Armani (SW3)
Enterprise (SW3)

Fifteen (N1)
Fifth Floor (SW1)
Fifth Floor Cafe (SW1)
Fino (W1)
Fish Shop/St. John (EC1)
Glasshouse (Kew)
Gordon Ramsay/Claridge (W1)
Gordon Ramsay/68 Royal (SW3)
Hakkasan (W1)
Harlem (W2)
Hush (W1)
Incognico (WC2)
itsu (multi. loc.)
Ivy, The (WC2)
Joe's (SW3)
Joe's Rest. (SW1)
J. Sheekey (WC2)
Kensington Place (W8)
Langan's Brass. (W1)
La Trompette (W4)
Le Caprice (SW1)
Le Cercle (SW1)
Le Colombier (SW3)
Les Trois Garcons (E1)
L'Etranger (SW7)
Livebait (multi. loc.)
Locanda Locatelli (W1)
Lola's (N1)
Lucky 7 (W2)
Manicomio (SW3)
Masala Zone (multi. loc.)
Mirabelle (W1)
Momo (W1)
Moro (EC1)
Nahm (SW1)
Nam Long-Le Shaker (SW5)
Nicole's (W1)
Nobu (W1)
Oliveto (SW1)
Olivo (SW1)
Orrery (W1)
Orso (WC2)
Osia (SW1)
Oxo Tower (SE1)
Pasha (SW7)
Pétrus (SW1)
Pizza Metro (SW11)
PJ's B&G (SW3)
Providores/Tapa (W1)
Putney Bridge (SW15)
Quo Vadis (W1)
Racine (SW3)
Randall & Aubin (multi. loc.)

Rasoi Vineet Bhatia (SW3)
Real Greek (multi. loc.)
Refettorio (EC4)
Richard Corrigan (W1)
River Cafe (W6)
San Lorenzo (SW3)
Savoy Grill (WC2)
Shumi (SW1)
Sketch (W1)
Smiths/Top Floor (EC1)
Sophie's Steak (SW10)
Spiga (W1)
Spighetta (W1)
Spoon+ (W1)
Square (W1)
St. John (EC1)
St. John Bread/Wine (E1)
Sugar Club (W1)
Taman gang (W1)
Timo (W8)
Tom Aikens (SW3)
Tom's Deli (W11)
Tsunami (SW4)
202 (W11)
Ubon (E14)
Vama (SW10)
Vingt-Quatre (SW10)
Wagamama (multi. loc.)
Wapping Food (E1)
Wells (NW3)
Wolseley (W1)
Yauatcha (W1)
Yo! Sushi (multi. loc.)
Zafferano (SW1)
Zaika (W8)
Zetter (EC1)
Ziani (SW3)
Zilli Fish (multi. loc.)
Zuma (SW7)

Views

Babylon (W8)
Belair House (SE21)
Belvedere (W8)
Blue Print (SE1)
Butlers Wharf (SE1)
Cafe Spice (E1)
Cantina del Ponte (SE1)
Canyon (Richmond)
Cigala (WC1)
Coq d'Argent (EC2)
Crivelli's Garden (WC2)
1802 (E14)

Fakhreldine (W1)
Foliage (SW1)
French Horn (Berks)
Gravetye Manor (W. Sus)
Greenhouse (W1)
Grissini (SW1)
Lanes (W1)
Le Manoir/Q.S. (Oxon)
Le Pont de la Tour (SE1)
Nobu (W1)
Orrery (W1)
Oxo Tower (SE1)
Oxo Tower Brass. (SE1)
People's Palace (SE1)
Plateau (E14)
Portrait (WC2)
Putney Bridge (SW15)
Quadrato (E14)
Ransome's Dock (SW11)
Restaurant 7 (SE1)
Rhodes 24 (EC2)
River Cafe (W6)
Rocket (SW15)
Royal China (E14)
Smiths/Top Floor (EC1)
Smiths/Dining Rm. (EC1)
Smollensky's (E1)
Tenth Rest. (W8)
Thai on the River (SW10)
Ubon (E14)
Waterside Inn (Berks)
Waterway (W9)
Windows on World (W1)

Visitors on Expense Account

Almeida (N1)
Angela Hartnett's (W1)
Asia de Cuba (WC2)
Aubergine (SW10)
Aurora (EC2)
Belvedere (W8)
Benares (W1)
Bentley's (W1)
Berkeley Sq. Café (W1)
Bibendum (SW3)
Blakes (SW7)
Boxwood Café (SW1)
Brian Turner (W1)
Capital Rest. (SW3)
Caravaggio (EC3)
Cecconi's (W1)
Chez Bruce (SW17)

Special Feature Index

Chintamani (SW1)
Christopher's (WC2)
Chutney Mary (SW10)
Cinnamon Club (SW1)
Cipriani (W1)
Clarke's (W8)
Club Gascon (EC1)
Coq d'Argent (EC2)
Criterion Grill (W1)
Daphne's (SW3)
Deca (W1)
Deya (W1)
Drones (SW1)
east@west (WC2)
Edera (W11)
1880 (SW7)
Embassy (W1)
Fat Duck (Berks)
Fifteen (N1)
Fifth Floor (SW1)
Fino (W1)
Foliage (SW1)
Glasshouse (Kew)
Gordon Ramsay/Claridge (W1)
Gordon Ramsay/68 Royal (SW3)
Gravetye Manor (W. Sus)
Green's (SW1)
Grill Room (W1)
Hakkasan (W1)
Incognico (WC2)
Ivy, The (WC2)
J. Sheekey (WC2)
Kai Mayfair (W1)
Lanes (W1)
Lanesborough (SW1)
Langan's Brass. (W1)
Launceston Pl. (W8)
Le Caprice (SW1)
Le Gavroche (W1)
Le Manoir/Q.S. (Oxon)
Le Pont de la Tour (SE1)
L'Incontro (SW1)
Locanda Locatelli (W1)
L'Oranger (SW1)
Matsuri (multi. loc.)
Mirabelle (W1)
Mitsukoshi (SW1)
Nahm (SW1)
Neal Street (WC2)
Nobu (W1)
Odin's (W1)
One-O-One (SW1)
Oriental (W1)

Orrery (W1)
Osia (SW1)
Oxo Tower (SE1)
Pétrus (SW1)
Pied à Terre (W1)
Plateau (E14)
Poissonnerie/l'Ave. (SW3)
Providores/Tapa (W1)
Quaglino's (SW1)
Quirinale (SW1)
Rasoi Vineet Bhatia (SW3)
Red Fort (W1)
Rhodes 24 (EC2)
Ritz (W1)
Riva (SW13)
River Cafe (W6)
San Lorenzo (SW3)
Santini (SW1)
Sartoria (W1)
Savoy Grill (WC2)
Shumi (SW1)
Sketch (W1)
Smiths/Dining Rm. (EC1)
Spoon+ (W1)
Square (W1)
Sumosan (W1)
Tamarind (W1)
Tatsuso (EC1)
Tom Aikens (SW3)
Ubon (E14)
Vineyard/Stock. (Berks)
Waldo's (Berks)
Waterside Inn (Berks)
Wilton's (SW1)
Windows on World (W1)
Zafferano (SW1)
Zaika (W8)
Zen Central (W1)
Zuma (SW7)

Winning Wine Lists
Angela Hartnett's (W1)
Aubergine (SW10)
Belvedere (W8)
Bibendum (SW3)
Boisdale (multi. loc.)
Cafe at Sotheby's (W1)
Cantina Vinopolis (SE1)
Capital Rest. (SW3)
Caravaggio (EC3)
Cecconi's (W1)
Cellar Gascon (EC1)
Chez Bruce (SW17)

Special Feature Index

Christopher's (WC2)
Clarke's (W8)
Club Gascon (EC1)
Criterion Grill (W1)
Cru (N1)
Drones (SW1)
Ebury Wine Bar (SW1)
ECapital (W1)
Edera (W11)
1880 (SW7)
Embassy (W1)
Enoteca Turi (SW15)
Fat Duck (Berks)
Fifth Floor (SW1)
Fino (W1)
Foliage (SW1)
Glasshouse (Kew)
Gordon Ramsay/Claridge (W1)
Gordon Ramsay/68 Royal (SW3)
Gravetye Manor (W. Sus)
Grill Room (W1)
Hakkasan (W1)
Il Convivio (SW1)
Isola (SW1)
Lanes (W1)
Lanesborough (SW1)
Langan's Bistro (W1)
Latium (W1)
La Trompette (W4)
Le Cercle (SW1)
Le Gavroche (W1)
Le Manoir/Q.S. (Oxon)
Le Pont de la Tour (SE1)

L'Escargot (W1)
Le Soufflé (W1)
L'Etranger (SW7)
L'Incontro (SW1)
Locanda Locatelli (W1)
L'Oranger (SW1)
Mirabelle (W1)
Odette's (NW1)
One-O-One (SW1)
Orrery (W1)
Pétrus (SW1)
Pied à Terre (W1)
Plateau (E14)
Prism (EC3)
Ransome's Dock (SW11)
Refettorio (EC4)
Rib Room/Oyster (SW1)
Richard Corrigan (W1)
Ritz (W1)
R.S.J. (SE1)
Sartoria (W1)
Savoy Grill (WC2)
Sketch (W1)
Square (W1)
Tate Gallery (SW1)
TECA (W1)
Tom Aikens (SW3)
Vineyard/Stock. (Berks)
Waldo's (Berks)
Waterside Inn (Berks)
Wilton's (SW1)
Windows on World (W1)
Zafferano (SW1)

Wine Vintage Chart

This chart is designed to help you select wine to go with your meal. It is based on the same 0 to 30 scale used throughout this *Survey*. The ratings (prepared by our friend **Howard Stravitz,** a law professor at the University of South Carolina) reflect both the quality of the vintage and the wine's readiness for present consumption. Thus, if a wine is not fully mature or is over the hill, its rating has been reduced. We do not include 1987, 1991–1993 vintages because they are not especially recommended for most areas. A dash indicates that a wine is either past its peak or too young to rate.

	'85	'86	'88	'89	'90	'94	'95	'96	'97	'98	'99	'00	'01	'02
WHITES														
French:														
Alsace	24	18	22	28	28	26	25	24	24	26	24	26	27	–
Burgundy	26	25	–	24	22	–	29	28	24	23	25	24	21	–
Loire Valley	–	–	–	–	24	–	20	23	22	–	24	25	23	–
Champagne	28	25	24	26	29	–	26	27	24	24	25	25	26	–
Sauternes	21	28	29	25	27	–	21	23	26	24	24	24	28	–
California (Napa, Sonoma, Mendocino):														
Chardonnay	–	–	–	–	–	–	25	21	25	24	24	22	26	–
Sauvignon Blanc/Semillon	–	–	–	–	–	–	–	–	25	25	23	27	–	
REDS														
French:														
Bordeaux	24	25	24	26	29	22	26	25	23	25	24	27	24	–
Burgundy	23	–	21	24	27	–	26	28	25	22	28	22	20	24
Rhône	25	19	27	29	29	24	25	23	24	28	27	26	25	–
Beaujolais	–	–	–	–	–	–	–	–	22	21	24	25	18	20
California (Napa, Sonoma, Mendocino):														
Cab./Merlot	26	26	–	21	28	29	27	25	28	23	26	23	26	–
Pinot Noir	–	–	–	–	–	26	23	23	25	24	26	25	27	–
Zinfandel	–	–	–	–	–	25	22	23	21	22	24	–	25	–
Italian:														
Tuscany	26	–	24	–	26	22	25	20	29	24	28	26	25	–
Piedmont	26	–	26	28	29	–	23	27	27	25	25	26	23	–

subscribe to zagat.com